Campaigns with Hill & Wellington

Campaigns with Hill & Wellington

The Reminiscences of an officer of the 92nd-
The Gordon Highlanders
in the Peninsula and at Waterloo
1809-1816

James Archibald Hope

*Campaigns with Hill
& Wellington
The Reminiscences of an officer of the 92nd-
The Gordon Highlanders
in the Peninsula and at Waterloo
1809-1816*
by James Archibald Hope

First published under the title
*The Military Memoirs
of an Infantry Officer
1809—1816*

Leonaur is an imprint
of Oakpast Ltd

Copyright in this form © 2010 Oakpast Ltd

ISBN:978-0-85706-202-4 (hardcover)
ISBN: 978-0-85706-201-7 (softcover)

http://www.leonaur.com

Publisher's Notes

In the interests of authenticity, the spellings, grammar and place names used have been retained from the original editions.

The opinions of the authors represent a view of events in which he was a participant related from his own perspective,
as such the text is relevant as an historical document.

The views expressed in this book are not necessarily those of the publisher.

Contents

Address	7
Walcheren	9
Ireland	29
Portugal	38
Arroyo-del-Molinos	46
Anecdotes of the Battle	54
Upon the Tagus	59
Almendralejo	62
Ciudad Rodrigo Falls	71
Medellin	76
Fort Napoleon	84
Villa-Alba	92
Towards Toledo	99
The Tormes	109
The Performance of the Army	117
The Second Division	124
The Storming of Bejer	134
Crossing the Ebro	141
Vittoria	146
Battle Vignettes	158
Maya	162

The Gallant 400	173
Vignettes of the Battle	179
La Zarza	183
The Pass of Donna Maria	191
Roncesvalles	197
The Last Battle	204
The Waterloo Campaign, 1815	217
Quatre Bras	226
Retreat to Mont St. Jean	235
The Battle of Waterloo	243
Brussels	253
Paris	260
Home	266

Address

The work now submitted to the public, contains an account of the author's campaigns during the most memorable period of the late french wars. it pretends to no eminence as a literary composition; but the author trusts, that it will not be found wanting in accuracy of detail, as to facts falling under his own notice. He trusts that no one who opens it in hope of being amused, will shut it disappointed; and he sincerely hopes that the junior members of his own profession will find in it something which may prove useful to them when they are called upon to suffer hardships—to encounter dangers—and to perform duties similar to those recorded in the following pages.

Perth, 20th March, 1833.

Walcheren

In the beginning of the summer of 1809, the whole European commonwealth—Austria, Spain, Portugal, and Sicily excepted, were arrayed in arms against the British Isles; and ere the autumnal sun had cheered the heart of the Austrian, husbandman, that powerful empire, after a series of sanguinary conflicts, was compelled to sue for peace, and join the ranks of the enemy. The latter unfortunate event reduced the number of our allies from *forty* to *sixteen* millions; and consequently gave to our haughty antagonist a numerical superiority of one hundred and fourteen millions—France and her allies forming a body of one hundred and fifty millions, while Britain, and her little band of faithful friends amounted to thirty-six millions of souls only! Such was the unequal division of power in Europe in July 1809, when the grand expedition under the present Earl of Chatham quitted the British shores, to assail the enemy in a quarter then looked upon as the most vulnerable point of his widely extended dominions.

During the awful period of preparation, the eyes of every inhabitant of these realms were directed to the place of rendezvous; while with breathless anxiety they watched the movement of every ship, and of every battalion, as if the fate, not only of the United Kingdom, but of the civilized world depended on the contemplated assault. From the Land's End to John O'Groat's, and from Donaghadee to the southernmost promontory of Erin's green isle, the interest excited on this occasion was everywhere the same. Throughout Scotland, England, and Ireland—in the mansion of the peer, and lowly abode of the peasant—one prayer only was heard, and that one was for the success of the expedition wherever bound, and a safe return to those embarked in it.

At Deal, Ramsgate, and Portsmouth, scenes of a most animated description were daily presented to the eye of a spectator, from the commencement of the vast preparations, till the last vessel spread her white sails to the wind, and bade *adieu* to the chalky cliffs of the sea-girt isle. During the whole of that interesting period, the embarkation of men, horses, artillery, and military stores, continued without intermission until all the ships in the fleet were filled with the munitions of war, and those gallant spirits who were destined to apply them to deadly purposes. At the embarkation of some of the battalions, it was truly heartrending to see the poor women taking leave of their husbands—many of them to meet no more. The agonizing cries,—the piteous lamentations, and the tears which flowed in copious streams down their care-worn cheeks, were more than sufficient to penetrate the hardest heart that ever lay incased in the breast of man.

The feelings of the soldiers, also, were on those occasions, not only such as to do them honour, but to convince every individual who witnessed the interesting scenes, that although soldiers may be said to live and move in a region of danger, and not unfrequently surrounded with scenes of horror, in every appalling shape which the field of battle can produce, yet their hearts are stored with a much larger portion of the finer feelings of the human breast, than people in private life have hitherto been disposed to give them credit for. The parting salutations of the distressed couples, no one could hear without being sensibly affected.—"God bless you, Mary; be kind to our babes;" or "Farewell, Betsy; think of me till I return;" were very generally the requests made by the soldiers, when they grasped the hands of their afflicted partners, to bid them *adieu*,—requests which the latter invariably promised to observe, and then sealed their pledge with a tender embrace.

Scenes of dissipation were also pretty numerous, particularly at Portsmouth, where it was nothing uncommon to see a jolly tar locked so fast in the arms of a help-mate on the beach, that it required considerable exertion to rouse them from their slumber, and not a little persuasive eloquence to make the happy mortals relinquish their unseemly couch on the shore, for one more secluded from public view.

For two weeks previous to the sailing of the expedition. Deal was literally filled to an overflow with naval and military officers of all grades, from the admiral to the little middy, and from the general to the jolly ensign. Every hotel and tavern, and numerous private houses, were so crowded, that four of my friends were one evening compelled to pay one pound four shillings for a *room* and *single bed*. Determined to reap a golden harvest, the *good honest* people of Deal, demanded most exorbitant prices for almost every article we required, and which, I am sorry to say, were but too generally paid, and without a grumble by the thoughtless, and almost countless host of purchasers. During the day, the principal shops were crowded almost to suffocation—particularly those confectionary establishments where the sparkling eyes of the fair shopkeepers formed a point of attraction too powerful for the youthful portion of our fraternity to resist.

By the bye, I should like to know the reason why so many confectioners and fancy snuff retailers, place pretty little interesting creatures behind their counters, for it is a system which I ever have, and will continue to condemn as one of a most pernicious tendency—the giddy and thoughtless portion of our youth viewing it in a light *favourable to immorality*. Now, this being a fact which no man can deny, and as it should be the grand object of all respectable tradesmen to stand fair with the world, and be at peace with their own consciences, those individuals who now employ *decoy ducks*, cannot too soon lay aside the practice, for they may rest assured, that no such barefaced attempts to procure a market for their commodities, will ever be patronized by any good or honourable man.

From the rising to the setting of the sun. Deal and its environs daily presented to the eye of a stranger, a singular and interesting picture. Afloat and on shore, the first disturbers of our nocturnal repose, were the morning guns, and reveille. By their united efforts, thousands of dormant spirits were daily roused into action, some to prepare for a long and a tough pull at the oar—others for a hard cruise on shore. From daybreak all was life and gaiety on board; and ere the sun had advanced far on his diurnal journey, hundreds of boats filled with naval and military heroes, were skimming along the surface of the briny deep, and with fearful velocity hastening towards the landing-place. The foraging parties returned to their ships on procuring the provisions of which they stood in need; those on pleasure remained on shore to enjoy the sports of the day.

On the departure of the former, stillness reigned through every corner of the town, till noon, when boats, as formidable in point of numbers as before, again approached the beach, and poured fresh cargoes of emigrants into it, to the great annoyance of all, save shopkeepers and publicans. On landing, each officer pursued the route which fancy pointed out. The politician retired to some place of entertainment, and scanned the pages of the newspapers; the sedate and prudent had an eye to their personal comforts; and the loungers made arrangements for a cruise through the town, to torment some unfortunate billiard marker, or make some confectioner, or milliner's shop girl fancy herself a goddess.

Engaged in similar *interesting* and *honourable* employments, the various groups promenaded the streets, till old father time, pointing to the hour of four, gave the whole a hint to retire and partake of Deal hospitality, or the good things which their friends had provided for them on board. From the latter hour, every hotel, and minor place of public resort, were crowded with warriors of every description, whence hundreds of them, after dedicating many a full flowing cup to those they had left behind, went daily reeling to their boats, as happy as the juice of the grape, or malt could make them, all the way singing,

How merrily we live who soldiers be.

Whenever the surf ran high at the landing place, these thoughtless mortals afforded their more reflecting brethren a very rich treat; for having generally dipped deeper into the cup of intemperance than prudence dictated, they had so much difficulty in stowing themselves into their skiffs, that a severe bruise or two on the leg, in addition to a complete ducking, were very frequently the fruits of their bacchanalian revels, before they accomplished their object.

A more unique, and on the whole, interesting mass of human beings, was perhaps never before collected within so narrow a compass. In Deal, were congregated men from every country, of every religious persuasion, and of every profession under the sun. So various were the costumes worn, and so numerous the languages spoken by the dense assemblage of naval, military, and civil characters, as they paraded the streets, that had that interesting personage, Mr Paul Pry, been then in existence, and dropped in upon us, ignorant of the cause which had drawn us together, he most assuredly would have taken it for granted, that it was our intention to build a second Babel on one of the heights between Deal and Dover.

Various as were the costumes of the multitude, their shades of character were not less diversified. Having occasion one day to wait upon Sir John Hope, (late Earl of Hopetoun) he, on my taking leave, requested me to carry a letter to Colonel Cameron of the 92nd regiment, who, with a portion of his battalion, was then on board of the *Superb* of 74 guns. On leaving Walmer, I proceeded to the quarter-deck of the *venerable* bark, and delivered my charge into the hands of the Highland chief. Knowing that Sir John Hope was to take his passage in the *Superb*, and that orders had been received for her to sail on the following morning, the colonel instantly communicated the contents of Sir John's note to Admiral ——, whose pendant floated in the wind from the mast of the "*Old Superb*" as the nautical gentleman generally denominated her. On hearing that Sir John Hope did not expect to embark for three or four days, the admiral then said he would write to Sir John on the subject, and requested me to forward his letter the moment I landed. The admiral then hurried into his cabin, and in a few minutes reappeared with the letter in his hand.

On receiving it, I again repeated my pledge to see the letter delivered, and was on the eve of turning round to regain my boat, when the admiral, without uttering a word, snatched the letter out of my hand, tore it in numerous pieces, and like a flash of lightning, darted into the cabin.

This comic scene drew smiles from many a weather-beaten countenance, while to me, the whole matter was totally inexplicable; and in this hopeful state of ignorance I might have remained to the present day, had not a naval friend the same day at dinner satisfied me, that with the exception of a few such occasional occurrences, there was no other drawback to as gallant and amiable a character as ever graced the quarter-deck of a British man-of-war.

To the same friend I am indebted for the following anecdote of another distinguished naval commander, who held an important command in the fleet, which wafted us to the pestilential marshes of the land of frogs.

A few days previous to the memorable battle of Trafalgar, Admiral Sir R. S, was detached on a special service by Lord Nelson, with several sail of the line. The gallant chief had not been long absent from the grand fleet, when one morning he observed an enemy's fleet of four sail of the line, bearing down, cleared for action. Our lads being as anxious for a bit of fun as their Gallic opponents, accepted the challenge, and to it they went, ship to ship. One of the British ships commanded by Captain ———, less distinguished for beauty than his unconquerable courage, grappled instantly with a French ship of superior force, and in a very short time made her opponent feel, that no enemy, however formidable, is at any time permitted to approach a British man-of-war with impunity; for

Firm are the sons that Britain leads,
To combat on the main.

On perceiving that the fire of his favourite ship was doing great execution, the Admiral, in token of his admiration, threw his hat on the deck, and remained uncovered, amidst dreadful showers of bullets.

The fire from the French vessel growing less vivid. Sir R.'s heart was so gladdened with this first prospect of victory, that he began to dance, and with the vigour of years gone by, kept it up, till his *hat* was turned into innumerable shapes; and in one of the most fantastic, removed from under the admiral's feet, and replaced on his head. A second favourable omen soon after appearing, the hat was again doomed to descend from its elevated station, to experience from its brave owner the same treatment as before. But fortunately for the *chapeau*, a third omen of victory soon followed the last, which operated so powerfully on the mind of the gallant admiral, that he ordered his *wig* to follow its friend, and in a twinkling again began to trip it on the light fantastic toe, and continued the youthful amusement till every one of the enemy's ships had successively hauled down their colours.

The day at length approached, when it became necessary for all and each of us to lay fun and revelry aside, and prepare for an early meeting with the enemies of our common country. Early on the afternoon of the 27th July, the ominous signal, *Blue Peter*, was hoisted on board of the head quarter ship. Although nothing had been permitted to transpire which could mark the exact point of debarkation, yet from various movements among the vessels of war, it was not very difficult to discover that our destination was Holland. This was rather a disagreeable discovery, for it was impossible to banish from our remembrance the dreadful hardships which our friends suffered in that country, during the campaigns of 1794 and 1795.

These unpleasant recollections, added to the disastrous dispatches which arrived from the banks of the Danube, a few days previous to the sailing of the expedition, produced an unfavourable impression on the minds of almost every individual in both services. But it may very fairly be questioned, whether the appointment of a titled general to a high command in the expedition, did not produce a much more baneful sensation. Report had been for some time particularly busy in assigning to this general the situation which he ultimately held in the expedition; but until the appointment actually appeared in the *London Gazette*, none attached the smallest credit to it; for there were more than one general officer then at home, not only well qualified for the command of such a force, but who having spent the greater part of their lives on foreign service, looked for such an appointment as a suitable reward for their long and faithful services.

That some of the best and bravest of our land felt severely the cold hand of neglect on this occasion, was not only currently reported, but *credited* in military circles. In fact, report went so far as to assert, that promises had been made in a high quarter to some of the gallant individuals, which, if kept, the noble Earl would have been compelled to remain at home, and live in expectation. Had the appointment of commander-in-chief rested with the troops, their choice would, no doubt, have fallen upon that general, whose military talents shone so conspicuously in the command of the British army in Spain, on the fall of his early and bosom friend, the lamented Moore. Can I adduce a stronger proof in support of this assertion, than the following little incident, to which I was an eyewitness. A private soldier of the 36th regiment, actually refused to embark at Portsmouth; and on being desired to give his reasons for disobeying the orders of his superiors, very coolly replied, *that it was because Sir John Hope was not to have the command of the expedition.* I may state further, that the soldier was placed in the boat by force; and on quitting the beach, cried, "*Sir John Hope for ever,*" to which the cheers of those on shore most heartily responded.

So confident were many of my friends that the fleet would never sail from the Downs, that when the signal of preparation was hoisted, hundreds were on shore, so totally destitute of the means of leaving it, that had the fleet got under weigh the same day, a considerable portion of them must eventually have been left behind. As it was, many officers did not get on board till four o'clock on the following morning, and then only on paying the *trifling sum of three and four guineas for a trip of half as many miles.*

The troops employed in this expedition, consisted of twelve squadrons of cavalry—forty battalions, besides portions of battalions, of infantry—and from eighty to one hundred pieces of artillery. The whole were formed into sixteen brigades, and the latter again into seven divisions as follows, *viz.*:

Lieutenant General Sir Eyre Coote's Division.
1st Brigade.—Colonel Mahon.
Three Squadrons.—9th Light Dragoons, part of 95th Rifle Corps, and Detachment of Royal Staff Corps.

2nd Brigade.—Brigadier General Rottenburg.
The 68th, 1st Battalion, 71st, and one Battalion of 95th Rifle Regiment.

Lieutenant General the Earl of Rosslyn's Division.
1st Brigade.—Major General Linsingen.
Three Squadrons 3rd Dragoon Guards—Three Squadrons 12th

Light Dragoons, and Three Squadrons 2nd Light Dragoons, King's German Legion.

2nd Brigade.—Major General Stewart.

The 2nd Battalions of the 43rd and 52nd, and Eight Companies of 95th Rifle Corps.

3rd Brigade.—Brigadier General Baron Alten.

The 1st and 2nd Battalions King's German Legion.

Lieutenant General Sir John Hope's Division, or Corps of Reserve.

1st Brigade.—Brigadier General Disney.

The 1st and 2nd Battalions First Foot Guards.

2nd Brigade.—Major General the Earl of Dalhousie.

The 1st and 2nd Battalions 4th Foot, and 1st Battalion 28th Regiment.

3rd Brigade.—Major General Sir William Erskine.

The 20th Foot, and 1st Battalion 92nd Regiment.

Lieutenant General the Marquis of Huntly's Division.

1st Brigade.—Major General Leith.

The 2nd Battalions 11th and 59th, and 1st Battalion 79th Regiment.

2nd Brigade.—Brigadier General Ackland.

The 2nd Foot, 76th, and 2nd Battalion 84th Regiment.

Lieutenant General Mackenzie Fraser's Division.

1st Brigade.—Major General Dyott.

The 1st Battalions of 5th, 58th, and 91st Regiments.

2nd Brigade.—Brigadier General Montresor.

The First Battalions 9th, 38th, and 42nd Regiments.

Lieutenant General Grosvenor's Division.

1st Brigade.—Major General Brown.

The 2nd Battalions 23rd, 26th, and 81st, and First Battalion 32nd Regiment,

2nd Brigade.—Major General Picton.

The 1st Battalion 36th, 2nd Battalion 63rd, and 77th Regiments.

Lieutenant General Lord Paget's Division.

1st Brigade.—Major General Graham.

The 3rd Battalion 1st Foot, and 85th Regiment.

2nd Brigade.—Brigadier General Houston.
The 2nd Battalions of the 14th and 51st, and 82nd Regiment.

Commander-in-Chief.
Lieutenant General the Earl of Chatham.
Second in Command.
Lieutenant General Sir Eyre Coote.
Commanding Artillery.
Major General M'Leod.
Chief Officer of Engineers.
General Terrot.

The naval part of the expedition consisted of from 300 to 400 vessels of all denominations, upwards of 100 of whom were ships of the line—frigates, sloops, and brigs of war, &c. The whole were placed under the command of Rear Admiral Sir Richard Strachan, who had Rear Admiral Sir R. G. Keates as his second, on this interesting and important occasion.

At daybreak, on the 28th of July, all hands were piped on deck to assist at the capstone, and most cheerfully did every man, soldiers and sailors, join in the good old British cry of "Yeo—heave ho!" In less than an hour, a considerable portion of the fleet had unfurled their white sails to the wind, and were ploughing their way towards the Scheldt, their decks covered with thousands of warriors, chaunting, as they cast a long and lingering look behind—

Ye beautuous maids your smiles bestow,
For if ye prove unkind,
How can we hope to beat the foe.
Who leave our hearts behind.

The vessels of war moved outside of the transports, and the gunboats, with the assistance of some buoys, marked the route of the whole. The appearance of the fleet this morning, was even more magnificent than when it rode at anchor in the Downs. Nothing could move more beautifully than the largest class of our men-of-war, as they dashed through the foaming billows, leading the way to the scene of action. For some hours I paced the deck of our little brig, admiring with feelings of national pride, the noble—the unrivalled spectacle before me; and on my eyes being sufficiently feasted, I descended into our little crib, and there craved from the Giver of Victory, success in some degree commensurate with the magnitude of the armament.

On weighing anchor, the wind was favourable, and blowing what our nautical friends called a gentle breeze; but as we receded from the British shore, it freshened, and during the rest of the day blew hard. A few hours after leaving our anchorage, and when something like order was restored on deck, we retired into the cabin to partake of our morning repast. The servants, however, having neglected to *lash* the table to the cabin floor, we had not been seated many minutes, when one dire hitch of our little jade, tumbled everything topsy-turvy. In an instant, away went seats and sitters, table, teapot, cups, bread, butter, and eggs, all towards one common centre—the portly person of our worthy quarter-master, a man nearly six feet four inches in height.

The latter no sooner felt an inclination to slide backwards, than he, like a drowning man grasping at a straw, rather unluckily caught hold of the table, which being as ready for a piece of fun as his own seat, at once yielded to the impulse of the venerable hero, and most cheerfully accompanied him in his trip to the then lower part of the cabin. Failing in this attempt to preserve his position, our messmate had now no other alternative than to permit matters to take their course, so down went the head, and up flew the heels of the warrior, who in a moment lay weltering—not in his blood—but in tea, and nearly suffocated with the caresses of his friends, who in their journey to the same quarter of the cabin, found the veteran an obstacle not to be avoided.

The wind had increased so much in the night of the 28th, that at daybreak on the 29th, the sailors called it a stiff gale. Two hours after sunrise, the sea presented to the view of all on board, such an unusual appearance, that every one fancied that the vessels in rear were descending a considerable declivity. As the day advanced, the wind increased, till the surrounding waters became so agitated, that when the masters of transports were plying between their own vessels and those of their respective commodores, they frequently appeared to us all but engulfed in the roaring element. The small craft rolled and pitched most fearfully, and the crews of the gunboats had work enough on their hands. The decks of the latter being raised very little above the surface of the water, almost every wave passed over them, drenching the crews so thoroughly, that the poor fellows, long ere night, had more the appearance of belonging to some amphibious tribe, than the human race.

In the afternoon, the cries of some of the latter for help, were truly deplorable. Previous to the sailing of the expedition from the Downs, the competition amongst the junior naval officers for the command of the gun-boats, was extremely keen, each candidate bringing into play all the interest he could command, to obtain for him the object of his ambition. But I am pretty certain, that had a sense of honour permitted them, not a few of those spirited individuals would, on this occasion, most gladly have made use of the same interest to have themselves removed back to their former situations.

About nine o'clock in the morning of the 29th, the person on the look-out duty, descried the Dutch coast a-head, and towards noon, a great many vessels dropped their anchors in the Room-Pot, but subsequently moved to a safer anchorage in the Vere-Gat, between the islands of Schowen, and North Beveland. Here the whole armament reassembled the same evening and following day.

Everything being ready for an immediate descent on the enemy's coast, part of the army destined to act against Flushing, were removed into flat bottomed boats; and at four o'clock in the afternoon of the 30th, moved off in beautiful order towards the shore. Under cover of a few bomb vessels and gun-brigs, the small craft advanced with great regularity, till within a short distance of the landing place, when a general cry of, "Devil take the hindmost," ran from right to left. The landing of troops in face of an enemy, being at all times a hazardous operation, considerable anxiety was apparent in every countenance, till the friends who had preceded us in the road to honour, had obtained a footing on the enemy's soil. Having effected a landing on the island of Walcheren, at a place called the Bree-sand, and about a mile from Fort Der Haak, part of the troops under General Fraser, were sent against the latter; which, on his approach, being evacuated by the enemy, he continued his offensive movement towards Ter-Vere.

The governor of this fortress shewing an unwillingness to resign his command, the place was regularly invested on the land side, and bombarded from the river, with great effect during the night of the 30th, and the whole of the 31st. These summary proceedings caused the commandant to listen to terms, and ultimately to surrender the *town*, garrison, and military stores, into our hands on the following day.

Middleburgh, the capital of this little island, surrendered to Sir Eyre Coote, on the 31st July, and Fort Ramakens on the 3rd of August, but not before the place was regularly invested, and our batteries about to open on its defences.

Pending these operations, a portion of the fleet under Sir Richard Keates, having on board the reserve, commanded by Sir John Hope, proceeded up the eastern branch of the Scheldt, and on the 1st of August effected a landing on the island of South Beveland, the whole of which fell into our hands, during that and the following day. The brigade of guards under General Disney, were pushed forward towards Fort Batz, a place of some strength, at the upper extremity of the island, which being evacuated by the enemy, was taken possession of by them on the 3rd of August. The brigade commanded by the Earl of Dalhousie, was directed to support the Guards in this movement, and Sir William Erskine's brigade occupied Ter Goes, the chief town, and some adjacent villages. A few days after, the latter brigade moved forward six or seven miles, and took possession of the towns of Capelle, Biesling, &c.

After a good deal of severe fighting between the troops under Generals Graham, Houston, Lord Paget, and the enemy. Flushing was closely invested on the 1st of August. From that day the duties of our companions engaged in the siege were unremitting; and owing to the natural dampness of the soil, and copious rains which daily deluged the earth around them, extremely severe. In constructing their batteries, and carrying forward their other field operations, the British troops had to contend with most unseasonable weather, and an active and enterprising enemy. But every individual bore his allotted portion of privations and danger, with a firmness and resolution which at once commanded the admiration and thanks of their superiors. Honour, country, liberty,—words to the military slave, or mercenary, unknown,—carries the British soldier through every danger and difficulty, and makes him lay down with pleasure even life itself, if by such a sacrifice, offered on the altar of his country, he can transmit to his posterity, untarnished and unimpaired, the liberties and honour of his native land.

From the 1st of August, daily affairs of posts took place between the besieged and besiegers—the French commandant allowing no opportunity of retarding the progress of his opponents to pass unimproved. His efforts to prolong the siege, or utterly defeat the plans of his antagonists, were ceaseless. His dreadful salvos of artillery from the ramparts, at one time, and his well-planned and ably executed sorties, at another, caused us a loss in time, as well as many valuable lives. But not- withstanding all his exertions, our batteries were constructed, and reported ready to open on the 12th of August.

Every moment of our time being precious, preparations were made for a combined attack on Flushing, by land and sea, on the following morning. The land batteries, accordingly, opened at ten o'clock, and were for some time gallantly seconded by a number of our vessels of war. But the fire of the latter not proving so effective as was anticipated, Sir Richard Strachan withdrew them from under the enemy's guns, resolved to make another trial on the succeeding day.

Accordingly, at ten o'clock on the morning of the 14th, Sir Richard Strachan again weighed anchor, and carrying six or eight ships of the line close under the enemy's batteries, instantly opened his fire upon the town, and by rapid and dreadful broadsides from his floating castles, assisted by the batteries on shore, soon set Flushing on fire in numerous places. For some hours General Monnet returned the salutes of our batteries and ships with much spirit and considerable effect; but towards four o'clock the flames had spread over the greater part of the town, and so many of his guns had been disabled, that before five o'clock his fire almost entirely ceased. Conceiving the moment favourable to transmit the governor a summons to surrender, Sir Eyre Coote accordingly sent in a flag of truce, about five o'clock, and gave him one hour to consider the conditions on which his submission would be accepted.

No answer having arrived at the expiry of the above period, the cannonade was instantly recommenced, and continued with unabated violence, till almost the whole of the devoted town was in a complete blaze. Being now fully convinced that it would only be a waste of human blood to continue the contest longer, General Monnet offered to capitulate, on condition of being sent into France. This offer being refused, he then agreed to accept the terms dictated by the British commanders, which in substance were,—that he should surrender himself, and all the troops under his command, prisoners of war, and deliver up all his cannon, and military stores, into the hands of the conquerors. The total loss sustained by the enemy on this occasion, consisted of 6079 men killed, wounded, and prisoners, 224 pieces of cannon, 2000 barrels of gunpowder, and an immense quantity of military stores.

The roaring of the artillery, in and around Flushing, had no sooner reached the ears of the good people in that quarter of South Beveland where I was then stationed, than the roofs of all the churches and windmills in our vicinity, were crowded with anxious spectators, almost all of whom had friends or relations residing in Flushing on that eventful day. Although the distance between us and the belaboured fortress was considerable, yet the spectacle produced by the operations of the belligerents, was forced upon our notice in the most magnificent, but melancholy form, which we could possibly have desired. None, however, but those who were close to the scene of action, can form any idea of the dreadful scene which followed in the wake of the last cannonade. But even at the distance at which we viewed the conflagration, its appearance was so truly appalling, that although there was no one thing which we more ardently wished for than the fall of Flushing, yet as men and as Christian soldiers, we could not refrain from dropping a tear of sympathy for the innocent inhabitants, who, surrounded with flames, and threatened with instant death by our shot and shell, had spent a day and a night of horror, which none but those who have been similarly situated can possibly describe.

At daybreak on the 15th, Flushing had all the appearance of a vast charnel-house, for whichever way a person turned his eyes, there was nothing to be seen but houses

Tottering in frightful ruins, as the flames
Had left them, black and bare;
And half burnt bodies, which allured from far
The wolf and raven,—and to impious food
Tempted the houseless dog.

Having all along looked forward to the fall of Flushing as a signal for the simultaneous advance of both army and navy, to prosecute, to a successful close, our ulterior operations against the enemy, language cannot express in terms sufficiently strong, the severe disappointment which all of us experienced, when, instead of being ordered to act a part worthy of the land of our birth, the whole army was kept in cantonments, and in the full enjoyment of an inglorious ease, till the troops became so sickly, that it seemed to be a *matter of doubt* how far *prudence* would lend the sanction of her name to any further military operations against Antwerp. To settle this point, however, a council of war was held, but not till *ten days afte*r the surrender of Flushing. The deliberations of the council were, as a matter of course, kept a profound secret. But report was busy on the occasion, and if it spoke truth, a naval officer of rank offered, with a given number of frigates, &c., to lead the way to Antwerp, and there take, burn, or otherwise destroy the whole of the enemy's fleet and stores, provided he was supported by Sir John Hope, with a mixed force of 22,000 men.

The offer, though not accepted, must have shewn the members of the council, that there was one of their number, who did not occupy that place at their board which his great military talents entitled him to fill. For on the *same day* it was also reported, that on the breaking up of the meeting of the general officers, *more than one* of them expressed an intention of returning to England, that they might no longer be an obstacle in the way of his appointment to the supreme command of the army in Holland. If none of the lieutenant-generals, *senior* to Sir John Hope, expressed themselves in the manner above stated, then report must have been amusing its auditors with a tale of fiction; but until the assertion is shewn to be groundless, by the testimony of one or more of the lieutenant-generals then present, (two of whom, *viz*. the Duke of Gordon, and Earl of Rosslyn, are still alive,) I shall consider myself entitled to hold the same opinion I have hitherto done in regard to this matter.

About the 20th of August, the troops were first attacked with fever and ague. Towards the latter end of the month it had appeared in the ranks of every battalion, but in some with more virulency than in others. A great part of the men being quartered in *barns*, it frequently occurred that all the inmates, (six or eight,) of some of those places, were seized with the disease in the same night. This, however, we were not much surprised at; for the natural dampness of the barn-floors, and the humidity of a Dutch atmosphere, were of themselves more than sufficient to engender disease, even had the barns been placed on situations of much greater altitude. As an antidote to the pestilential vapours incident to the climate, a *wholesale* system of bathing was recommended by our medical friends. When it was intended to indulge the soldiers with a little of this cooling amusement, they were generally marched down to the right bank of the Western Scheldt about midday.

At a given sound of the bugle, the lads of our battalion undressed, but not a man durst move into the water, till the shrill notes of a second bugle intimated to the *interesting* group that they had permission to do so, dressed in *Adam's first covering*. The scene which followed can only be portrayed by the pencil of a Cruickshank,—language would fail in the attempt. Some were highly amused with the exhibition; but I must confess that I looked upon the whole proceedings with loathing and disgust, I most readily concede, that the feelings of a considerable portion of the private soldiers are not of a very refined description,—but as men of various characters are to be found in every mixed society,— who will assert that there were not many individuals in the battalion, whose feelings were deeply wounded on these occasions, by making them figure in an exhibition, no less novel than indecent. It is bad policy to place men in situations, where, if any change in their conduct is produced, that change must be for the worse.

But Sir William Erskine, who was intimately acquainted with the nature of the malady, strongly recommended to our notice the following recipe,—one glass of brandy before dressing, one at breakfast, one after dinner, and another in the evening. This antidote, being much more congenial to the habits and tastes of a great majority of his brigade, than an ablution in the Scheldt, raised the fame of Sir William as a son of Æsculapius, far above others of greater pretensions.

But regardless of all our antidotes, death appeared in our ranks about the latter end of August. His power continuing to increase, it was deemed advisable to remove all our sick to England, on the 1st of September. On the 2nd, our division, the reserve, received notice to prepare for embarkation; and on the following morning we marched to the left bank of the Eastern Scheldt—went on board of transports ready to receive us, and afterwards dropped down to the anchorage of the Vere-Gat. Here, by some of those unaccountable occurrences which but too often follow the failure of a military enterprise, we were detained nearly a week, inhaling infection at every breath, when we might have been enjoying the healthful breezes of our native land. The consequences were such as any man of common understanding would have anticipated. Fever and ague, in its worst form, increased so rapidly, that before we reached our own coast, more than a-half of the men were under medical treatment, and the whole as uncomfortable as our most inveterate enemy could wish.

On the morning subsequent to our re-embarkation, between twenty and thirty of the men on board of the transport in which I took my passage, were attacked with the pestilence. To prevent it spreading, the worst cases were removed from the hold, into boats placed under an awning on deck. In one of these temporary hospitals, ten or a dozen fine fellows were confined on the evening of the 5th September, when the first victim on board ship, a tall, handsome grenadier, took leave of this world. His companions taking it for granted that their dissolution was also approaching, became so agitated, that it was with the utmost difficulty they could be prevailed upon to remain in their berths. Being on deck when the grenadier died, and perceiving the state into which his melancholy exit had thrown them, I endeavoured, but unsuccessfully, to soothe their excited feelings, and banish the dreadful notions which seemed to haunt their minds; but the prospect of immediate dissolution, and its attendant horrors, stared them so fully in the face, that no language I could use seemed to have the smallest effect.

Their situation, at length, was so truly deplorable, that one of the party, a tall, robust non-commissioned officer, started to his feet with the agility of the hare, leaped from the boat, and then with the countenance of a maniac, ran along the deck, crying in all the bitterness of despair, that he was a dying man, and continued in this state of temporary delirium, till a fresh attack of ague compelled him to resume his place in the boat.

In the same group of patients, there was a grenadier, a man of a most athletic form, but of weak intellect. On perceiving the serjeant leap from the boat, honest Willie Mill attempted to follow his example, but was prevented by the sentry on duty. Early next morning I went on deck, expecting to find Willie in the last stage of the disease, but to my utter surprise I found him soliciting, not the grim king of terrors for a short respite, but the pay-sergeant of his company for a morning repast. Willie's appetite being always keen, he pressed his suit with so much ardour, that the sergeant was frequently on the point of yielding. A sense of duty, however, at length prevailed, and Willie's request was refused. Foiled in his attempt to obtain a substantial breakfast of beef and bread, Willie turned round, and with a look that would have sunk deep into the heart of a savage, very gravely said,—"Weel, weel, sergeant M'Combie, if ye think thae things are o'er strong for my weak stamach, just gang to the cook, and tell him *to mak me some stir-about, and to mak it gay'n thick."*

I need scarcely add, that Willie's second request excited considerable merriment on deck, in which some of his boat-companions, ill though they were, heartily joined. Willie's last appeal was too powerful to be resisted; his appetite was gratified; he recovered, and I believe still lives to enjoy the bounty of his sovereign, which enables him to indulge in a daily allowance of his favourite stir-about.

On the 8th September, the transports containing our regiment, quitted their anchorage on the Dutch coast, and on the 10th cast anchor in the Downs. On the following morning we sailed for Harwich, where, by reason of foul winds, we did not arrive till the afternoon of the 13th. Early on the 14th our worst cases were landed and consigned to the care of the medical staff at Harwich, and a few of those who could with safety be removed farther by water, were transported in boats to Ipswich. In the afternoon the rest of the battalion, including all the remaining sick, landed at Land-Guard Fort, and proceeded to Woodbridge barracks—the former on foot, the latter on waggons. Never did I witness a spectacle more heart-rending than the removal of the sick from the transports to the shore, and thence to Woodbridge. The emaciated figures, and long thin pale visages of the poor sufferers as they lay stretched in the boats and on the waggons,—the piercing shrieks and agonizing groans which the jolting of the latter drew from their death-like lips, forced tears from my eyes as I moved along with the melancholy throng.

This scene however, distressing as it was, was soon to be eclipsed by others of a still more mournful description. For several weeks after our arrival at Woodbridge, our sick-list daily increased, till upwards of *four hundred* of our men were immured within the cheerless walls of an *hospital*. Of these, two, three, and even four, were frequently removed in one day to the place of interment, and there consigned to the silent tomb, by those few whom a merciful Providence was pleased to bless with health and strength. At first the dead were buried with military honours; but this mark of respect was latterly withheld, on a representation being made to the commanding-officer by the medical attendants, that the loner-roll of the muffled drum operated so powerfully on the minds of the sick, as to renew the alarming symptoms which had previously yielded to the power of medicine. As each mournful procession crossed the barrack-square, the lamentations of friends, or the wailings of a widow, and her orphan children, struck upon every ear, and penetrated every heart. Never, no never, shall these distressing scenes, the fruits of rashness and mismanagement, be banished from my remembrance.

During the first two months of our residence in Woodbridge, the duties of the regimental medical staff were unremitting and severe—particularly those of assistant surgeon Dunn, whose humanity would never permit him to absent himself from the bed of the poor sufferers, so long as his medical advice could be of service. For this praiseworthy attention to those under his charge, the blessings of the soldiers saluted him at every step, and no doubt encouraged him to persevere in the same laudable conduct throughout. I have been induced to notice these facts, in order to shew my young medical friends that it is only by a humane, diligent, and faithful performance of their duties, that they can expect to obtain the grateful and sincere respect of those whose comforts and happiness, on similar occasions, are generally increased or lessened, in exact proportion to the zeal with which the surgeon and his assistants discharge the duties of their stations.

With regard to the loss which we sustained in this most disastrous expedition, I may remark that the effective strength of the battalion, which, on landing in South Beveland, was 998 rank and file, was so much reduced by the Dutch pestilence, that, in the month of October following, between 200 and 300 only were fit for duty. One morning, indeed, the grenadier company could only bring *two* non-commissioned officers, and *three* privates, to the public parade. But had the deaths, numerous as they were, constituted the whole of our loss, a few additional recruiting parties would very soon have made good the deficiency. Unfortunately, however, in our battalion, as in almost every other employed on the same service, the deaths formed but a small portion of our *real loss*. For the repeated attacks of the malady had made such inroads on the constitutions of the survivors, that, when put to the test in the Peninsula, they were found to be no longer the same men. Their frames had become so enervated, that exposure to the night air, or a heavy shower of rain, sent many of them shivering to their beds; then to an hospital, where they but too frequently led a life of suffering and misery, till they sank into a premature grave.

Placed in Woodbridge under the circumstances just now stated, it cannot be considered surprising that the months of October and November should have appeared to us cheerless, and have passed slowly away. Indeed I believe, that but for the grand jubilee parade, subscription ball, and dinner, on the 25th of October, we should have died of perfect *ennui*. In the afternoon of that day, the garrison, consisting of four battalions of infantry, a considerable body of artillery, and some German cavalry, were marshalled in the barrack-square, by Baron Alten, and almost immediately on the troops taking their stations, the thundering of the cannon right and left,—the volleys of musketry,— the cheers of the soldiers, re-echoed by dense masses of the populace, proclaimed to the surrounding country, that George the Third, the Father of his people, had completed the fiftieth year of his eventful reign.

At the conclusion of this interesting pageant, the officers threaded their way towards Woodbridge, where, at five o'clock, they sat down to an elegant dinner, consisting of all the varieties and delicacies of the season. Almost every officer in the garrison was present, and for some time everything went off with *éclat*. On occasions of this kind, however, it but too frequently happens that the young and inexperienced allow reason to resign her seat to folly, and are then betrayed into actions the most extravagant and absurd. Inexperience has, no doubt, been often permitted to be pleaded in mitigation of the offence of an unfledged youth; but some young men are led to the commission of offences which even youth cannot palliate. This being the case, I trust I shall be permitted to express a hope, that in future the young and thoughtless portion of our military youth will attentively listen to, and ponder over the advice of their more experienced brethren, before they place themselves under the guidance of a tutor reared in the school of folly. For by doing so, they may rest assured that they will at all times glide along the surface of life as smoothly as a little bark, skimming along the surface of unruffled water, and like her, at length find their way into port without meeting with anything materially to lessen the pleasure of the voyage of life.

On the 6th of March, 1810, I bade *adieu* to Woodbridge, and proceeded to Scotland, on my way to join the second battalion of my regiment in Ireland. Being in a delicate state of health, I amused myself a few weeks in Edinburgh, and then proceeded to the country to inhale the air of my native hills.

Ireland

Completely restored to health, I took leave of the Land of Cakes for that of true hospitality, in the very centre of which I beat up the quarters of my friends in the second battalion, in the latter end of June 1810.

It was originally my intention to take no other notice of my services in this part of the world, than what is to be found in the above paragraph, and perhaps a similar one on my taking leave of the second battalion for the Peninsula. But a much-valued friend, conceiving that the *Memoir* would be incomplete, without a few articles descriptive of the duties which soldiers are but too frequently called upon to perform in Ireland, and of the enemies against whom they generally act, has pressed me so strongly on this point, that I have, in deference to his opinion, selected the following for insertion.

Athlone is a very ancient town, and stands on both banks of the river Shannon, over which there is an old, ugly, ill-built, narrow bridge. The general appearance of Athlone is extremely antiquated, and far from prepossessing. It is just what we may very aptly denominate a finished town. Dull and lifeless, however, as everything appeared during the day, yet with the kind attentions of the families residing in the town and vicinity, we contrived to pass the monotonous hours of a soldier on home service pleasantly enough. But pleasant as the private parties generally were, they did not constitute our only sources of amusement. We possessed within our own circle others no less captivating, amongst which I may mention a garrison weekly club, as not the least attractive. The expense was limited to half-a-crown, for which each member was entitled to supper, and a couple of tumblers of punch. The officers of the different corps always assembled at seven o'clock, played cards, chess, or backgammon, till ten;—then attacked the pandowdies; and after destroying a few hundreds of them, and doing ample justice to the poteen, retired to our respective cages before the midnight hour, always in good humour with ourselves, and all those friends who five hours before we were happy to meet, from whom we were sorry to part, but with whom we would be happy to meet again.

Since that time, I have heard many individuals who arrogated to themselves a larger share of common sense, or worldly wisdom, than their neighbours, inveigh with considerable asperity against regimental messes and garrison clubs, on the plea that they were apt to lead the young officers from the path of temperance to that of dissipation. Had those people taken a less superficial view of military society, they would have come to a very opposite conclusion. Young officers, like the young men in every civil society, are no doubt in danger of being led astray by the seductive orations of the dissolute portion of their fraternity. For the latter, on finding themselves lowered in the estimation, and shunned by their discerning and more honourable-minded brethren, invariably employ every stratagem they can think of, and all the most fascinating language at their command, to induce the inexperienced and unsuspecting youth to quit the paths of virtue and honour; and this is too often done under the specious, but false pretext, that dissipation, and its accompanying vices, are most becoming the officer and gentleman.

From this candid acknowledgment of the dangers to which officers are exposed on joining their corps for a first time, some may think it totally impossible for a youth to escape the wiles of the enemies of virtue. But I request all those to bear this in remembrance, that the moment an officer joins his regiment, he is from that time surrounded with men of high character and honour, who are ever ready to throw a protecting shield round the head of a junior brother, against which the shafts of vice, from whatever quarter they may be directed, usually prove pointless. Yes; I repeat that five-sixths of the officers are always ready to act in this manner; for as the misconduct of any one member of a battalion never fails to cast a deep shade over the characters of the others, it is evidently the interest, no less than the duty, of all those officers who have any regard for themselves or their profession, to check every attempt made by a brother officer to swerve from the paths of duty, of virtue, and of honour, and endeavour to impress on the mind of their frail friend the important truth, that those paths alone lead to rank and military renown. From whatever motives, therefore, the great body of British officers may act,—whether from a high sense of honour or interested feeling,—it is quite obvious that their youthful associates are equally safe, for in either case their heads must at all times be so protected, as to render the utmost efforts of the profligate to lead them into a ruinous course of low and degrading pleasures, altogether unavailing.

In almost every newspaper we open, we find detailed the proceedings of some religious meeting, convened for the purpose of raising funds to send missionaries into foreign parts to convert the heathen to Christianity. Now, though I readily admit that this is a most laudable and praiseworthy object, yet I cannot help thinking, that before we expend any more of our British gold in attempts to convert the heathen inhabiting the burning sands of Asia and Africa, or the cold and inhospitable wilds of Europe and America, we should endeavour to bring the British heathen to know and adore the infinite goodness of the All-wise and Omnipotent Ruler of heaven and earth.

Some of those pious individuals who have assisted to fill the coffers of foreign missions, will no doubt read "British heathen" with surprise, if not with the eyes of a sceptic. But to those who have doubts that such people really reside within the British isles, I at once say, take a trip to the other side of the Irish Channel and have them fully removed. Lest, however, it may not be convenient for every one of them to take this step, I beg to state for their information, that on every fine *Sunday evening* during the summers of 1810 and 1811, an immense concourse of people assembled a little north of the batteries at Athlone, where two roads intersect each other, and there, to the sounds of the Irish bag-pipe and violin, danced and gambolled till night spread her sable mantle around the heathenish groups, and put an end to their unholy sports.

Now, as this unhallowed sport was not confined to Athlone, but was equally common in various other parts of Ireland, I was then of opinion, and I have seen no reason to change it, that to this open profanation of the Lord's day a great proportion of the outrages which have so long disgraced that country must be ascribed. For when people of either sex totally disregard these sacred duties which the day of rest imposes on them as Christians, it is not to be expected that they will be more attentive to the moral and political duties of their station. When a man once breaks the Sabbath, he is then easily led on from one crime to another, until he becomes so involved in the vortex of vice, that all other pleasures, save the most sinful and detestable, are at length perfectly abhorrent to his nature.

Whenever religion loses its hold in the mind,—when the day set apart for rest, prayer, humiliation, and thanksgiving, is converted into one of dissipation, riot, and profanity, what check remains, I ask, to curb the unruly passions of men, and restrain them from the commission of every description of crime, but the dread of a capital punishment on earth? Now, as the man who knows not the great Author of his being, cannot be supposed to dread the power of his Almighty arm, and as men, when engaging in any criminal enterprise, generally indulge the hope of eluding the lynx-eye of justice, they,—on having their hopes realized, are frequently so much elated with their good fortune, that they gradually get rid of that terror which the law inspires, and are soon prepared to execute the most hazardous and most atrocious offences. Have we not lamentable proofs of this afforded us every day, by the confessions of those whose lives have become forfeited to the laws of their country?

One market-day, a countryman all in his glory, with a "sprig of shilellah" poised above his head, and a "shamrock so green" neatly entwined in the band of what had once been a hat, made his appearance at the upper part of the market-place of Athlone, challenging to mortal combat all and sundry the lieges, from the veteran of threescore and ten, down to the stripling of sixteen. After capering and vapouring for some time, to the great terror of egg and crockery merchants, and no one appearing inclined to volunteer a tilt with him, Pat, afraid that he would be done out of a customer, knocked a neighbour down for pure love, in order to procure the grand object of his ambition—a row. The whack had scarcely been given, when more than fifty shilellahs flew like flails round as many heads, with which they instantly came in contact.

A few of them fell on the head of the aggressor, but, as on all similar occasions in Ireland, the principal object of the belligerents is to keep up the row at whatever expense, the greater proportion of the weapons came in collision with the craniums of individuals, who were no otherwise interested in the matter than that their skulls lay rather more convenient for a crack than that of the object of their rage. One man after another continuing to join in the grand fracas, the combatants at length became so numerous, and their conduct so extremely outrageous, that the local authorities found it necessary to apply for military aid. One hundred men were instantly dispatched from the barracks to the scene of action, and by charging along the market-place, separated the combatants, and caused a suspension of hostilities. Pat, however, far from being satisfied with the issue of the conflict, embraced the earliest opportunity, after the soldiers retired, to renew the sport. To it again they went as gallantly as before. For the following half-hour there was no scarcity of men—of shilellahs—of blows—or of blood, which ultimately flowed copiously from numerous wounds. Heads were cracked—arms damaged—and many an odd bone complained of fractures—and yet none thought of yielding.

Everything in fact was progressing as favourably as Pat could wish, when the same party of "lobsters," as Jack would say, put an end to the glorious sport, by charging a second time the motley assemblage, which, but for the officers, would have received a hearty drubbing from the soldiers, as a proper reward for their barbarous foolery. After clearing the market-place, the soldiers retired, and left the combatants to bind up their wounds, and splice their fractured limbs in the best manner they could. As for the unfortunate wretch, the *sole cause* of the bloodshed, he was found in the evening on the banks of the canal, close to the town, beat almost to a mummy, but in life; and such was his ghastly appearance, that it was with the utmost difficulty that any person could be prevailed upon to admit him within their door, even for a single night.

With a party of fourteen men, and an excise-officer, I left Athlone one evening at a *still*-hunting excursion. At daybreak we seized upon one of the delinquents engaged in the illicit traffic, who, with all his apparatus, but no whisky, we lodged in safe keeping in Athlone. This duty every officer most cordially detested, but it was much relished by the greater portion of the men, who, for *every still captured*, received, in addition to their pay, serjeants 18s., corporals 10s. 6d., and privates 7s. In the spring of 1811, a party of our corps, and a few dragoons, captured in thirty hours, no fewer than twenty-two stills, and for each every man received payment in the foregoing proportions. These are no doubt startling facts, and ought, I think, to convince those who have the Irish revenue laws in their keeping, that a system which requires so much money to keep it in a working condition, must be founded on principles radically unsound.

Parties of the lawless portion of the peasantry then denominated *Carders*, having administered an unlawful oath to a considerable number of rather respectable people in the counties of Roscommon and Galway, detachments were ordered from our garrison in the month of February 1811, to various places from fifteen to thirty miles from Athlone, in order to put a stop to their treasonable proceedings. Those parties having been recalled, and others ordered out to replace them, I, at the head of one of those detachments, marched from Athlone on the 11th of April, and having taken an early dinner with a brother officer at Roscommon, proceeded in the evening to Ballymoe Bagot, in the county of Galway.

In this village my quarters were of the most miserable description, the only apartments I could procure, being a small room and closet, neither of which had any ceiling. In fact, the only thing between the clay under my feet, and the thatch above my head, was large quantities of soot, so neatly suspended from the roof, in long and beautifully curled rows, that the whole dangled in nearly as becoming a manner, as the black feathers on a Highlander's bonnet. Notwithstanding this, it was with more than ordinary regret that I quitted Ballymoe, after a six weeks residence, for I never experienced more genuine hospitality than I did during my stay in that rural village.

Soon after I parted with my friend at Roscommon, a large assemblage of town and country people attacked his barracks, broke all his windows, and threatened to break his head also, and those of the men under his command. These threats, and the entire demolition of his windows, raised the temperature of my friend's blood to such a degree, that, regardless of the consequences, he moved his band of twenty out of the barracks, fixed bayonets, charged along the market-square, and in an instant cleared it of the rioters, one of whom received a deep probe in the breech. Called upon for a detail of his operations, the *gallant commander* transmitted to General Sir James Affleck, then commanding the western district, a long and whimsical dispatch, in which, after enumerating the names of all those who had distinguished themselves in the engagement, (and which I believe included every man in the detachment) he concluded, "It now only remains for me to express my sincere regret, that the nature of the service on which I have lately been engaged, will not permit me to recommend any of my brave followers for promotion." Poor L——! he fell in a more memorable conflict—that of Quatre Bras.

One afternoon, during my stay in Ballymoe, a brawny, squat, real son of Erin, came running to my quarters all covered with mud and perspiration, and foaming at the mouth like an enraged mastiff. Hat or shoes he had none; and his inexpressibles, and other toggery, as the members of the fair-play club would say, were such as would have secured him ready employment as a scarecrow in any part of Ireland. Conceiving that something was wrong, I hurried to meet him, and rather eagerly inquired the cause of his visit, but the only answer I could obtain was, Och! murder—murder, your honour! And as he continued to return similar answers to my subsequent interrogatories, I was at length in- duced to look upon the frightful figure before me as a murderer, craving protection from a host of pursuers.

Under this impression, I inquired if my suspicions were well-founded. At first he made no reply; but on the question being repeated, he stammered out,—"Och! is it me, your honour, that is a murderer? No, no; I am no murderer; but a murder, and a bloody-murder too, your honour, has been committed in my presence within the last half-hour, and I am come to ask your honour for five or six of your men, to help us to take the vile murderer."

On requesting him to favour me with the particulars, he informed me, that a few men and women being at work together in a field between three and four miles from Ballymoe, one of the men raised a pitchfork, and without the smallest provocation, plunged it into the bowels of a bosom friend. On hearing these facts, I instantly dispatched a sergeant and six men to the scene of blood, but previous to their arrival, the monster had unfortunately escaped.

A few days after this melancholy affair, my assistance was required to root out a band of freebooters, who were so entrenched in the affections of a village peasantry, from ten to twelve miles from Ballymoe, that they committed offences with impunity, and bade the law defiance. At eleven, p.m. I left Ballymoe, taking with me a sergeant, corporal, and sixteen privates. About three o'clock, a. m., I received an addition to my force of eighteen strapping young Irishmen, armed with shilellahs, all of whom had some knowledge of the parties against which we were marching. At daybreak we arrived in sight of the abode of the lawless banditti. On approaching which, I detached four of my own men, and six of my auxiliary corps to the right, and as many to the left of the village, to watch the motions of the nine individuals we were in search of, and with the rest of the soldiers and Irishmen, I pushed forward into the centre of the village to take the whole napping. In this, however, I was disappointed, for early as it was, they had obtained intelligence of our approach, and had all left their houses, save one woman whom we secured.

But the non military part of my detachment, who were well acquainted with the village, had their eyes riveted on the avenues of escape, and consequently, that portion of them who filed round the town, were ready to pounce upon their game, as soon as they made their appearance. The latter being completely rigged for a flight, flew like lightning across dub and mire, and over hedge, ditch, and dykes, till they reached the summit of a gentle acclivity, when, being considerably blown, and seeing some of their bare-kneed assailants gaining rapidly upon them, three of them joined, and with their backs to a stone-wall, offered battle. The challenge being accepted, a bloody affair ensued, which ended in the capture of those three, and another of their associates. All the others escaped.

By this time all the village population had turned out, and hundreds were fast approaching us from all quarters, and as I soon learnt, for the express purpose of releasing the prisoners. Being of opinion that it is at all times infinitely better to prevent crime than to punish it, I caused the men to load, and on doing so, to shew the deluded creatures their *balls*, before ramming home their cartridges, in hopes of deterring them from making the meditated attempt, which could only have produced streams of blood. And I am happy to state, that the object I had in view was completely obtained, for in a few minutes the whole multitude retired peaceably to their respective places of abode, and left us at liberty to remove the prisoners wheresoever we pleased.

Having dispatched the prisoners to a place of safety, we retraced our steps towards Ballymoe. Ravenous as wolves, we took the liberty to walk into a snug-looking cabin, where two riddles, well filled with smoking *Murphy's*, appeared in a most inviting condition for hungry men. Having asked and obtained permission to join the rustic party at their frugal morning repast, we were not long in seating ourselves, and doing ample justice to the *praties* and butter-milk. During our operations, I could scarcely refrain from smiling at the innocent simplicity which played on the countenances of the little half-clad urchins, who, as each potato disappeared, looked wistfully, first at the riddle, then at their mother, and finally, cast a significant glance towards us, as much as to say, "Bad luck to you, be off, or we shall be compelled to honour Duke Humphrey with our company to breakfast." On preparing to resume our journey, I tendered the poor woman a trifle for her excellent fare; but so determined was she *not to accept* of anything in the shape of remuneration, that I had no alternative left, but to sprinkle a few small pieces in such a manner on the floor, that they could not he collected till we were completely out of the reach of pursuit.

I shall conclude this chapter with the following anecdote, which was related to me by the gallant major himself.

Major C——, on joining the regiment in November 1810, being

obliged to take lodgings in town, was, one morning before daybreak, roused by a hideous noise under his windows. Conceiving that this proceeded from a body of *carders*, on their way to attack the barracks, the major paced the floor in a twinkling, decorated in his military paraphernalia. John, whom the sonorous voice of his master had awakened from dreams of earthly bliss, to ruminate on the troubles of the other world, entered the major's apartment just as the latter was buckling on his sword, and with extended mouth, and eyes half open, eagerly inquired what had happened. "The *carders* are by this time at the barracks," replied the major.

"Did you see them, Sir?" said John, rather anxiously.

"Why, no," answered the major, "but I heard their unearthly screams as they passed under the windows." Here a considerable pause ensued; for John, having some doubts on the subject, scratched his head, shrugged his shoulders, and with an unmeaning grin on his I countenance, stood as if anxious to state them, but yet afraid to do so. Silence being at length broken by the major inquiring the cause of John's grimaces and shrugs, the latter instantly replied, "I have just been thinking, Sir, that what ye ha'e ta'en for the cheers of thae blackguards, the *carders*, has probably been the skirlings of some country lassies at a funeral." The morning being uncommonly dark, and the major totally unacquainted with the mode of conducting funerals in Ireland, John's remark, instead of producing any change in I the major's original intention, only tended to convince him, that his servant was better fitted for a snug berth in Bedlam, than the one which he held near his person.

Fully satisfied, therefore, that the garrison would derive but little assistance from John, Major C——, after bestowing on his servant a few well dove-tailed epithets, was descending the stair on his way to the barracks, when his landlord, who had overheard the latter part of the conversation, pursued his gallant tenant, and soon succeeded in convincing him, that the noise was nothing more than the mellifluous notes of a few of his fair countrywomen accompanying some departed friend to the place of everlasting repose.

Having thus gratified the wishes of my friend, though perhaps not to the extent he may have expected, we shall now, with his permission, take a temporary leave of Erin, and by easy stages, proceed to the theatre of war in the Peninsula,

And join the gallant quarrel.

Portugal

With a detachment, consisting of one major, two captains, four subalterns, one assistant-surgeon, and 248 rank and file, I took leave of Athlone on the morning of the 17th of August 1811, and proceeded to Fairbane, on our way to the place of embarkation. On the 18th we moved forward to Birr—next day to Roscrea—on the 20th to Thurles—and on the 21st to Tipperary, where we halted on the following day. On the 23rd our route led us to Mitchelstown, and to Fermoy on the 24th. Here an order had preceded us for forty-eight of the detachment to return to Athlone, they being considered too young to undergo the fatigues of a Peninsular campaign. The poor young lads, on being made acquainted with their new destiny, absolutely shed tears of sincere heart-felt sorrow. Two hours before daylight, on the morning of the 30th, they commenced their retrograde movement; and about as long after daybreak we also bade *adieu* to Fermoy,—proceeded to Cork,—and on the following morning embarked at Monkston, on board of the *Minerva* transport.

Having previously purchased a competent stock of provisions for our little voyage, we weighed anchor at seven o'clock on the morning of the 7th of September, and shortly after quitted Cove harbour, under a gentle breeze from the land. Continuing to scud along with a favourable gale, we descried the Rock of Lisbon a little after sunrise on the 19th. About two o'clock a pilot paid us a visit, and carried the old bark up the majestic Tagus in fine style, to a berth opposite Fort-Belem. At three o'clock, p.m. on the following day, we disembarked at the Blackhorse square. The men were quartered in a convent, and the officers upon the inhabitants.

The exterior appearance of Lisbon from the Tagus is extremely beautiful, vieing in splendour with the finest city in Europe. But the interior view of it is so truly disgusting, that we are forced to place it in a scale beneath the rank of the very lowest. The streets, which are narrow and ill-paved, are filthy beyond description. But how can it be otherwise, when every night, between nine and ten o'clock, everything, no matter how disgusting, is tumbled from the windows and balconies of the houses into the streets, and with so little warning, that the ominous *Garde-del'eau* seldom reaches the ears of the passengers till they have been completely soused by their brethren in the upper regions. Now, to remove this abominable nuisance, which offends the eye, as well as the nasal organs of every stranger, none of the inhabitants ever contribute either personal service, or pecuniary aid.

What, therefore, can be expected in a city such as Lisbon, but filth, particularly when it possesses no scavengers, save the rains of heaven which occasionally descend in torrents, and hordes of half-starved dogs, which are confined all day without meat, and in the evening turned adrift to find food as they best can, to satisfy the cravings of hunger. The piteous howlings of those wretched animals, as they crawl along the streets, would wring a tear of sympathy from the heart of a savage; and yet it produces no other effect on that of a Portuguese, than to excite a laugh at the expense of the individual who may have the humanity to commiserate the cruel fate of the poor four-footed scavengers.

A little before our arrival at Lisbon, a party of officers, on landing from England, agreed to dine together previous to retiring to their respective billets. Happy to meet, and sorry to part, they continued to while away the time so pleasantly, that the clock told nine before they were aware that more than seven hours of the last half of the day had passed away. As their quarters lay in different parts of the city, each individual at parting had to act as his own guide. In the group there was one, who, to an amiable, added rather a timorous disposition. This officer had proceeded but a short way on his journey, when the usual cry, *Garde-del'eau*, struck his ears from various quarters at the same time. Being alike ignorant of the language, as of the customs of the Portuguese, he fancied himself surrounded by individuals who intended doing him some bodily harm. Pausing a moment, to see if any friendly hand was near, or any loop-hole by which he could effect his escape, he was glad to observe but few people in the street, and that the greater portion of his enemies were several stories above him.

This discovery led him to try if a good pair of heels would remove him to a place of greater safety. He accordingly started at a pace which would not have disgraced any of the winners of the Great St Leger, but in the hurry, his foot unfortunately struck the corner of a broken flag, when down he tumbled, amidst shouts of *Garde-del'eau*, and the contents of numerous mortars from the batteries above. In a twinkling he started to his feet, and bounded along like a deer, he knew not whither, every now and then receiving the partial contents of an additional mortar. At length worn-out, and observing something resembling a guard-house, he walked in. His appearance, however, being a little cadaverous, the officer of the guard (a Portuguese) shewed at first a disinclination to hold converse with him; but on the British hero making his hair-breadth 'scapes known to his foreign brother, the latter, though he deeply commiserated the fate of his visitor's uniform, yet enjoyed a hearty laugh at his expense, in which not only the guard, but the subject of merriment himself, ultimately joined.

From the immense number of British officers and soldiers that were continually parading the streets of Lisbon, a stranger not knowing the cause, would, on first witnessing the novel spectacle, have been apt enough to exclaim, "What! has Portugal become a colony of Great Britain?" From morning to night the adjutant general, quarter-master general, and town-major's offices were constantly filled with officers and non-commissioned officers. Some reporting their arrival from England—others from the army. Some were applying for a passage to England—others for a route to the army on the frontiers. Some were necessarily and usefully employed in copying extracts from the general orders of the army, regarding the marching of detachments to and from the army,—others were in quest of billets,—and the whole were in close pursuit of the commissary.

Having received our camp equipment, and every other article we required, we embarked in boats at six o'clock on the morning of the 28th of September, and both wind and tide being favourable, the whole disembarked at Valada, forty miles above Lisbon, at two o'clock in the afternoon. This small village stands on the right bank of the Tagus, and at that time almost every house in it bore ample testimony of the friendship which the ruthless invaders entertained for the proprietors.

When Lord Wellington retired from Almeida to the far-famed position of Torres-Vedras, the inhabitants were invited to remove their persons and property to a place of security in rear of the allied army. *Amongst the few* who were deaf to all entreaty, was an elderly man, who, with his wife, and a beautiful daughter, occupied a house in Valada. On Massena's progress being arrested at Torres-Vedras, the whole country was instantly over-run with his legions, in search of shelter from the inclemency of the weather. Valada, as a matter of course, was occupied, and a party quartered on the obstinate old man. They had not been many days in the house before the sparkling eyes of the beautiful Maria had so far captivated the hearts of the foreign inmates, that two of them successively paid their addresses to her, which, however, she rejected with marked disdain.

This so irritated the villains, that from that day they sought the ruin of the family. The eyes of the father being at length opened, he, with the most sincere and poignant grief, beheld for the first time, his daughter standing on the brink of inevitable destruction. But alas, it was too late to retrieve the error into which his obstinacy had betrayed him. An order arriving for the detachment to proceed to Santarem, one of her lovers again made Maria a tender of his hand, which was rejected as before. This was conclusive of her fate. In an instant the innocent girl was dragged from under her father's roof, and he, in an attempt to rescue her from the grasp of the ruffians, received a wound from one of their bayonets, of which he soon after died. Her mother was afterwards maltreated, and the house plundered; in fact nothing was left but the bleeding trunk of the once happy father—the wretched mother—and the once beautiful and happy, but thenceforth the miserable and unhappy Maria. The former then lay hid from the sight of men, but the other two I saw in Valada; the widowed mother mourning over the loss of a beloved husband, and the misfortunes of an only daughter; and poor Maria, deprived of a parent's fostering care, sat brooding over her misfortunes, with misery staring her in the face, being unable to render any assistance to her mother from the barbarous treatment she experienced at the hands of the vile miscreants.

How often since that time have I fancied that I heard this interesting girl repeating, in all the calm utterance of despair.

―――― *O cover not*
His blood, thou earth; nor ye, ye blessed souls
Of heroes, and of murdered innocence,
O! never let your everlasting cries
Cease round the eternal throne, till the Most High,
For all these unexampled wrongs, hath given
Full overflowing vengeance.

Our route led us on the 29th to the once beautiful city of Santarem, but then little better than a heap of ruins. That part of it denominated the New Town, stands on the summit of a considerable eminence, and commands a most extensive and delightful view of the vale of the Tagus, and country on its left bank. The Old Town is built along the eastern base of the hill, close to the bank of the river.

When Marshal Massena retired from before Lord Wellington at Torres-Vedras, he selected the position of Santarem as one admirably adapted for a defensive post, against an assailant moving from the side of Lisbon. The left of the French army rested on Santarem, and the right extended westward a considerable distance. What nature had left unfinished to render the position formidable, Massena endeavoured to accomplish. Field-works of various kinds crowned the eminence, while the face of the hill was studded with innumerable breastworks, from which thousands of Gallic soldiers for some time looked down upon their opponents with the scowl of defiance. From the plain the allied troops could advance by one road only to the assault of the left of the enemy's position, and that was so completely commanded by the works above noticed, that thousands of them would have bit the dust before they could have made the smallest impression in that quarter.

For not attempting to drive Massena from this position, the British general was roundly but most unjustly censured by various classes in England. At first the troops were a little disappointed in not being allowed an opportunity of measuring weapons with the enemy; but before Massena finally relinquished his hold of Santarem, I believe there was not a man in the British army but was convinced that their chief acted on that occasion with his usual prudence and caution, in not attacking the crafty marshal in his almost impregnable post, defended as it was by a numerous and veteran army, and commanded by a general, who, from his numerous successes, had been dubbed by his *Imperial Master*, the "*Child of Fortune.*"

On the 30th we moved forward to Gallegao, fourteen miles from Santarem. During the last invasion of Portugal, some hundreds of the inhabitants of this large village were turned adrift on the world by the French, who subsequently ransacked and pillaged their houses, and then either threw them down, or burned them. But even these barbarous acts did not always satisfy the enemy. No: when it suited their convenience, murder was added to their long catalogue of crimes.

See yonder cottage, once the peaceful seat
Of all the pleasures of the nuptial state.
The sturdy son, the prattling infant there,

And spotless virgin blessed the happy pain
In gentle sleep undreaming ill, they lay;
But, oh! no more to see the cheerful day.

Observing a young man of genteel appearance walking rather hurriedly, and apparently in deep meditation, behind the counter of a very small coffee-shop, we stepped in under pretence of purchasing a cup of that excellent beverage, but, in reality, to obtain information relative to the conduct of the French troops during their sojourn in that town and vicinity. After enumerating various acts of uncommon barbarity, he informed us, that before the French invasion, his father, mother, brother, and two sisters, occupied one of the neatest cottages in Gallegao, where, blessed with a competency, they lived in the full possession of every earthly comfort, which a family united within itself, and possessing the esteem and love of its neighbours, could enjoy. Being the reputed possessor of riches, the enemy naturally conceived that the old man would have a portion of his cash secreted near his person, but how to lay their talons on it, they were for some time at a loss to invent a proper excuse.

At length, however, the happy thought struck them, that as our informant was then in the ranks of the Portuguese army, nothing could be more plausible than a charge of *treason* against his father and brother. Accordingly they were seized, tried, and on a charge of corresponding with the British, condemned and executed. Their once happy abode was plundered and unroofed, and his beloved sisters were dragged from their native village, and compelled to accompany the murderers of their parent and brother. Of their fate he was then totally ignorant; but his opinion was, (and tears trickled down his cheek as he spoke,) that if they had escaped the fate of the former, it was not improbable but that both of them, rather than survive their dishonour, had put a period to their wretched existence.

Next morning we occupied Punhete, once a neat village, but then almost a ruin. It stands on a piece of level ground, at the confluence of the Tagus and Zezere, and is completely surrounded with hills, as barren as they are uninteresting to the eye. To those who have not witnessed the distressing spectacle, no language can properly convey the most distant notion of the destruction of property by the enemy at Punhete, in spring 1811.

Almost every piece of furniture, and every door and window in the village was removed to the French bivouac, in its vicinity, but not one article ever returned; for everything was consigned to the flames, when the enemy took a final leave of Punhete. The village church was not even held sacred by the unhallowed crew. No: from under the sacred roof everything portable was removed, and the interior of the building was then converted into a place of repose for mules and asses. God grant that a similar calamity may never befall the sacred edifices of our own happy isle!

On the 2nd of October, we entered Abrantes. This ancient city crowns the summit of a hill, two sides of which, the south and the east, are extremely steep and difficult of access. The base of the eminence on these sides, and part of the west, is washed by the Tagus, over which there was then a bridge of boats, by which all reinforcements and stores for the army, proceeding from Lisbon by Abrantes, crossed to the left bank, up which, those intended for General Hill's corps, ascended as far as Alpalhao, and turned to the right; and those for the main army, as high as Villa-Velha, where they again crossed the noble stream by a similar conveyance, and then proceeded to their destination by Castello-Branco. The claims of Abrantes to rank high as a military station, will be taken into consideration, along with those of Elvas and Castello-Branco.

Having rested our limbs on the 3rd, we advanced to Gavao on the 4th. Crossing by the bridge before mentioned, our route led us two leagues over a sandy plain, studded with cork trees; and then a similar distance over a heath as barren and uninteresting as any spot I had ever before traversed. In a morning when a little fog is skimming along the surface of the ground, the country around Gavao, when viewed from the spire of the village church, or any other building of equal height, presents a singular appearance—its *natural undulations* giving to the whole surrounding space, as far as the eye can reach, all the appearance of the mountain waves of a watery expanse, when violently agitated by a dreadful gale of wind.

At Alpalhao, on the 5th, the people complained bitterly of their poverty; but when they found that we required nothing from them, they praised the English and cursed the French, as roundly as the greatest enemy of the latter could have wished.

Early on the following morning we quitted Alpalhao, and moved forward to Portalegre, then the headquarters of General Hill, as well as of our first battalion. Our march was a very dreary one; but the warm reception which we met with from our friends, who on our arrival hastened to welcome us to share their dangers and their glory, soon banished all traces of it from our remembrance.

On the breaking up of the allied army from its encampment in the vicinity of Estremoz, on the 1st of August, the main body under Lord Wellington, proceeded towards Almeida, and the remaining portion of it was formed into a corps of observation, which, at the date of our arrival at headquarters, was composed of the following brigades of artillery, cavalry, and infantry, under the command of Lieutenant-General Rowland Hill.

Allied Artillery.
Three Brigades, British and Portuguese.

Allied Cavalry.
Commanded by Lieutenant General Sir William Erskine.

British Brigade.—Major-General Long.
The 9th and 13th British Light Dragoons, and 2nd Hussars King's German Legion.

Portuguese Brigade.—Colonel Campbell.
The 4th and 10th Light Dragoons.

2nd Division, Allied Infantry.
Under the temporary command of Major-General Howard.

1st British Brigade.—Major-General Howard.
The 1st Battalions of the 50th, 71st, and 92nd Regiments, and one company 5th Rifle Battalion 60th Regiment.

2nd Brigade—Colonel Byng.
The 1st Battalions of the 3rd and 57th, and 2nd Battalions of the 31st and 66th Regiments.

3rd Brigade.—Colonel Wilson.
The 1st Battalion 28th, and 2nd Battalions of the 34th and 39th Regiments.

4th, or Portuguese Brigade.—Colonel Ashworth.
The 6th and 18th Regiments of the Line, and 6th Caçadores.

General Hamilton's Division of Portuguese Infantry.

1st Brigade.—Brigadier-General Campbell.
The 2nd and 14th Regiments of the Line.

2nd Brigade.—Brigadier-General De Costa.
The 4th and 10th Regiments of the Line.

Arroyo-del-Molinos

General Morillo having advanced from the frontiers of Portugal, towards Caceres in Spanish Estremadura, for the double purpose of procuring recruits, and supplies for the 5th Spanish Army under his command;—the Count D'Erlon, on the first intelligence of these movements reaching him, instantly detached General Gerard with a division of the 5th French corps, and a considerable body of cavalry, from Merida, to arrest his progress. The belligerents came in sight of each other a short distance from Caceres, but no serious collision took place, for Morillo's force being far inferior to Gerard's, both in point of numbers and discipline, the former conceived it prudent to withdraw his troops towards Malpartida, and subsequently to Arroyo-del-Puerco and Aleseda.

Oil these facts being communicated to Lord Wellington, he instantly transmitted instructions to General Hill to advance and drive the enemy behind the Guadiana. General Hill accordingly broke up from his cantonments at Portalegre on the 22nd of October, and with a portion of his troops moved towards the frontier. Two leagues from Portalegre, we passed Allegrete, the last Portuguese town in this direction, and three leagues farther we arrived at Codeceira, the first Spanish village, where, under torrents of rain we bivouacked. The whole of the officers being in light marching order, many of them were but ill prepared for such a visitation. A few, who were really very slenderly covered, formed a circle round a blazing fire, and each with his head resting on the legs of the friend immediately before him, they endeavoured to make themselves as comfortable as men whose bodies are two-third parts frozen, and one-third part roasted, can expect to be.

Next morning we advanced to Albuquerque, an ancient city, built on the northern slope of the Sierra-de-Montanches. On a rock, a little above the town, stands a castle, which, from its antiquated appearance, must, I should imagine, have braved the buffeting of the pitiless storm, from a period anterior to the introduction of gun-powder. Its situation is commanding, and could a full supply of good water be introduced within its walls, it might become a useful military station.

Our brigade, and three pieces of Portuguese artillery, moved forward to Cantallana on the 24th, and on the following forenoon, a league farther to Aleseda, where we found the Third Brigade, other three pieces of artillery, and some Spanish cavalry, commanded by Colonel Downie. The road between Cantallana and Aleseda, was so miserably bad, that the guns had to be removed from their carriages, and carried up a considerable acclivity by a party of our brigade.

On arriving at Aleseda, we were ordered to cook with all expedition. This we subsequently found to be rather an ominous order, being generally the precursor of a long march, or a sharp battle; and not unfrequently of both. At this time, the bullocks on which we were to dine, were running and jumping around us, as free as the air of heaven, but in less than an hour, they were amusing us with more interesting leaps in our camp-kettles. The soup, just removed from the fire, having been placed before us, at the same time that the bugle called us to arms, we were compelled by dire necessity to despatch it into the regions of the stomach, in a state little colder than boiling lead.

"This is comfortable employment for a cold day," said I to a friend near me, as we gulped down the boiling liquid.

"True, but don't you think," said he, "that the comfort would be greatly enhanced, if we could lift up the veil which hides the future from our view."

"Quite the reverse, my friend," replied I, "much wiser and better for the human race, has it been ordered by an all-wise and over-ruling Providence—who—

From all creatures hides the book of fate,
All but the page prescribed their present state;
From brutes what men, from men what spirits know:
Or who would suffer being here below?
The lamb, the riot, dooms to bleed today,
Had he thy reason, would he skip and play?
Oh, blindness to the future! kindly given,
That each may fill the circle marked by heaven.

On leaving Aleseda, about four o'clock, p. m. the evening was rather mild; but as the sun dropped behind the western curtain, the clouds began to lower, and soon after, the sluices of the heavens were opened, and with great violence poured their fury on our heads, as we groped our way towards Malpartida. Marching under the cloud of night, even in the finest summer weather, is a most unpleasant operation. How much more unpleasant, therefore, must it be to a poor soldier in a dark stormy night, on a road covered to the depth of several inches with mud and water, and a surface so uneven, that every twenty or thirty yards the foot either sinks deep into a rut, or comes bump upon a stone, throws the owner completely off his balance, and precipitates him headlong into the puddle. Such were the pleasures we enjoyed on our trip from Alesada to Malpartida, which occupied the whole of the night. So pale and worn-out were some of the men at dawn, on the 26th, that had the enemy been at a greater distance, not a few of them would have laid themselves down, and waited the coming of the morning sun to guide them on their cheerless course.

The enemy having given us the slip, by retiring from Malpartida before daybreak, the German hussars were sent in pursuit of the fugitives, who retired to Caceres, and subsequently to Torra-Mocha. There being no prospect of bringing the French to action, General Hill ordered us under cover in Malpartida. Early on the 27th, we resumed the offensive, and finding that the enemy had retired from Torra-Mocha to Arroyo-del-Molinos, we marched first to Aldea-del-Cano, then to Casa-de-Don-Antonio, and subsequently a forced march to Alcuesca, three miles from Arroyo-del-Molinos.

Fully resolved to attack the enemy on the following morning, all the troops, save the 71st, were placed in bivouac, in rear of the village, and completely out of the enemy's view. No fires were permitted; and the 71st regiment which occupied the town of Alcuesca, placed piquets all around the village, to intercept any spy, or disaffected person that might attempt to carry to Gerard any intelligence of our movements. About six in the evening the rain again descended on our heads in perfect torrents, and continued with unabated violence throughout the whole of the ensuing night. On being desired to make themselves as comfortable as they could, without the aid of fires, the troops, without a murmur, consigned themselves to rest, and bore their allotted portion of misery like men and soldiers.

At two o'clock in the morning of the 28th, the sergeants went round their respective companies, and in a whisper bade their men prepare for action; the utmost silence being indispensably necessary to ensure the success which our general anticipated. A few minutes were sufficient to put the column in motion, and a few more to shew us the enemy's fires, at the appearance of which our poor fellows were quite overjoyed, being to them a sure indication that the birds had not flown. Although the distance between the belligerents was little more than three miles, yet from the broken state of the road, the darkness of the morning, and the inclemency of the weather, we were fully four hours in traversing that space. The whole moved in one column, right in front, until we arrived within half-a-mile of Arroyo-del-Molinos, when the various battalions closed up, and under cover of a little eminence, were formed into the following columns of attack:—

The left column, commanded by Lieutenant-Colonel Stewart, 50th Regiment, was composed of the 1st brigade, 50th, 71st, and 92nd Regiments, one company 60th, and three field-pieces; and the right column, led by Major-General Howard, consisted of the 28th, 34th, and 39th regiments, one company 60th, 6th Regiment of Portuguese Infantry of the line, 6th Portuguese Caçadores, two field-pieces and a howitzer. The centre was formed of the 9th and 13th Light Dragoons, 2nd German Hussars, and the Conde-de-Penne Villamur' Spanish cavalry, and was commanded by Sir William Erskine.

The formation being completed, the columns advanced in the following order:—The 71st and 92nd Regiments, and 60th Rifle Company, moved direct upon the village, at quarter-distance, and the 50th in close column, with the artillery a little in rear as a reserve. The right column, having the 39th Regiment as a reserve, moved to the right, crossed the plain to the right of the town, in order to cut off the enemy's retreat by any of the roads leading from Arroyo-del-Molinos to Truxillo, Medellin, or Merida, The centre column moved between the other two, and was kept in readiness to act wherever its services might be required. General Morillo, with the Spanish infantry, supported the left column.

The 71st and 92nd Regiments entered the village at a quick pace, and, at the point of the bayonet, soon cleared it of the enemy, who were quite unprepared for such an unceremonious visit. One brigade of the French infantry had unfortunately marched from Arroyo to Medellin previous to our arrival, and the others were filing out of the village for a similar purpose, when the British huzza fell on their ears, and arrested their progress. Finding it totally impossible to escape without giving battle, Gerard faced to the right-about, and made the best disposition in his power for a determined resistance. The infantry he formed into two squares, on the roads leading to Merida and Medellin. The right square was posted not more than one hundred yards from the village,—the other was at a greater distance, and had its left flank protected by their cavalry.

On arriving at the eastern extremity of the principal street, the 71st moved to their left—lined some of the village garden walls, and peppered their antagonists in very good style. The 92nd Regiment following close on the heels of their companions, filed to the right, formed line, prepared to charge, but were not permitted to fire a single shot. This was extremely galling to the soldiers, who saw their officers and comrades falling around them without daring to retaliate upon the enemy. This was no doubt an unpleasant situation to be placed in, but knowing that the success of an enterprise frequently depends on the manner in which orders of this description are attended to, the Highlanders, with a praiseworthy forbearance, resisted every temptation to commit a breach of their orders, and with a patience not very peculiar to their countrymen, waited the arrival of the decisive moment.

During the time occupied by the 92nd Regiment in completing their new formation, the three pieces of artillery were brought forward, and on being posted on our right, fired with terrible effect on the enemy's masses, carrying death into their thickest ranks. In a few minutes the French troops appeared extremely uncomfortable, and in a few more something like a wavering in their squares was observable. The moment so anxiously looked for having now arrived, the Highlanders moved forward to the charge, but the French declined the honour intended for them, wheeled to the right-about, and with rather a hasty step retired towards a steep hill in their rear, over which their general fancied he should be able to conduct them to more comfortable quarters.

Pending these operations against the enemy's right. General Howard manoeuvred round their left, and after cutting off their retreat upon Merida and Medellin, endeavoured to interpose his whole force between the enemy and the mountain in their rear. Our cavalry were also very actively employed. On perceiving it to be General Gerard's intention to gain the rock with his mixed force, they advanced, cut off the French cavalry from their infantry, charged them repeatedly, routed them, and captured all their artillery. These movements reduced the French general to the choice of two very bad alternatives—unconditional surrender, or a hazardous flight across the mountains. Giving a preference to the latter, he retired upon the most inaccessible point of the hill, which his troops ascended, and then fired down upon us from behind the rocks, with which the whole face of it was thickly covered.

To prevent the enemy from reaping all the advantages which he anticipated from this movement, General Howard pushed them closely with the 28th and 34th Regiments, and detached the 39th, and Colonel Ashworth's Portuguese, round the eastern corner of the mountain, to charge the fugitives in flank. The left column also kept close to the enemy on their retreat; and the Spaniards prepared to ascend the hill considerably to our left, to assist in the capture of the flying host. By these various movements, the latter became so sensible of their own inability to continue the conflict, but at a very unnecessary sacrifice of human life, that after throwing away their arms, or rendering them useless, they attempted to escape from our toils; but the great proportion seeing that to be impossible, a white flag was at length hoisted on the point of a sword, in token of submission. The remainder continuing their retrograde movement across the mountain, and the British troops being much in want of repose. General Hill gave over the pursuit of the fugitives to General Morillo, who followed them twenty miles—killed a number, and made many prisoners.

Our loss in this admirably conducted affair, was extremely trifling, compared with that of the enemy. We had only seven killed, fifty-seven wounded, and one officer, Lieutenant Strenuwitz, *aide-de-camp* to Sir William Erskine, missing.—That of the French, consisted of one general (Brun), Colonel the prince D'Aremberg, two lieutenant-colonels, an *aide-de-camp* of General Gerard's, thirty other officers, and from thirteen to fourteen hundred non-commissioned officers and soldiers prisoners. The whole of their artillery, money, baggage, and provisions, also fell into our hands. Their loss in killed must have been severe, for besides those who fell in action, Morillo found upwards of *six hundred dead* in the woods and mountains, when in pursuit of the remains of this little army, which in the action and pursuit, was reduced from 3100 to 300, who with their wounded chief, effected their escape.

The 18th Regiment of Portuguese Infantry, and Brigadier-General Campbell's brigade of Portuguese infantry, having joined us at the close of the action, these corps, together with General Long's brigade of cavalry, and the 50th, 71st, and 92nd Regiments of British Infantry, quitted the field of battle, immediately after the prisoners, &c. were collected, and moved forward to St Pedro, two leagues from Arroyo-del-Molinos.

We had not been long in camp, before a party of twenty-three

French dragoons were observed scampering across the plain in our front, in the direction of Medellin. As no time was to be lost, one of our cavalry piquets, consisting of seventeen men, dashed across the plain to intercept them. In a few minutes the two parties stood in the presence of each other, and without much ceremony, proceeded to *business*. The action, however, was of short duration, for the enemy, after a feebler resistance than was anticipated, agreed to accompany our dragoons into camp, where they were received with three hearty cheers. Both parties being in full view the whole time, the scene was altogether extremely interesting.

At three o'clock in the morning of the 29th, we quitted our bivouac at St Pedro, and after a march of fifteen hours, under torrents of rain, entered Merida, wet, weary, and hungry. The following day being one of rest, all the horses, mules, and asses, captured on the 28th, were sold by auction in the square of Merida, the produce of which, together with the money found in Gerard's military chest, was ordered to be divided at a subsequent period amongst the troops actually engaged on that day.

Our mission into Estremadura being ended, the whole of the troops in Merida, retired on the 31st to Montejo, and on the 1st of November, to Campo Major. The distance being fully seven leagues, we marched two hours before daybreak, and at twelve o'clock, halted to refresh the soldiers. Having a few minutes before crossed a deep, rapid, narrow river, which struck some of our men a little under the armpits, our situation at the time was not very comfortable. However, a two hours vest, before a rousing fire, aided by a glass of grog, and the rays of a powerful sun, soon banished all traces of our ducking. In high spirits, therefore, we quitted our temporary bivouac.

But we had not proceeded above four hundred yards, before another river, broader, deeper, and more rapid than the other, crossed our path, and again drenched us to the neck. How we came to halt in such a position, none could form any notion; but all were agreed, that however amusing the spectacle of a few thousand men standing in water to the neck may be to members of the quarter-master general's department, those individuals must be told that mistakes such as this cannot be tolerated, for to the weary, and but too often heated pedestrians, duckings such as those just mentioned, are the prolific sources of almost every disease, which on service, hurries the young soldier into a premature grave.

We remained in Campo-Major on the 2nd of November, and

on the 3rd moved to Arronches, an old fortress, the walls of which seemed tottering to their base. Resuming our retrograde movement next morning, we re-entered Portalegre about one o'clock, amid the loud acclamations of a grateful and delighted populace. Satisfied that the spontaneous and grateful effusions of the multitude on this occasion, flowed from hearts untainted with hypocrisy, we received them as a people's thanks—the noblest reward a soldier can receive.

Thus terminated our memorable trip into Spain, the success attending which very far exceeded the expectations, either of the noble individual who planned it, or the gallant and truly amiable general who carried the plan into execution. And it is but justice to the soldiers to state, that by a praiseworthy exercise of those military qualities—patience, firmness, and valour, in a manner peculiarly their own, their general was enabled to surmount every obstacle which attempted to arrest his progress.

Anecdotes of the Battle

If General Gerard required evidence to convince him that it is easier to prevent a surprise, than to banish the effects which are generally produced by this worst of all military misfortunes, the issue of the conflict on the 28th of October must have furnished him with proof of the most ample description. Prolific as the page of history is in examples of surprises of a similar nature, yet I doubt much whether it affords one where the officer surprised, reposed in a more criminal security than General Gerard did on the above occasion. When first informed that the British troops were in motion, and advancing upon the town in order of battle, the French chief who was then in bed, raised himself on his elbow, and said to his informant, "Pooh, pooh, the English troops will not march in such a morning as this!" and then threw himself into his former position.

Almost the greatest military blunder which any officer can commit, is that of allowing himself to be surprised. When a general loses a battle, his honour and reputation remain unsullied, provided he has discharged the duties of his office with fidelity and zeal. But the very reverse befalls that general, who through carelessness, or a gross dereliction of the duties confided to him, permits himself to be surprised and beaten. Any general may have the laurel torn from his brow, however conspicuous his military talents may be; but a shameful defeat is rarely the reward of that individual, who, as far as his means will permit, provides against every contingency; who adopts every precaution in his power to prevent a surprise; and who never for a moment leaves anything to chance, lest fortune, if trusted too far, may prove faithless; and, as in the case of General Gerard at Arroyo-del-Molinos, entail on himself and followers, defeat, and an overwhelming load of disgrace.

The military annals of the world exhibits to our view a long list of commanders, who by forming too high an opinion of their personal military qualifications, and spurning the advice of generals of inferior rank, have placed themselves and followers in situations of imminent peril. In this list, I fear we must insert the name of General Gerard. At all events, his conduct at Arroyo-del-Molinos should serve as a beacon to warn all officers of the dangers to be apprehended from the smallest neglect of duty, from whatever cause it may arise, and also to convince them of the folly of rejecting the advice of an experienced or talented friend, simply because he may be junior in rank to themselves.

The necessity of British troops being instructed in every description of field and camp duty, previous to quitting their native shore, was never more clearly developed than in our bivouac at Codeceira on the 22nd of October. Our arms were no sooner piled, than the old stagers flew like lightning through the woods in search of comforts. But our poor *Johnny Raws*, as all young soldiers were denominated, instead of imitating their brethren in their laudable vocation, formed themselves into little groups, and seated on their knapsacks, sat shivering in expectation that fire, water, and beef would be provided them without any personal trouble. The fruits of this gross ignorance of camp duty were soon obvious. In two hours the experienced soldiers were called to dinner—the young ones had not then placed their camp-kettles on the fire.

It would be an act of gross injustice, however, to throw the smallest blame on the shoulders of those young men, for the ignorance exhibited by them on that occasion. Totally uninstructed in field-cookery, or any other portion of camp duty, what else could be expected of them? But, should the British soldiers be longer permitted to embark for a foreign clime in this state of ignorance? Should they not rather be marched regularly as the state of the weather will permit, to a convenient piece of ground in the vicinity of their cantonments, then encamp, and after being instructed in every description of camp duty which they can be called upon to perform in the face of an enemy, return to their quarters in the evening. Some such plan as this is indispensably necessary, for it is principally owing to their total ignorance in the mode of cooking in the fields, and sheltering themselves from the surly attacks of the midnight hurricane, that so many of our best and bravest spirits are hurried into hospital in the early stages of a first campaign. Some individuals would, no doubt, grumble and growl like bears at the new duty, but these would always be few in number; for there are but few officers or soldiers who would not willingly exchange a little inconvenience at home, for health and some little comfort when roughing it at a distance from their native land.

On crossing an extensive plain between Malpartida and Aldea-del-Cano on the 27th of October, the troops were highly entertained by the mounted officers of the corps, the latter having accidentally started a hare, all the greyhounds belonging to the corps, were instantly put in requisition to run down poor puss. The little, timid, short-legged elf, ran hard for existence, but notwithstanding all its arts and stratagems, it at length fell under the snouts of its numerous pursuers. Perceiving that the soldiers were highly delighted with the sport, the officers set about coursing in earnest, and continued to amuse their companions, till they arrived at the extremity of the plain.

Trifling as this little piece of attention may appear, it produced a much greater effect on the spirits of the men, than the most sanguine promoter of the sport anticipated. Time was so wonderfully beguiled, that on the arrival of the column at Alcuesca, many of the men conceived that they had not marched above half the distance they had really done. Should not this tend to convince us that much good may at times be effected by the officers finding harmless amusements for the soldiers under their command?

The 34th French Infantry having preceded their commandant to the field of honour at Arroyo, the latter who was still in his quarters when we passed through the town, mounted his charger soon after, and with his powerful arm raised for mischief, galloped along one of the principal streets, resolved to rejoin it, or perish in the attempt. Colonel Cadogan, 71st Regiment, happening to be in the same street, attempted to stop him, but in making a cut at the head of his opponent, Cadogan completely neglected to guard his own, which the former perceiving, returned the favour of his antagonist with such effect, that, but for the tough materials surmounting it, the head of Cadogan would have been severed in two. The gallant Frenchman, however, was made prisoner, and having on various occasions shewn a great deal of disinterested kindness to British officers who had had the misfortune to be made prisoners, the same marked attention was shewn to him at Portalegre.

As a more memorable reward for his humanity towards our countrymen, he, soon after his arrival in England, received permission to return to the bosom of his family in France. Were all officers to act a similar part to those who fall into their hands, the horrors of war would be considerably mitigated, and much of that ferocity which but too frequently characterizes the actions of men in the field of strife, would be altogether unknown. The numerous escapes which soldiers have had from instant death in the field of battle, would, if collected and published, form a most interesting volume. Buttons, pen-knives, stocks, pencil-cases, keys, watches, pocket-combs, sword-handles, and pieces of old paper, would be found recorded as instruments made use of by Divine Providence to prolong the lives of thousands of them. Amongst those whose lives have been thus preserved by the kind interposition of the Divine Being, I may name Colonel Cameron of the 92nd Regiment.

The captain of the grenadier company of his regiment having been wounded early in the action, the senior lieutenant, on assuming the command of it, made a false movement, on perceiving which, the Colonel greatly irritated, repeated his former orders in a voice of thunder, and as was his usual custom when displeased, he struck his left breast with his right hand, which then grasped the hilt of his sword. The last syllable of his orders had just been delivered, and his right hand had scarcely touched his breast, when a bullet, dispatched by one of the enemy's riflemen, struck the colonel on the first joint of the middle finger, shattered the bone, passed through the handle of the sabre, and then struck the breast so violently, that he relinquished the command of the battalion to Major Mitchell, in the full conviction that the ball had passed into his body.

On being undeceived, however, the gallant colonel instantly rejoined his battalion, and with his middle finger dangling by a small piece of skin only, and the blood flowing from the wound in copious streams, he remained at the head of his Highlanders to the close of the engagement.

A few days previous to the battle of Arroyo-del-Molinos, a private soldier of very weak intellect, named Brown, lost his firelock, but where, or in what manner, he could give no proper account. On the circumstance being reported to the commanding officer, he was so enraged, that he ordered Brown to be taken into the first action without arms. The captain of his company, however, feeling for the situation of the poor fellow, ordered him to fall out when close to the village of Arroyo. But no: the proud spirit of the half-witted creature would not permit him to accept of the kind indulgence tendered him. Brown continued in his proper place in the ranks, during the whole of the engagement.

Seeing some firelocks without owners, Captain D—— desired Brown to arm himself with one of them, but the latter replied, "Colonel Cameron having been pleased. Sir, to order me into action without arms, here I will remain unarmed until the action is over, or poor Jack Brown is sent into another world;" which resolution the heroic simpleton faithfully kept.

Upon the Tagus

The commanding officer conceiving that five of us who had accompanied the detachment from Ireland, properly belonged to the 2nd Battalion, applied to Lord Wellington on our return to Portalegre, for permission to send us home. Leave being granted, we, after mutual expressions of regret, parted with our friends at Portalegre, on the 22nd day of November, and proceeded to Gaffeta. Next day we moved to Gavao, but finding an officer there taking quarters for Colonel O'Callagan, and the First Battalion, 39th Regiment, we departed instantly for Villa Franca, a small village two leagues from Abrantes.

On approaching the residence of the chief magistrate, in order to procure billets, that worthy personage testified his joy at our arrival, by throwing the door in our faces. Enraged at the insult offered us, it is possible we might have adopted a summary mode of obtaining an interview with this truly *amiable personage*, had not a most interesting and ladylike woman introduced herself, and kindly offered us all the shelter of her rural abode for the night. Having previously invoked a blessing upon our *patrona* and her interesting family, for her genuine hospitality, we bade *adieu* on the following morning to the residence of this most excellent woman, and proceeded to Abrantes.

After stowing away our baggage, and putting everything in a fair train for dinner, we strolled about the streets and ramparts of Abrantes for a couple of hours, and then returned to headquarters, where we fancied a nice dish of soup and a beef-steak would greet our return. Our disappointment therefore may be more easily conceived than described, when I state, that instead of such excellent fare greeting our entrance, we were welcomed by two servants with rueful countenances, and each relating, in a plaintive strain, tales of woe, sufficient to melt a heart of adamant. Moving as these were, however, they proved but a poor substitute for dinner. To work, therefore, we went; and partly by threats, and partly by entreaty, procured from the inmates a few culinary articles, which they very *kindly* had refused our servants.

Our disappointments, however, were not yet at an end, for when everything was ready, the amiable couple refused us even a single piece of earthen- ware to put it on. Had *Cruickshank* witnessed the infernal pair standing sentry over their stoneware, the wife at one cupboard, and the husband at the other, he must have acknowledged that a finer subject for his pencil was never afforded, for truly they had more resemblance to the inhabitants of Pandæmonium, than of this world.

After disposing of our baggage animals, we embarked at Abrantes in a small commissariat boat on the 20th, and with a gentle breeze, glided down the surface of the majestic Tagus, till the shades of night made it dangerous to proceed farther. On arriving at a point opposite to the neat, clean village of Chamusca, we hauled our boat ashore, and proceeded to the town, where we were treated with true hospitality. On the following day we dropped down to Valada, where, on the 28th, we embarked in a large boat, and after spending a rather uncomfortable night, landed at daybreak next morning, at the Black Horse Square in Lisbon.

On the 2nd of December, thousands of handbills were circulated in Lisbon, intimating that at one o'clock on the following day, a British officer, accoutred in cork-boots, would walk across the Tagus, from Fort Belem, to the nearest point of land on the opposite shore. Conceiving this to be the project of some hair-brained or unfortunate individual, who, tired of life, was about to solicit the assistance of old Neptune to carry him into another world, I walked down to Belem to view the sports of the day. By eleven o'clock, the various streets leading from the city to Belem, were literally crammed with people of all nations and conditions, from the peer to the peasant, hurrying along to the starting-post, some on foot, and the rest on every kind of conveyance, from the humble donkey, to the carriage-and-four.

Being admitted into Belem Fort, I had a fine view of almost every person, place, and thing in the vicinity. The fort was filled to an overflow with officers and ladies. Belem Castle was crowded with Portuguese nobility and gentry, and the whole space around, and be- tween these two places, was completely covered with carriages, equestrians, and pedestrians. Of the former, I at one time counted four hundred and fifty. The river, for a considerable distance around the spot whence the hero was to start, was covered with hundreds of boats, carrying immense numbers of ladies and gentlemen, a great proportion of the latter wearing the naval and military uniforms of Old England. Six, eight, and even ten dollars were given for the hire of a boat from Lisbon, on this occasion—the ordinary fare of which was only about two shillings.

As the hour of one was announced by the bell of an adjoining clock, the dense masses on shore pushed and jolted each other so much, in order to get a peep at the cork accoutred hero before he set out on his perilous excursion, that the company of Portuguese militia stationed to preserve an opening for the officer to get to the river, kept their ground with great difficulty. Soon after one, a voice announced the hero's approach, but the intimation was premature. Two o'clock was chimed, still he was absent. Three o'clock was at length tolled, but he was not forthcoming. Not long after this, the people, whose appetites were getting a little keen, whetted, no doubt, by the fresh breeze from the Tagus, began to steal slyly away, and by four o'clock the greater proportion of the immense multitude, between forty and fifty thousand, had retired to their respective domiciles, fully satisfied that they had been completely hoaxed, and vowing vengeance on the British officer and his cork-boots.

Having received a letter of recall from my commanding-officer, I parted with my friends of the second battalion on the evening of the 4th, and early next morning embarked at Belem, with a detachment which had just landed from England, and after spending an uncomfortable night, we landed at Valada next day at noon. On the 7th we marched to Santarem—on the 8th to Gallegao—9th to Punhete—the 10th to Abrantes, where we halted the 11th and 12th. On the 13th we proceeded to Gavao—the 14th to Gaffeta—and on the following morning bade our companions in Portalegre all hail.

Almendralejo

The well picked bones of a Christmas goose had scarcely been removed from our mess-table, when an orderly entered, and announced the unwelcome intelligence that our attendance was required at the alarm-post next morning before daybreak,—and worst of all, in light marching order. Had this personage been the bearer of a warrant for the execution of the whole party, our countenances could not have presented a more rueful appearance. We could have wished the evil day put off for twenty-four hours, but as any memorial to that effect would only have been productive of further disappointment, we at once resolved to make a virtue of necessity, and accordingly retired to our respective quarters, and made the necessary preparations for another excursion into Spain.

A little before sunrise on the 26th December, the whole of the troops quartered in Portalegre bade a temporary *adieu* to that friendly town, and in the evening our brigade occupied Codeceira. Next day we moved to Albuquerque, and on the 28th quitted that city for Merida. Two leagues from the former we passed to the right of the Castle of Zagala, beautifully situated on the summit of a hill, from which there is a delightful view of the surrounding country. Three leagues farther we passed through the miserable village of La Rocka, and on the western slope of an eminence, a few hundred yards in front of it, we went into bivouac. General Dombrowski being in possession of Merida, with a mixed force of 1500 men, General Hill requested commanding-officers of corps to have their fires as much under the hill as possible, in order to favour the design he then meditated of taking the Pole napping. The object, though not expressed, was so obvious to everyone, that the order was readily and most cheerfully obeyed.

Next morning at daybreak we quitted our bivouac, and under cover of a dense fog, moved towards the point of attraction. General Hill not being aware that the enemy had, the previous evening, pushed forward a party of 150 cavalry, and 300 infantry, to the village of La Nava, about half-way between our bivouac and Merida, the cavalry, under General Long, were permitted to precede the infantry some miles. This movement turned out unfortunately; for General Long being also in ignorance of the proximity of this body to his own, came bump upon one of the enemy's *videttes* close to La Nava, and made him prisoner, but not till by discharging his carabine he had made his friends aware of the danger that threatened them. The density of the fog at the time rendering it impossible for either party to ascertain the others real numerical strength, the French troops rushed to arms, and in a few minutes were formed ready for action, on an eminence in rear of the village; but the British cavalry halted so long, that before General Long *finally resolved to attack*, the favourable moment had fled—never to return.

The fog soon after this first collision began to disperse, which enabled our advanced guard to get a peep of their opponents. Continuing to clear away. General Long was at length enabled to draw near to the enemy without any fear of being surprised. Although formed in square, the general resolved to attack, and if possible compel them to surrender; but the little band of French infantry received his charge with firmness, and finally beat him off. This success gave the enemy some idea of their own strength, for they instantly commenced a retrograde movement towards Merida, fully convinced, no doubt, that they could effect their escape, should no other opponents take part in the deadly feud. Charge succeeded charge,—but from each our cavalry were forced to retire with loss, and without making the least impression on the little column. These repeated assaults proving ruinous to us, the dragoons were ordered to hang on the flanks of the retiring foe, and take advantage of any opening that might occur, either from the inequality of the ground over which he had to retire, or the fire of two pieces of artillery, which latterly joined in the pursuit.

Accordingly, a gap no sooner appeared, than our cavalry instantly prepared to renew the assault; but before any advantage could be taken of it, some other brave spirits had stepped forward and filled it up. Not one of the enemy's infantry ever once appeared to shrink from the terrible conflict; on the contrary, the whole party, individually and collectively, exhibited throughout the action a degree of coolness and firmness which none but the truly brave can possess in the hour of danger. In the manner now described the parties traversed several miles, till the French being reinforced from Merida, our cavalry gave over the pursuit, more than satisfied that a body of well-disciplined infantry, when under the guidance of an officer of courage, experience, and prudence, has nothing to fear from a body of cavalry of double their numerical strength. In the evening our corps closed up, and bivouacked in front of La Nava, and next morning moved forward to Merida, which the enemy had precipitately evacuated during the night, leaving behind them a considerable quantity of corn.

The conduct of the French captain and his little band at La Nava, affords to all officers and soldiers one of the noblest examples for imitation on record. It is when placed in situations such as this, that the prudence of an officer, and the courage of himself and soldiers, is put to the severest trial. It is on occasions of a similar kind that the soldier who combats for honour and glory, possesses such decided advantages over him whose mercenary propensities lead him to look upon honour and military renown as secondary objects. Bear this then in remembrance, my brave fellow-countrymen, that it is when duty calls you to defend a post against great numerical superiority, that your courage is put to the severest trial; but never forget, that it is also on those occasions you may expect to reap the richest harvest of military renown.

When honour does the soldier call
To some unequal fight,
Resolved to conquer or to fall,
Before his general's sight.
Advanced—the happy hero lives,
Or, if ill-fate denies,
The noble rashness heaven forgives,
And gloriously he dies.

The 31st was a day of rest; but at daybreak on the 1st of .January 1812, the whole corps crossed the Guadiana, and moved towards Almendralejo, where we expected our arrival would be announced by a royal salute from the field artillery of the Count D'Erlon. For a league and a-half our route led us over a very barren heath, then across a large, rich, but partially cultivated plain. As the road between these two places rises with a gentle acclivity for at least five miles from the banks of the river, the leading battalions enjoyed a delightful view of the long and party-coloured columns, as they winded along the heath towards their destination; and I have no doubt but the spectacle would have appeared still more gratifying, could we have banished from our recollection the object of our movement—the destruction of our fellow-creatures. But notwithstanding this, shall I say, almost only drawback to a military life, we enjoyed the interesting scene while it lasted; and when deprived of that, we jogged along the plain as cheerily and merrily, as the fatiguing nature of the march would permit us, till our proximity to the enemy told us to prepare for battle.

It was now one o'clock, and a dense fog so enveloped every surrounding object, that it was quite impossible to discover anything beyond a few paces from where we stood. As this unfavourable state of the atmosphere prevented General Hill from ascertaining whether the enemy held possession of Almendralejo, with *five hundred*, or twice as many thousands; the cavalry, a few pieces of artillery, and the 1st brigade, moved towards the town in order of battle. We had not proceeded far, when the cavalry came into contact with the French piquets, which were instantly attacked and driven in. To be prepared for whatever might occur, the rear brigades quickly moved up on our left, and occupied the stations assigned them.

When the first collision took place, the French troops in Almendralejo were busily engaged in preparing their dinners, and consequently had their thoughts riveted on something more palatable than either gunpowder, bullets, or bayonets. Part of them instantly moved to the support of the piquets, and the remainder retreated to a rising ground in rear of the town. The former, on receiving a few shots from our artillery, wheeled also to the right about, and in a few minutes were alongside of their friends. On the re-union of the two bodies, the whole retired towards a height a considerable distance from the town, over which runs the roads to Villa-Franca, and Fuente-del-Maestre. Our light troops pursued the fugitives closely, skirmishing with them all the way, and we followed, in hopes that the Count would make his appearance at the head of his corps, ready to receive us. In this, however, we were disappointed, for on the fog clearing away, we were sorry to find that he had withdrawn to Zafra with the main body, leaving behind him a strong rearguard only to cover his retreat.

As the fog died away, the rain which began to fall about one o'clock, continued to increase in violence, till about three, when one would actually have supposed that it was falling from buckets. Under these circumstances, night approaching, and there being no chance of bringing the enemy to close quarter, General Hill gave orders for strong piquets to be posted on all the roads around Almendralejo, and the rest of the troops to march into the town—which were obeyed with the greater cheerfulness, that not one of them had a dry jacket or shirt on their backs.

On taking possession of the quarters allotted to another officer and myself, the poor people instantly pointed to the dinners of seven Frenchmen, which in their hurry, they had found it necessary to leave behind in a stew-pan by the fire. Preferring, however, a little tea, to a mess of beef, pork, beans, garlic, and oil, we desired the family to make use of it themselves. Permission was no sooner granted, than the contents of the stew-pan was emptied into a large stone bason, into which, sixty fingers and thumbs were instantly plunged, and then, grasping a piece of the delicious morsel, carried to the mouth, streaming with grease, like as many candles receiving a polishing touch at the hands of their maker. The scene was a laughable one, but very short, for in two or three minutes not a vestige of any part of the dinner was visible.

The enemy shewing a reluctance to retire from Villa-Franca and Fuente-del-Maestre, two detachments were despatched from Almendralejo on the 3rd of January to dislodge them. The one which moved against Villa-Franca, consisted of the 9th and 13th Light Dragoons, two pieces of artillery, the 50th, 71st, and 92nd Regiments, and 60th Rifle Company, and was commanded by Major-General Howard. The other which was under the command of the Honourable Lieutenant-Colonel Abercromby, 28th Regiment, was composed of the 2nd Hussars, King's German Legion, the 4th and 10th Portuguese Cavalry, and 28th British Regiment of Infantry. Both detachments moved from Almendralejo, at twelve o'clock. On a height about half way between the latter place and Villa-Franca, we first obtained a view of the enemy, drawn up on a commanding piece of ground, a few hundred yards from the town, on the road to Los-Santos.

Soon after this, the detachment was formed into two columns, the right composed of the 92nd Regiment, 60th Rifle Company, and one piece of artillery, was placed under Colonel Cameron; and the left, which consisted of the remainder of the detachment, was led by Major-General Howard in person. The left column moved direct upon the town, in order to attack their right flank and centre, while the right was to co-operate with the right battalion of the left column, in its assault on the centre, if it could not throw itself in rear of the left wing. The enemy not only appeared prepared for a visit from us, but for some time gave most unequivocal indications that they would pepper us well before they retired. Indeed so satisfied were we all of this, that we looked forward to a tight little affair with them.

But appearances on this, as on many former occasions, proved deceitful;—for just as we had approached that point from which we intended to apply those means, by which British soldiers are accustomed to remove every obstacle which attempts to arrest their progress, the French chief considering it imprudent to stake the fate of his little corps on the issue of a brush with us, faced about, and walked off towards Los-Santos, pursued by our cavalry.

Lest the enemy should attempt to pay us home in the coin of Arroyo-del-Molinos, piquets composed of whole companies were posted on every road branching from Villa-Franca. The rest were thrown into the town, with orders to remain accoutred, to be ready to turn out at a moment's warning, and to be on the alarm-post two hours before daybreak. From nine o'clock in the evening, till seven o'clock on the following morning, rain and hail fell in such prodigious quantities, and was forced to the earth with such violence by the wind, which blew a perfect hurricane, that all those who were on piquet, joined their battalions in the morning in a most deplorable condition. One of the officers in particular, was to all appearance a perfect maniac. Two hours before daylight, we who were in Villa-Franca proceeded to the alarm-post, where, in ten minutes, we were as thoroughly drenched as if we had just emerged from a six months ablution in the Bay of Biscay. Never before did I witness such a tempest. After a four hours exposure to its utmost fury, we departed from Villa-Franca, and returned to Almendralejo.

The detachment under Colonel Abercromby was more successful in killing and maiming than we were. On the road to Fuente-del-Maestre, a French regiment of cavalry crossed the path of the detachment. On coming in sight of the enemy, the 2nd German Dragoons flew at them like as many bulldogs, and being supported by the Portuguese, the enemy was defeated with the loss of twenty killed and wounded, and thirty-one taken prisoners. Our loss was trifling. This detachment also rejoined the main body on the 4th, and the whole retraced their steps to Merida on the following day.

None but those who were present can have any idea of the fatigue which the soldiers endured from the 1st to 5th January, from the wretched state of the roads from Merida to Villa-Franca. On returning to Merida, they had more the appearance of troops that had been six months under canvass, than men returning to cantonments after a ten day's campaign. On the marches of the 1st, 3rd, 4th and 5th, a great many of the soldiers sunk deep into clay of such an adhesive quality, that in extricating themselves from its grasp, many of them tore their gaiters to pieces, and some of them actually left their shoes behind them, and trudged along in their stockings.

On these occasions I seldom had less than four pounds of clay at my feet, which fatigued me so much, that on retiring to rest each night, I dropped asleep without the aid of any stimulant. Such then being my situation, who had neither musket, knapsack, canteen, or haversack to carry, what must the soldiers have suffered who had to march encumbered with all these, weighing altogether nearly three stone ?

To those who are eternally croaking about the half- pay and pensions of those officers, non-commissioned officers and privates, who served in the late war, I wish no greater punishment than to be made to serve but one short campaign in a country where hardships and dangers, similar to those the British troops encountered in Spain, may stare them in the face at every step, and where their only comforts, when summed up, may, as in the Peninsula, consist of a daily allowance of one pound of tough beef, and a similar quantity of hard biscuit; being well convinced that on their return to their native land, they will have tasted so freely of the sweets of a soldier's life, when engaged in the active operations of the field, that they will be prepared to convert their hoarse murmurs of disapprobation of the half-pay and pension-list, into a sweet-sounding and rapturous applause.

In the suite of General Hill, on the 1st of January, moved the Marquis of Alemeida, a Spanish nobleman, between fifty and sixty years of age. Having suffered severely from French rapacity, the marquis, as may be supposed, was one of their bitterest enemies. Being a warm admirer of the British character, he not only accompanied us in all our wanderings, but laid aside his *native habit*, and assumed the *scarlet*, in humble imitation of his friend, our worthy General. In addition to a long scarlet coat, the marquis generally wore a cocked- hat, always decorated with one, sometimes with two, and not unfrequently with *three* long red and white feathers dangling to his shoulders, in as many different directions. His appearance altogether was rather odd, but the singularity of his costume soon ceased to attract notice, and in a little time he became a considerable favourite with all classes.

On arriving in front of the enemy's piquets, the marquis had no idea that he was so close upon the enemy, until the unexpected intelligence was announced to him by one—two—three from our artillery, a few yards in front. Neither the worthy nobleman or his horse being prepared to accede to this mode of conversing with the plunderers of his estates, the former stared, and the latter reared and plunged, as if anxious to get quit of its burden, fancying, no doubt, that the marquis was the sole cause of his being in such noisy company. On the third gun being fired, the marquis, with a countenance which at once denoted the fervour of his prayer, exclaimed,—"Oh, Jesus, Maria, Jose!" and then casting a glance towards those around him, as much as to say, "I am off," put spurs to his willing nag, which being as anxious to get out of the scrape as its master, flew like lightning in the direction which it was supposed the marquis wished him, and in a twinkling both were lost to our view in the fog.

A private soldier of the 28th Regiment having sipped rather freely of the juice of the grape, previous to our departure from Almendralejo on the 5th of January, fell out of the ranks unperceived, laid himself down to banish all traces of the copious draught, and enjoyed his nap so comfortably, that night's sable shroud had shut every earthly object from the view of man before he awoke. Alone, enveloped in darkness, and in a part of the country totally uninhabited, the poor lad frequently fancied during the stillness of the night, that he saw his name as a deserter to the enemy, handed in to the adjutant-general—the members of the court-martial assembling to try him—the sentence of death passed, and the provost-marshal at the head of his party, ready to carry the sentence into execution. With such thoughts as these darting across his mind, the victim of dissipation rose from his cold and cheerless couch at dawn, on the 6th, and bended his steps towards Merida. Afraid to join his corps, however, the *bragge slasher* proceeded to a small village about three miles from headquarters on the opposite bank of the Guadiana, in hopes that some humane individual would intercede for him at headquarters.

Receiving information soon after his arrival that there were two French soldiers concealed in the village, the worshipper of Bacchus proceeded with a few of the natives to their residence, and after securing them, and fastening their hands, he marched them off in triumph for Merida. Strolling on the bridge with a few friends, when the trio were first observed, and considering it rather an odd circumstance to see a British soldier marching two Frenchmen as prisoners from the left bank of the Guadiana, where there were no British soldiers then quartered, we inquired at the worthy Hibernian where he became possessed of the friends in his company.

Shewing some disinclination to satisfy our curiosity, we repeated our query in a more peremptory manner. We had scarcely done so, however, when we perceived the poor man struggling hard to give utterance to his inward thoughts, but notwithstanding his utmost exertions, he could not utter a syllable, till his heart was relieved by a few pearly drops trickling over his weather-beaten cheeks. On these drying up, the repentant soldier related to us the foregoing particulars, and then with a palpitating heart, (the vision of the previous night being still before his eyes,) he moved into town with his prisoners. He was of course placed in confinement, and but for this singular adventure, would have paid dearly for his libations to Bacchus at Almendralejo.

If the various members of the British army would reflect for a moment on the consequences; which but too generally follow in the train of dissipation, before seating themselves to taste the pleasing, but intoxicating beverage, numerous crimes which now stain the pages of the character-books of every regiment in the service, would never be heard of. The conduct of the Macedonian conqueror on various occasions, shews us to what a degrading condition this most detestable vice some- times reduces the most celebrated individuals, and his death furnishes a memorable example, that dissipation hurries all its votaries to the narrow house, without any regard to age or station in society.

On launching into the world, therefore, all military men should ever be on their guard against the assaults of dissipation, for by dipping deep into the cup of intemperance, they will not only destroy their mental faculties, ruin their pecuniary resources, as well as their constitutions, but may at length be led to commit crimes, for which, like Alexander on the death of Clitus, they may be made to suffer all the horrors which a conscience, burdened with the murder of a fellow-creature, and that individual a bosom friend, can inflict upon them.

Ciudad Rodrigo Falls

Sir Rowland Hill having received an order early in the morning of the 12th of January, to retrace his steps to Portalegre, we marched from Merida at nine o'clock, a. m. and in the afternoon bivouacked behind La-Nava. Next evening we reposed on the bank of a little river, under the castle of Zagala, and on the 14th returned to Albuquerque. We retired to Alegreta on the 16th, and to Portalegre on the 17th. On the succeeding day, the men were busily employed in renewing their stock of clean linen; and on the 10th, we moved to Alpalhao, on our way to the North, to tender Lord Wellington our assistance, should his lordship require it. We reached Niza on the 20th, where, on the following morning, we received the glad tidings of the fall of Ciudad-Rodrigo.

As Marmont, however, still shewed a disposition to give battle, we advanced from Niza to the Tagus on the 25th, crossed that river by a bridge of boats at Villa-Velha, and then moved two leagues farther, and occupied a few miserable villages. Next day we entered Castello-Branco, where we had the pleasure of meeting with the French garrison of Ciudad-Rodrigo, on their way to British transports.

Marmont having withdrawn his army to Salamanca, to wait an opportunity of resuming the offensive, when his chances of success should appear more inviting, we bade *adieu* to Castello-Branco on the 1st of February, and retraced our steps as far as Villa-Velha, where we bivouacked. On the 2nd, we occupied Niza, the 3rd Alpalhao, and re-entered Portalegre the following morning.

The siege of Ciudad-Rodrigo, forms one of the most glorious achievements of the late Peninsular war, and marks in an eminent degree the consummate military talent of the General who brought it to a successful conclusion.

The Marshals Marmont, Soult, and Suchet, viewing the inactivity of the allied army in the latter months of 1811, as something tantamount to an acknowledgement on the part of the British chief, that he was not in a condition to undertake any offensive movement of importance, formed a triple league, by which Marmont appears to have agreed to favour his brother Marshals with a few of his brigades during the winter months, on condition of receiving a *similar* favour from them in the following summer. Marmont's reinforcements quitted the banks of the Tormes and Tagus in the end of November and beginning of December 1811, and moved towards the seat of war in the east and south of Spain. On the approach of their friends, Soult laid siege to Tariffa, and Suchet to Valencia.

Having instantly discovered the deep game which his powerful opponents were playing, Lord Wellington took measures to render it a losing one. With the eye of the eagle, he watched their every movement, but never attempted to derange their plans, or arrest the progress of the brigades, till the latter had arrived at a point so distant, that they could not return to the banks of the Agueda in time to prevent his Lordship carrying into execution his designs upon Ciudad-Rodrigo. But on Marmont's troops arriving at that point, instructions were immediately transmitted to Sir Rowland Hill, to carry into execution the first part of those admirably planned operations, which terminated in the capture of that important military post.

No better proof can be adduced of the ability with which the whole of these operations were planned and executed, than the signal advantages which resulted from them to the common cause. Sir Rowland Hill's grand object in marching upon Merida, being to draw the attention of the enemy to a point far distant from that to be assailed, his movement was attended with all the success which could have been anticipated. The Count D'Erlon no sooner heard of our arrival on the banks of the Guadiana, than he withdrew precipitately from Almendralejo, and for a day or two after, dispatched a courier to Soult every two hours, soliciting immediate assistance, otherwise he would be inevitably devoured by the "*Arroyo-del- Molinos devils,*" who were in close pursuit of him.

Being totally ignorant as to the number of "devils" that were following his friend D'Erlon, Soult, on receiving a few of these applications for succour, transmitted instructions to General Laval, commanding before Tariffa, to raise the siege of that place, and at the expense of all his battering-train, &c. fly with all possible celerity to the count's relief, which instructions were implicitly obeyed. From these proceedings of the enemy in Andalusia, and the subsequent tardy movements of Marmont on the side of Ciudad-Rodrigo, it appears quite evident that the eyes of the two were riveted too long upon our movements, for before they recovered from the panic which our march created amongst them, they thus allowed the British flag proudly to wave over the turrets of Ciudad-Rodrigo.

With all deference to the experience and high military characters of the three marshals, it seems evident that their plan of operations was based on a capital military error,—that of under-rating the strength of their opponent. By adopting this view of Lord Wellington's forces, Marmont denuded himself of the means of affording the necessary protection to that portion of the Spanish territory which his Imperial Master had placed under his charge, and as a natural consequence of such conduct, lost possession of Ciudad-Rodrigo. Soult, on the other hand, committed another error, little inferior in magnitude to the one just mentioned, that of over-rating the force under General Hill.

By doing so, Soult not only raised the siege of Tariffa in a disgraceful manner, but allowed his attention to be completely abstracted from that point towards which the eyes of every Frenchman in the Peninsula should have been directed. These facts, I conceive, shew us the folly of any general either under-rating or over-rating the numbers, courage, or discipline of an opponent's forces. For although I most readily admit that it may be a little difficult at times for a general to banish from his breast the timidity of a Druet, who exaggerated the danger that threatened him, or the temerity of a Marmont, who as much under-rated them; yet I am quite satisfied, that unless a general's experience and knowledge of his duties are such as will enable him to steer clear of timidity on the one hand, and temerity on the other, he should be held incapable of conducting any field operation, if the result is expected to have any influence on the issue of the campaign.

On passing a church one morning during our residence in Portalegre, a melancholy sound struck my ear,—it was a funeral dirge. In a few minutes the mournful procession entered the portal of the church, and being anxious to observe the ceremony, I followed. Around the bier stood an assemblage of priests and friars, who for a considerable time chaunted hymns for the soul of the deceased. At the conclusion of the service I stepped forward to view the coffin, and the piece of inanimate clay it contained. The coffin being open, I beheld a female figure laid out in the usual manner, with her face uncovered, and decorated in a rich muslin dress. The countenance, though then in ruins, exhibited marks of beauty.

The junior priests having removed the corpse to a grave dug for its reception in the body of the church, the bottom of the coffin was withdrawn, when the body descended into its place of repose, in a manner the most revolting I ever witnessed. But distressing to the feelings as was this disgusting mode of depositing the body of a fellow-creature in the silent tomb, the subsequent operations of the sexton was ten times more so. The latter, after sprinkling a little mould over the body, instantly began to pound it with a log of wood, resembling a paviour's mallet, and continued to do so, after every additional layer of earth, till the whole of the latter had been so far replaced in its original position, as to permit the flag which surmounted the grave to be laid on a level with those around it.

During the latter part of the ceremony I remained close to the grave, gazing in silent astonishment at the scene before me. At length, however, I was roused from my reverie, by a most offensive effluvia proceeding from the depository of the deceased. I did not, however, for some time, desert the post which I had assigned to myself; but being at length completely overcome, I made the best of my way towards the door, lest the exertions of the grave-digger might impose on his superiors the disagreeable duty of bearing me to my lodgings.

There being no places of public amusement in Portalegre, time, long before the end of February, had become such a drug on our hands, that the collective wisdom of the garrison was frequently reduced to its last shift to devise a rational mode of employing it. Our walks being few, and miserably bad, and having no books "save the devil's," by scanning the pages of which we could hope to spend a few hours each day with pleasure and advantage, not a few of the idlers paid more visits to a place denominated *hell*, than were at all profitable either for their purses or their morals.

When officers are once induced to give up their time to play, and employ all the powers of their mind to gratify the low, grovelling ambition of acquiring wealth at the expense of those whom they consider their friends and brothers;—when the love of play leads officers to prefer the amusements of the card and billiard-tables, and the rattling of dice, to the faithful discharge of their public and private duties; when they become so wedded to their favourite pursuits, as to consider it a punishment to eat, drink, and sleep, they must be held as totally useless to the service,—to be worthless members of society,—the slaves of vice,—and of that low cunning and chicanery which borders upon villainy.

Accursed game! thy blight is everywhere,

Thy lawless lingers pilfer every purse;
The smart mechanic, and the pamper'd peer,
Endure alike the pressure of thy curse.
When hopeless ruin hath dissolv'd thy snare,
The pistol or the bowl are things of course;
And few can from thy gripping fangs depart
Without a blighted name or broken heart.

Medellin

Lord Wellington having finally resolved upon the siege of Badajoz, the advanced guard approached our cantonments on the 2nd of March. Next day we moved forward to Alegreta, and on the 4th to Albuquerque. Here we remained until every preparation was made which our *generalissimo* considered necessary to ensure the success of the enterprise.

On the 16th of March we bade a final *adieu* to Albuquerque, and with the exception of one Portuguese brigade, the whole of Sir Rowland Hill's corps moved upon Merida. That evening we bivouacked near Zagala, next afternoon at La Nava, and on the 17th we entered Merida.

Sir Rowland Hill finding Merida in possession of a few of the enemy's dragoons, and that the latter were supported by a battalion of infantry, encamped about a mile from the town, on the opposite bank of the Guadiana, gave orders to General Long to cross the river a little below the bridge, with his brigade of cavalry, in order to capture those of the enemy in Merida, and keep the infantry from retreating too quickly, till we could get up to them. On the first alarm, however, the French cavalry fled from Merida, some by the bridge, others by a ford a little above it. The former, by discharging their carabines on the bridge, gave their friends in the wood intimation of their danger. As no time was now to be lost, the 1st brigade, 50th, 71st, and 92nd Regiments, moved towards the town at a trot.

In a few minutes we were on the bridge, and a few more carried us across it. Here we halted a minute, and then renewed the pursuit with renovated strength; but notwithstanding all our efforts, and those of our mounted friends, to bring them to action, the enemy retreated at such a goodly pace, that fast as our brigade ran, the fugitives always continued to run faster. Success at length appearing hopeless, and our men being completely blown, we gave over the pursuit, and retraced our steps to Merida, carrying with us a few prisoners, whose joints being less supple than their more fortunate friends, were obliged to fall behind, and were consequently taken.

Sir Thomas Graham crossed the Guadiana on the 16th, at the head of the right wing of the covering army, consisting of the greater part of the cavalry, the 1st, 6th, and 7th Divisions of Infantry, and then directed his march upon Santa Martha, Zafra, and Llerena. On Sir Thomas' arrival at the latter, the right wing of the covering army rested on the heights on the south of Llerena, and the left on the Guadiana at Don Benito.

Lord Wellington also crossed the Guadiana on the 16th, invested Badajoz the same evening, and broke ground before the fortress on "*St. Patrick's Day*"

At daybreak on the 18th, Sir Rowland Hill's corps crossed the Guadiana at Merida, advanced to Almendralejo, and retraced their steps on the 21st. In the afternoon of the 26th, we again crossed the river, moved up its left bank to La Zarza, and next morning still farther to Quarena. On the 28th, the cavalry, one brigade of artillery, and the 1st Brigade of Infantry, advanced to Medellin and Don Benito. On the march the detachment was formed into two columns, the left consisting of the 92nd Regiment, and two pieces of artillery, moved against Medellin; and the right column, commanded by General Howard, and composed of the cavalry, 30th and 71st Regiments, one company 60th Rifle Corps, and remaining pieces of artillery, against Don Benito. Medellin was occupied about sunset without opposition.

Informed that the enemy had retired from Don Benito, General Howard, on arriving close to the village, dispatched Captain Blacier with his rifles into the town, to see that none of the enemy lurked in it, and to obtain an interview with the chief magistrate regarding quarters. The gallant captain was plodding his way through the streets, thinking on the good things of this world, when all at once his thoughts were riveted on the things of the world to come. Unconscious of their contiguity to the British, a French cavalry patrol had entered the village on a reconnoitring excursion, and like my friend the captain, were thinking of everything but what was before them. Each party was therefore moving along in conscious security, when, on turning the corner of a street, they unexpectedly met.

With eyes looking amazement, they gazed at each other for a few moments, and then proceeded in the usual manner to extricate themselves from the dilemma into which false intelligence had led both parties. A pretty little skirmish ensued, in which the balls of the rifles made a suitable return for the favours showered upon their heads by the Gallic sabres. After a few mortal wounds had been given and received, the enemy, suspecting they had got into the wrong-box, wheeled to the right-about, retired rather precipitately, and left the gallant captain in possession of the well-won honours of the street.

Medellin is built along the base of a *lonely* hill, on the left bank of, and close to the Guadiana. On the summit of the little conical mount, stands a castle, better calculated to repel the assault of a pop-gun, than a twenty-four pounder. On our arrival, we threw a strong piquet into it, which was followed by the whole battalion two hours before day-break next morning. On ascending the eminence, the air was disagreeably cold, but the scene which opened to our view at sunrise, soon I banished past miseries into the shades of forgetfulness.

Twelve miles to the west lay before us the memorable plains and surrounding hills of Arroyo-del-Molinos, where hundreds of Gerard's followers f breathed their farewell sigh on the 28th of October 1811. From the ramparts of Badajoz, the continual rolling of Phillipon's thunder, reminded us every minute that the work of mutual destruction was proceeding with unabated violence. A few miles to the east we had a most commanding and beautiful view of the memorable field of Medellin, where Victor and Cuesta contended for victory in 1810, and where, before the close of that memorable day, victory perched on the standard of Victor, which on that fatal evening soared over the inanimate forms of thousands of warriors, who ever since have soundly slept on the plains of Medellin.

> *There shall they rest—ambition's honour'd fools,*
> *Yes, honour decks the turf that wraps their clay.*
> *Vain sophistry! in these behold the tools—*
> *The broken tools that Tyrants cast away*
> *By myriads, when they dare to pave their way*
> *With human hearts—to what? a dream alone.*
> *Can despots compass aught that hails their sway?*
> *Or call with truth one span of earth their own,*
> *Save that wherein at last they crumble bone by bone.*

The troops in Medellin rejoined their friends in Don Benito on the 29th, and on the 31st, the whole retreated to Quarena. On the 1st of April, we retraced our steps to La Zarza, and next morning to Merida. Sir Thomas Graham being under the necessity of withdrawing his troops from Llerena, retired slowly towards Albuera, where it was generally understood the covering army was to assemble. On the afternoon of the 5th, we again crossed the Guadiana, marched to St Servan, and on the 6th, to a small eminence near the village of Lobon.

Aware that the capture of Badajoz was to be at tempted that night, the most intense anxiety pervaded our encampment, for the issue of the terrific conflict. Throughout every corner of our gloomy bivouac, the opinion of almost every individual seemed to be, that our friends would *not* be able to surmount the numerous obstacles which the besieged had provided to obstruct the passage of the besiegers into the place by the practicable breaches. It was therefore with feelings which I shall not attempt to describe, that we waited the commencement of the struggle in which our companions were about to engage, in order to rescue a suffering people from the iron grasp of a hateful and grinding tyranny.

On the signal being given, the various columns moved forward to the points of attack with extraordinary spirit, but the whole were ultimately beat back with considerable loss. Again they attempted to force a passage into the body of the place, but with no better success. Again and again the intrepid assailants mounted the breaches— renewed the sanguinary conflict with renovated courage, and at these points, maintained the murderous conflict, till the ditches were literally filled with dead, dying and wounded, piled above each other in one undistinguished mass. The scene at length became one of horror; numbers every moment breathed their last, while the heartrending cries of the wounded in the ditches, intimated to their more fortunate companions, that if they were not soon removed from their dreadful situation, death by suffocation would be their inevitable fate.

Appalling as this state of affairs was, yet none seemed inclined to yield till victory should entitle them to decorate their brows with the wreath of the conqueror. All therefore being alike determined to perish rather than yield, it was with no small reluctance that they ultimately obeyed an order of recall to prepare for another and final effort to wrest the place from the enemy. This effort, how- ever, was not required, for General Picton having rather unexpectedly obtained a footing within the castle. General Philippon, the governor, on perceiving the fruits of his own folly, in leaving this part of the fortress without a sufficient body of troops to defend it, retired into Fort St Christoval, and at daybreak on the 7th, surrendered himself and garrison prisoners of war.

The loss of the enemy during the siege, was 1200 killed and wounded, and 4000 prisoners; ours amounted to 3860 British, and 1010 Portuguese killed and wounded.

Early on the 7th, Sir Rowland Hill moved from Lobon, to a field on the left bank of the Albuera, a short distance from Talavera la-Real. Marshal Marmont having dispatched a small body of infantry to the assistance of his friend Soult, Lord Wellington gave orders for two arches of the beautiful bridge of Merida to be destroyed, that their junction with the army of Soult might be retarded to the latest possible period.

Marshal Soult who had arrived in the vicinity of Zafra, Los-Santos, &c. on his way to the relief of Badajoz, became perfectly frantic when he received the first intelligence of the fall of that important fortress. Being seated at breakfast when the unlooked for and unwelcome intelligence reached him, the gallant Marshal raised his foot, and after wishing all the "*Leopards* at the bottom of the sea," dispatched the breakfast table to the opposite side of the apartment, and made the china, under which it groaned, fly into a thousand pieces.

As soon as this unseemly fit of passion had subsided, Soult gave orders for his followers to wheel to the right-about, and retrace their steps into Andalusia. On being informed of the marshal's intentions, Sir Stapleton Cotton was ordered to harass the enemy's rear with the allied cavalry.

Coming up with a strong body of their dragoons near Villa-Garcia, a sharp conflict ensued, which terminated in the defeat of the French, with a loss of 300 killed, wounded, and prisoners.

On the 10th, the Northern army set out on its return to the banks of the Agueda, to keep Marshal Marmont in order; and we advanced to Almendralejo, to look after Druet,—the Count D'Erlon.

Strolling at a short distance from our bivouac, in company with two friends, on the 6th of April, we perceived a Spanish peasant reposing under the cooling shade of a large tree. After a few preliminary questions, we inquired whence he came, and his business in the vicinity of our camp. To: these interrogatories he unhesitatingly replied, that he was an inhabitant of a mountain village, twenty miles distant, and that his only object was to kill as many Frenchmen as he could, *after*, not *in*, the great battle which he imagined had become inevitable, from the proximity of the army of Soult to ours.

And to prove that such was his intention, he pulled a tremendous knife from his side-pocket, with which he assured us, he sent *eleven Frenchmen* to sleep with their fathers on the morning subsequent to the battle of Albuera. On upbraiding him for his cruelty, and inquiring how he could perpetrate such cold-blooded atrocities, he very coolly replied, that it was the duty of every loyal; Spaniard like himself, to send as many Frenchmen into another world as they could, wherever they might find them, whether in the field of battle, or in a private retreat—whether armed or unarmed—or whether they might be in the enjoyment of health, or writhing under the effects of severe wounds. From this doctrine, we not only most decidedly dissented, but endeavoured to convince him that conduct such as his was highly derogatory to his character as a man; for either revenge or inhumanity towards an enemy, when he can no longer offer resistance, was no less an insult to human nature, than it was contrary to the laws and usages of war. Finding, however, that we could not bring him to coincide with us in opinion, we bade the Albuerian assassin *adieu*, in the fervent hope that we might never again find ourselves near his polluted person.

Having formerly alluded to the battle of Medellin, I now proceed to make a few remarks on the conduct of the Spanish General Cuesta, on that occasion, conceiving that a great proportion of those reverses which subsequently befell the Spanish arms, are to be traced to the unfortunate issue of that engagement.

On retiring behind the Guadiana, Cuesta took up an excellent position between Medellin, and Don Benito, with his right resting on the Guadiana, and his left on an almost inaccessible mountain. In fact, it was so well chosen, that Victor was compelled to use stratagem, before he could with prudence make any attempt to drive his opponent from his stronghold.

Anxious, therefore, to bring Cuesta to action, but yet afraid to do so in his position, Victor, in order to rouse the pride of the haughty *Don*, detached one party after another, close up to his front line, with instructions to use every effort in their power to draw their opponents into the plain. For some time, the Spaniards bore all the insults and degrading epithets gratuitously bestowed on them by the French, with considerable humour, but the same species of abuse and insult being continued day after day, and hour after hour, Cuesta's wrath at length waxed so hot, that he was induced to depart from the defensive system which he had hitherto adopted, and to risk the fate of his army, I may add, his country, on the issue of a general engagement.

Were we called upon to estimate the character of Cuesta as a military leader, by the talents displayed by him on this occasion, I fear that the utmost praise, I should feel myself warranted in bestowing on him, would amount only to this, that had the fate of the day depended on the personal courage of the Spanish chief, *perhaps* the result might have been less disastrous for his country. But unfortunately for Spain, the fortune of the day did not depend on the personal courage of either of the military chiefs, but on courage, aided ' by military talent and experience, tempered with prudence, and guided by a clear and sound judgement, none of which military qualifications Cuesta possessed.

Had the Spanish *generalissimo* taken a proper view of the duties which of necessity devolve upon the commander-in-chief of an army, he never could have permitted this important truth to escape his recollection, that a general who is appointed to command the armies of his country in times of peril, is entrusted not only with the lives and honour of those under his immediate command, but with the lives, honour, liberties, and property of all his fellow-countrymen. Had Cuesta not lost sight of this fact, he never would, for the sake of a little ephemeral praise, have placed in jeopardy the lives of his followers, and the best interests of his country, by attempting to accomplish that which ages yet unborn will look upon as a rash, hazardous, and totally uncalled for military enterprise; for had the attack been delayed but a few days longer, the French soldiery, who frequently can brook no delay, would have compelled their leader to attack his opponent, when Victor's defeat must have been as inevitable as Cuesta's appeared to be on that fatal morning, to almost every person but himself.

Situated as Cuesta was, one of two things appears to me quite evident—he must either have been totally incapable of commanding-in-chief on such an occasion; or he must have grossly betrayed the trust reposed in him by his country, otherwise he never would have yielded up the many and important advantages he possessed, and unnecessarily placed himself on a footing of equality in point of ground with his antagonist—a piece of infatuation not only without a parallel in the history of Spain, but one which might have shaken the pillars of his country to their very foundation. O Spain! Spain! how many thousands of your bravest sons were in those times offered up as sacrifices to the pride, ambition, ignorance, or hateful personal feelings of your generals.

In the early ages of the world, a victory obtained by stratagem, did not confer much honour on the victor, for everything then was attempted! and achieved by force alone. But as men improved in military science, they perceived that there were, occasions, when, by sacrificing the lives of a few of their followers, a less bloody and more complete! victory was obtained, than when they exposed to hazard the lives of every man under their command. They became convinced, that by using stratagem, much time was saved, and many an advantage gained, which open force would never have accomplished. So satisfied were the Spartans of this, that, in order to make their officers endeavour to achieve everything by stratagem, they ordered that every general who obtained an advantage by stratagem, was to be permitted to sacrifice an ox, but those who succeeded by open force, a cock only. This shews us how much that gallant people preferred the wiles of war, to open force, and I trust may induce my military friends to follow their example, being of opinion, that as the performances of the mind are preferable and superior to those of the body, so in exact proportion is stratagem to be preferred to open force.

Fort Napoleon

We remained quietly cantoned in Almendralejo, from the 13th of April to the 11th of May. At daylight, on the 12th, the 13th Light Dragoons, one brigade of artillery, the 28th, 34th, 50th, 71st, and 92nd British Infantry, the 6th and 18th Portuguese Infantry, 6th Caçadores, and two companies 60th Rifle Battalion, moved from Almendralejo for Almarez to break a link or two of the enemy's chain of communication, between the French army under Marmont, and that of the south commanded by Soult. That evening we encamped about a mile from Merida, on the left bank of the Guadiana. The arches of the bridge which were destroyed during the siege of Badajoz, having been temporarily restored, the infantry passed the river by the bridge on the 18th, all the rest of the troops, including the baggage, crossed by a ford above it. In the evening we halted at St Pedro; next morning advanced to Villa-Macia, and on the 15th entered Truxillo.

At eleven o'clock, the same evening, we proceeded to our alarm-post, and soon after moved off towards Almarez. By sunrise, our main body was ensconced in the bosom of a wood, three leagues in advance, so that the enemy neither got a glimpse of our persons or arms. Here we cooked; and those friends who were to lead the storming party, had their limbs pretty well exercised, by running one hundred and one times up ladders placed against the front of an old stone bridge. On hearing one of the party, a jolly ensign, afterwards complain of stiffness of the joints, a friend of his, who overheard him, turned round and said, "Be thankful, my good-fellow, if your *limbs are not suffer to-morrow*; what you have received today, is only in part payment of what you, as a member of the *Forlorn Club*, may expect to receive at daylight tomorrow morning." Being a married man, the joke was not at all well received.

There being three distinct points of attack, the troops were formed into as many columns. The left column consisted of the 28th and 34th

Regiments, and 6th Portuguese Caçadores, and was placed under the command of Lieutenant-General Tilson Chowne, who had a short time before assumed the command of the second division. The centre commanded by Major-General Long, was composed of the 13th Light Dragoons, the 6th and 18th Portuguese Infantry; and the right column led by Major-General Howard, consisted of the 50th, 71st, and 92nd Regiments, and one company 60th Rifles. Each column was provided with scaling ladders.

The works against which the right column moved, consisted of a pontoon bridge, thrown over the Tagus by the French, near the village of Almarez, defended by a *tete-du-pont* on the left bank, rather strongly entrenched. On a height above the latter, the bridge was farther defended by a fort called Napoleon, mounting ten guns; and on the right bank by another fort, named Ragusa, mounting eight guns. Four miles from the bridge, the road from Truxillo runs through the pass of Mirabete, at the highest point of which the enemy had a fort, and so judiciously was it erected, that its guns not only swept the Truxillo road many hundred yards, but flanked the various turnings of the road, which, on the opposite side of the mountain, winds along the face of it in a zigzag manner all the way from the base to the very summit of the long and very steep ascent.

The centre column was ordered to attack this point. On the very summit of a rugged peak, which, from the fort just mentioned, rises several hundred feet, in an almost perpendicular manner, an old convent had, by French ingenuity, been converted into a place of strength, and dignified with the title of "Castle of Mirabete." The guns of this fort were so planted, as to bear upon that part of the road from Truxillo, which was out of range and view of those at the pass; and so great was the altitude of the castle, that it could be seen from points many leagues distant both on the south and the north. To capture this formidable little castle, was the portion of labour allotted to the left column.

Formed in this manner, the whole corps moved from their bivouac in rear of Jaracejo, about eight o'clock in the evening of the 16th, towards the several points of attack. But a body of troops, when marching in the night, frequently meet with obstacles against which no human foresight can provide, particularly when cross roads, or difficult passes intersect, or branch out from the principal line of march. One of those obstacles most unfortunately interposed its baleful influence on this occasion, between the right column and the enemy, and so effectually, that when the hour arrived at which the works were to be assaulted, the column was still five miles from its destination. Under these circumstances, Sir Rowland Hill deemed it prudent to halt the right column on the summit of a bleak ridge called the Lina, which overlooks the vale of the Tagus, and to order the other columns to withdraw from under the guns of Mirabete.

There being no road by which artillery could be transported across this chain of hills, but that in possession of the enemy, Sir Rowland had now the choice of two rather bad alternatives, *viz.* either to carry the works at the pass, and open a passage for his artillery, or attack the bridge and forts without the latter, and carry them by escalade. Giving a preference to the latter, the 17th and 18th were spent in reconnoitring the road leading from our encampment to the bridge, which was little better than a sheep path, and in many parts so narrow, that not more than one man could move along it at a time.

About ten o'clock in the evening of the 18th, the 50th, 71st, and 92nd Regiments, two companies 60th Rifles, and 6th Portuguese Infantry, descended the Lina, and moved towards the banks of the Tagus, with the intention of attacking their opponents a little before daylight, on the following morning. But owing to the darkness of the night, and the narrow and broken state of the foot-path, the sun had appeared, before the rear of the column had closed up, and formed for the attack. This second disappointment caused a temporary depression of our spirits, but on it being made known that Sir Rowland was resolved to attempt the capture of the works, by an immediate assault, the men resumed their usual gaiety.

The circumstances in which the detachment was thus again unfortunately placed, caused Sir Rowland Hill to abandon the original plan of attack, and substitute the following. The detachment was divided into three columns. The 50th, and one wing of the 71st, composed the column destined to attack Fort Napoleon, and was placed under the command of Major-General Howard. The 92nd Regiment, and the remaining wing of the 71st Regiment were ordered to support the former, and to be in readiness to move to the assistance of their friends, or to attack the *tete-du-pont*, and Fort Ragusa, and the 6th Portuguese, and 60th Rifle Company formed the third column, or reserve.

Formed ready for the assault, behind a little height, one hundred and fifty yards from the fort, the 50th, on a given signal, moved from their hiding-place between six and seven o'clock, a.m. on the 19th, and, covered by the 71st Light Infantry, advanced with great firmness to the attack, the enemy all the while pouring on them grape, round-shot, and musketry, in quantities sufficient to gratify the appetite of the most determined fire-eater. On descending into the ditch, some of the ladders were discovered to be too short. This unfortunate obstacle was soon removed by the presence of mind of General Howard, who led the assault, and whose cool and intrepid conduct on the occasion, was the subject of general admiration.

This little check, however, instead of blunting the courage of the assailants, tended rather to increase their ardour in the pursuit of victory. The first that ascended the ladders, met with a warm reception; and not a few of them tumbled from the top of the ladders into the ditch head foremost—some dead, others to die, and the rest to fight some other day. The bravery of the assailants was most conspicuous; and for a little time that of the assailed was not less deserving of praise. But the French officer in charge of the artillery having retired from the fort *without leave* from his commanding officer, the arms of the private soldiers became paralyzed, and after a sharp conflict of *eleven minutes*, the "*Old Dirty Half-Hundred*," and their friends of the *Seventy-First*, fairly established themselves in Fort Napoleon.

Pending these operations, the second column was moved forward in a zigzag manner round every little knoll which afforded them protection from the fire of Fort Ragusa, until they arrived at a point, nearly opposite to the left flank face of Fort Napoleon, when turning to the left, they advanced direct upon the *tete-du-pont* at a quick pace. Perceiving that our object was to cut off their retreat, the enemy, on retiring from Napoleon, rushed towards the bridge in order to escape. But some of their own people having previously cut the bridge, and drawn two or three of the pontoons to the right bank, a great many of them to preserve their liberty, threw themselves into the dark rolling current, where, instead of that inestimable blessing, not a few of them found a watery grave. All the others surrendered at discretion.

The head of the second column had arrived within a few yards of the chasm, before it was discovered that the bridge had been cut. This was rather an awkward situation to be placed in, and one which, but for the panic which seized the governor of Fort Ragusa, might have produced disagreeable consequences. But fortunately the latter, instead of attempting to add a hundred more to our list of killed and wounded, very considerately retired towards Almarez, leaving us at liberty to get out of our dilemma in any manner most convenient for ourselves.

As soon as the enemy had fairly taken to their heels, permission was given to our troops to help themselves to some of the good things which had fallen into our hands. In a few minutes, wine, brandy, and rum, flowed in abundance, while bacon hams, and pieces of pickled pork and beef decorated hundreds of bayonets, many of which were still tarnished with the blood of the enemy. Some of the knowing ones obtained valuable prizes from the officers mess-room, but by far the greater part of the men were amply satisfied with a haversack well stuffed with bread, or a canteen filled to an overflow with some of the heart-moving liquids just mentioned. At the close of this extraordinary scene, the troops were moved back about half-a-mile, and ordered to bivouac.

The attention of the victors was now directed to the fallen brave, who in and around Fort Napoleon lay in considerable numbers. Our loss amounted to 177 killed and wounded, and that of the enemy to 450 killed, wounded, and prisoners. Parties from every regiment were employed during the remainder of the day in removing the wounded, destroying the forts, cannon, bridge, and such stores as we could not carry off. Everything being accomplished to the entire satisfaction of Sir Rowland, we quitted the bloodstained eminence at eight o'clock next morning, and retired, first to the Lina, and thence, the same afternoon, to our former bivouac behind Jaracejo.

On the 21st we re-entered Truxillo, where we halted during the 22nd and 23rd. On the 24th we bivouacked at Villa Macia, and on the 25th retraced our steps to St Pedro. On the following day we retired to a ridge half-way between Medellin and Merida, and on the 27th re-entered the latter place amid the cheers of the populace, and the warm gratulations of those friends who were left to protect that part of the country in our absence.

Soon after the British troops entered Fort Napoleon, a French soldier begged his life from one of the 50th, just as the fatal weapon was on the point of performing its office; the honest Briton at once, and with pleasure, granted the boon of the petitioner. But the gallant fellow had soon but too good cause to repent the generous deed, for on turning round to follow his comrades, his ungrateful and unworthy antagonist endeavoured to bury his bayonet in the breast of his preserver. On perceiving the danger to which he was exposed, the British youth wheeled about, and received the bayonet of the cowardly wretch in his arm. Irritated at such conduct, the former raised his musket, and instantly plunged his bayonet into the body of his dastardly opponent, who, on uttering a few inarticulate sounds, took leave of all earthly things.

When the French colonel commanding in Fort Napoleon perceived that farther resistance was fruitless, he adopted the prudent course of surrendering himself a prisoner of war. Being permitted to retain his sword, the commandant was leaning on his best friend and companion in many hard-fought fields, and ruminating on the mutability of everything below, when, little dreaming that he was so soon to receive a farther confirmation of it in his own person, an officer belonging to the storming party entered the fort, and being equally ignorant of the French language, as of the terms on which the colonel had been permitted to retain his sword, made a lunge at him, which the other being totally unprepared to parry, a mortal wound was the consequence of this extremely thoughtless, rash, and ill-judged act. Lingering in great agony for ten days, the commandant expired, and two days after was buried in the Great Church of Merida with military honours, the whole of the British officers assisting at the ceremony.

Lieutenant Theile, of the German artillery, having been instructed to destroy the enemy's works at Ragusa, his people had the whole mined at an early hour on the 20th. On being informed that everything was ready, Theile proceeded to apply the match to the train. The powder, however, being longer in igniting than he expected, he hastened to the fort to ascertain the cause. But, alas! Theile had scarcely entered the fort when the mine exploded, and carried him into the air.

About an hour after the capture of Fort Napoleon, I observed a private soldier of the 50th Regiment, bending over the lifeless trunk of one of his comrades, and apparently wiping away the tear from his eye. Anxious to ascertain the cause of. his grief, I stepped forward, and diverted his attention from the melancholy scene before him, by inquiring the name of the deceased. Till I spoke, the poor man imagined he was pouring out his grief in secret, for on lifting his head he blushed, and instantly dried up the fountain of tears. In answer to my query, I was informed that the deceased was my informant's brother, and the third of the family who had given their lives for their country. Perceiving that previous to my arrival he had been endeavouring to dig a grave for his brother on the counterscarp, with nothing but his fingers and his bayonet, I, on moving away, kept my eyes upon him for some time, and was not less astonished than delighted to see him succeed in forming a grave sufficiently capacious to contain the mangled remains of his beloved brother.

On re-entering Truxillo from Almarez, we found the inhabitants busily engaged in preparing to treat us to a grand bull-fight, as a small mark of respect and gratitude for the services rendered at Almarez by the British general and his humble followers.

The market-place being the grand arena where the two and the four-legged combatants were to contend for victory, every street leading from the square was barricaded with waggons, carts, ploughs, etc. to prevent the escape of the poor animals. In a house adjoining the square, the bulls were kept in durance, till released in order to appear before those for whose amusement they were to be tormented in every possible manner which the ingenuity of man could invent.

The Spaniards who were to act the most conspicuous parts in this extraordinary drama, entered the theatre of action about seven o'clock, each carrying a pike in his right hand, and a brown cloak in the left. As soon as they had moved to their respective stations, one of the bulls was released from prison. On entering the scene of action the air rang with the loud acclamations of thousands of delighted spectators, while the poor animal, astonished at his reception, surveyed the surrounding multitude with an eye of fury. With that bold and determined frown so characteristic of his species, he first gazed on his tormentors, and then with a wildness in his countenance altogether inexpressible, scampered around the square, bellowing hideously, until he perceived an opening under a waggon, at the lower part of it, when darting towards the port of liberty, he endeavoured to obtain that which is alike dear to bulls as to men The waggon being *crowded* with men and women the whole on the approach of the furious animal were precipitated in various curious and somewhat laughable attitudes, from their elevated station to the same level with the object of their fears.

At this crisis, the Spanish combatants advanced and with a war-whoop equalled in wildness only by that of the savage, pursued their antagonist and probing him in the hip, made him stop short in his victorious career. Turning round to resent this act of cruelty, and seeing five or six men all equally near, he spent a few moments in deliberation, before he selected an antagonist, on whom to wreak his vengeance. Having at length made choice of a tall, dark, powerful opponent, he pursued the latter with such speed, that the female spectators, trembling for the consequences, uttered the most horrific screams imaginable.

The life of the man certainly appeared to be in imminent danger, but at the very moment when his fate seemed to be decided, he made use of the *weapon*, which above almost all others is the best calculated to avert the dreadful collision, I mean the *cloak*. By throwing that at the head of the bull, the latter seldom fails to stop short, conceiving he has his antagonist in his power, and in order not to let the animal get too close to him before he takes this step, the Spaniard always runs, with his cloak at *full arms' length from his body*. Just as the bull had tossed the cloak in the air, one of the Spaniards, from an opposite corner, went unperceived behind the poor brute, probed him in the hip, then made off, hotly pursued by his four-footed antagonist, until stopped by the cloak of the fugitive, and pike of one of his friends before. Thus the fight continued till the animal could neither shake his head nor wag a foot. On recovering a little, he was removed to make room for another, which afforded no sport.

The third, on making his appearance, seemed completely out of humour. Foaming and bellowing, he made the circuit of the square several times. From eyes sparkling fire, the bull darted looks of scorn upon the surrounding spectators, and after frisking and capering a little, and attempting to pay home his tormentors for their acts of cruelty, at length effected his escape, and made room for others, none of which afforded much amusement.

A similar exhibition took place the following evening, but the sport was bad. Three soldiers, more expert at handling a musket than the horns of a bull, were, on their endeavouring to seize upon one of the infuriated animals, tossed into the air and dreadfully injured.

This savage-like amusement is considered a refined one in Spain, by all classes, from the peer to the peasant. Even the fair *donnas* think so. I suspect, however, that but very few of my fair country-women will feel inclined to join their Spanish sisterhood in their admiration of a sport, the principal feature of which is cruelty.

Villa-Alba

After spending the 4th of June in a manner worthy of the day, we took leave of Merida for the last time, at one o'clock in the morning of the 5th, and marched to Almendralejo. Intelligence having been received a few days after, that Marshal Soult intended paying us a visit. Sir Rowland Hill deeming it prudent to concentrate his little army at a more advanced point, the whole of the infantry moved forward to Zafra, Los Santos, and Sancho Perez, on the 12th and 13th.

On the 11th of June, a severe, gallant, but unfortunate action was fought near Llera, between the French cavalry under General L'Allemand, and our heavy dragoons commanded by General Slade. In the early part of the conflict our troops were completely victorious, but from some unfortunate I cause, they were ultimately beaten back with great loss to themselves, besides the loss of all the prisoners they had previously taken from the enemy. To whom the heavy cavalry brigade were indebted for this drubbing, I shall not affirm, but it was reported that Sir Rowland Hill was highly displeased with the issue of the affair.

This disastrous affair cast a deep gloom over every battalion in the division; but fortunately it was of short duration, for Sir Rowland Hill having received intelligence, on the 12th, that the men General Slade had lost on the preceding day, were then in the village of Meguila, under a slender guard, instantly despatched fifty of the heavy brigade of cavalry, under Lieutenant Strenuwitz, to recapture them. This was exactly the kind of thing for Strenuwitz, for as he frequently told us, "he was so fond of *de fight*" that he was sure to be killed some day or other. Away the whole party went in high spirits. In their principal object, however, they were unsuccessful; but having fallen in with a detachment of French cavalry, consisting of eighty men, the British, notwithstanding the great disparity of numbers, instantly attacked them, and after a tight little brush, defeated them with the loss of many killed and wounded, and twenty prisoners, and completely established the superiority of our heavy cavalry over that of the enemy.

The enemy's cavalry in front of Llerena having been reinforced, and their every movement indicating an intention of attacking us, the allied cavalry were withdrawn from Llerena on the 14th June. The latter continuing to fall back, and the French to advance, the 50th and 92nd Regiments retired from Sancho Perez to Los Santos on the 16th, and at sunset, on the following evening, the whole corps retired towards Santa Martha, behind which we halted at sunrise on the 18th. Resuming our retrograde movement on the 19th, we marched to a wood a mile and a half in front of the position of Albuera, and encamped on the right bank of the little river of that name, where, on the 20th, we were joined by the 5th, 17th and 22nd Portuguese Regiments of the line, and one battalion of *caçadores*, which raised our force to upwards of 21,000 men.

Fully convinced that Soult intended to attack him. Sir Rowland Hill lost not a moment after going into camp, in making such preparations as he considered necessary to give the marshal a warm reception, on the same ground from which Marshal Beresford so unceremoniously drove him on the 16th of May 1811.

The ground denominated the position of Albuera, is a ridge covered with heath, the left or lower part of which is washed by the small river Albuera. From the river, it runs in a southerly direction about three-quarters of a mile, and all the way rises with a gentle acclivity, till it terminates abruptly at a deep ravine, which separates the position from a high range of mountains farther to the right. The slope on each side of the ridge is long, but not steep. The stands on the lower part of the ridge, at a short distance from the river; and the high-road from Zafra to Badajoz runs through the centre of it. The extreme right being considerably higher than the other parts of the ridge, must be considered as the key to the position.

As this part of the ground, therefore, was likely to become the grand bone of contention, an engineer and strong working parties were instantly ordered to the spot, to increase its natural strength by all the artificial means in their power. Accordingly, by dint of hard working, day and night, a most respectable looking redoubt crowned the summit of the ridge in course of a few days. Another redoubt was raised on an eminence a little lower down, and a third one begun still farther to the left. The parapet of the bridge over the Albuera, a little in front of the village, was thrown down; the road broken up; the streets were barricaded; many of the houses loop-holed; and numerous breastworks graced the slope of the ridge.

An officer from each regiment proceeded to the position, under the quarter-master general, who pointed out to them the ground which their respective battalions were to occupy, in case of an attack, as well as the particular fords of the river, where each corps was to cross on its way from the encampment to the position. Cavalry piquets were posted in front of the wood where the infantry were encamped. These were supported by some companies of infantry, placed within an abattis, and the first brigade, 50th, 71st, and 92nd Regiments, were ordered to be in readiness to proceed to the front of the wood, on the first appearance of the enemy, and to retard their progress till the other brigades had taken up their ground. Such were the precautionary measures adopted by Sir Rowland Hill at Albuera in June 1812,—measures which every individual present characterized as the offspring of caution, prudence, and a very considerable portion of military talent.

On taking possession of the ridge of Albuera, we were a good deal astonished to find a trench, forty yards in length, nearly half filled with human skeletons, without so much as one handful of mould sprinkled over them, to screen them from the eye of the eagle, the vulture, or carrion crow. "*Look*" cried the men, one to another, on first beholding the horrifying spectacle, "*behold our reward!*" In order to quiet their minds, we threw out a hint that the skeletons were those of the French soldiers who had fallen in battle the previous year. But our oratory produced very little effect;—and no wonder, for that circumstance formed anything but a good apology for the conduct of those to whom Marshal Beresford had entrusted the duty of burying the dead. That the dead were ordered to be buried, we require no other proof than the existence of the trench;—for had no order been given, that tomb of many warriors would never have been made.

Now, as an order to bury the dead is all that can be expected from a general commanding an army, no blame can possibly be attached to the general who commanded the allied army at Albuera, in May 1811. To suppose for moment that he gave no orders to bury the dead, would be a foul aspersion on his military character; for every general whose breast, like his, glows with humanity, will, after completing the rout of an enemy, invariably endeavour to enhance his victory, by extending mercy to all those who are in his power, and consigning to the tomb, with becoming solemnity, all those, whether friends or foes, who may have fallen in battle.

"Did you ever hear a good reason given why Marshal Beresford did not either destroy, or capture the remains of the French army after the battle of Albuera?" is a question which has been privately put to me more than a hundred times, and to which I shall now endeavour thus publicly to return a satisfactory answer.

In the height of their patriotic frenzy, the inhabitants of these realms are but too apt to anticipate from their naval and military armaments, a degree of success far beyond what they can possibly achieve. In forming these extravagant notions of success, it often happens that the sanguine people lose sight of a great many facts, which, if kept in view, would assist them materially in forming a correct estimate of the advantages which may be expected from any particular body of troops. On the occasion alluded to, the querists must unquestionably have forgotten, that when an army is composed of troops drawn from various nations, it is almost impossible for a general to infuse into the breasts of all his followers the same daring spirit, the same ardour, and the same praise-worthy disposition, to emulate in deeds of valour, those who have gone before them in the path of danger, of honour, and of glory. Let him do his utmost, he will not succeed; for so long as the troops of each nation possess, as they now do, a separate and distinct species of courage from the others, there will, there must be a secret enemy at work in the shape of jealousy and envy, which will prevent the soldiers of different nations from co-operating so heartily, and so effectually with each other, as the different corps of an army composed entirely of native troops do.

Even in a native army, trivial causes have frequently been known to produce jealousy, hatred, and envy. It often happens that a particular battalion, brigade, or division is engaged in many and successive combats, while others have no opportunity of displaying their prowess, and all without any premeditated arrangement of the general commanding. This succession of partial combats, seldom fails to draw down upon the general, a charge of partiality, and upon the troops engaged in them, the envy and hatred of their less fortunate companions. This again produces ill-will between the different battalions, brigades, and divisions, which, in the end, tends to destroy confidence, and of consequence, unity and strength in an army.

That the victory would have been more complete, had the general placed the key of his position in the keeping of the British troops, instead of those of Spain, there can be but one opinion; for the great loss of the former did not arise from defending their own portion of ground, but in *retaking that* which the *Spaniards* had *too tamely* yielded up to the enemy. That the original plan of operations on that day was forced on the general, I believe there cannot be a doubt. But whatever may have been his reasons for agreeing to the arrangements, the issue shews us, that to place implicit confidence in foreign troops, is, to say the least of it, s bad and dangerous policy. Let us, therefore, hope that the fate of the key of the position of Albuera on the 16th May 1811, will forever operate as a warning to every British general or officer in command of a mixed force, never to place a post of importance in the keeping of foreign troops, but on all occasions to give the preference to the troops of that nation, whose army he commands.

A troop of one of our light cavalry regiments being on outpost duty one morning during our stay at Albuera, one of the horses bestrode by an honest Hibernian became so restive, that the rider was ordered to fall out to the rear, and make it quiet. Pat being more anxious for a trip in another direction, requested permission to take the horse to the front. Leave being granted, Pat, on leaving the ranks, said to his comrades, "Now, by J——, lads, I will shew you something you never saw before." Every eye was instantly fixed upon the son of Erin, while he belaboured the head and sides of the poor horse in the most unmerciful manner. Neither the smart reproofs of his officers, nor the coarse jokes of his comrades, had any effect in lessening the punishment of the animal. In defiance of everything, Pat kept whipping, spurring, and swearing, till he had gained a hundred yards from the troop, when, conceiving himself out of danger, he turned the head of his horse towards the enemy, gave him the reins, and the spurs at the same time, and at full speed gained the French lines, before any of his companions could overtake him.

For ten days the enemy gave us very little trouble, but in the morning of the 30th, a body of their cavalry approached our advanced posts, apparently with an intention to give us a meeting. Our brigade being busily employed in preparing their breakfast when the alarm was given, the camp-kettles were instantly emptied, and away we went to dispute with the enemy the passage through the forest. After waiting two hours for them, we were informed they had retired, and at the same time received permission to follow their example.

On returning to our camp, we put our culinary articles again in requisition, but most unfortunately, just as the kettles were about being removed from the fire, a second alarm called us again to the front, when as before, we were forced to leave our dinners behind us—the soup to fertilize the soil, and the beef to feed the carrion crow. This movement was equally unproductive of incident as the former, as far as we were concerned. The Spanish cavalry were less fortunate however, for in addition to the loss of breakfast and dinner, not a few of them lost their lives in an engagement with a body of the enemy's dragoons. In the early part of the action, the Spaniards were successful, but having advanced farther than prudence warranted, they at length fell into an ambuscade, and suffered severely. On this occasion the Conde-de-Penne-Villamur and his cavalry, fought in very good style.

Finding that the enemy were only amusing him, until he could draw off the main body of his army, Sir Rowland Hill abandoned the defensive and assumed the offensive on the 1st of July. Moving in one column, we arrived in the afternoon at Santa Martha, and encamped. On the following day, the corps advanced in two columns. The left, consisting of General Long's brigade of British, and Colonel Campbell's brigade of Portuguese cavalry, one brigade of artillery, the First Brigade of British, and Brigadier-General Campbell's brigade of Portuguese infantry, was placed under the orders of Sir William Erskine, and moved against the enemy at Villa-Alba. The remaining brigades of artillery, cavalry, and infantry, advanced along the high road to Zafra, under the command of Lieutenant-General Tilson Chowne.

The whole moved from Santa Martha, about nine o'clock, a.m. The German hussars, who led the advance to Villa-Alba, hearing that the French were quite unprepared for a visit, dashed into the village, cut down a number of them before they mounted their chargers, and would have taken or destroyed the greater part of them, had the Portuguese cavalry behaved equally well. But unfortunately, neither the threats nor promises of Colonel Campbell and his officers, could induce their men to take part in the fray, till the favourable moment had for ever fled. Attacked at length by a superior force, the hussars were compelled to retire, I until the light dragoons advanced to their assistance, when they once more became the assailants, and drove the enemy from the village to a height a short distance from it, where the whole skirmished very beautifully for some time after our brigade arrived at Villa-Alba.

When the enemy finally retired, we crossed the Guadacia, moved a few miles up its right bank, then recrossed the river, and lay down under arms. Towards evening, we were moving from the banks of the Guadacia to encamp, when the enemy brought forward a few pieces of artillery, and cannonaded us from an opposite height. Our artillery returned the fire of the enemy from a rising ground, close to the river, across which the 71st Light Infantry were thrown, to take possession of a height half-way between us and our opponents. After a mutual interchange of civilities, the affair was brought to a close by the French withdrawing their artillery, and leaving us to bind up the wounds of a few of our artillerymen, and some Portuguese infantry, in peace and quietness.

In the engagement at Villa-Alba, one of the Second German Hussars was assaulted by a powerful French dragoon. Both being dexterous swordsmen, it was sometime before either could claim an advantage. Another Frenchman conceiving his friend in danger, flew to his aid, but when he arrived, his companion was heaving his last convulsive throe at the feet of his conqueror. The fatal result of this rencounter did not however deter the second antagonist from making an attempt to revenge the fall of his friend. To it they went gallantly. Cut succeeded cut, and thrust succeeded thrust, till both were considerably weakened. At length a third opponent approached the scene of action, and in seconding his friend, buried his sword in the body of the German hero, just as the sabre of the latter had performed a similar favour to his antagonist.

In the afternoon of the 3rd of July, we quitted the banks of the Guadacia, marched two leagues through a close country, and bivouacked on the left of the road from Santa Martha to Zafra.

Next morning we advanced to Los Santos and bivouacked, and at sunset the same day resumed our march, and at sunrise on the 5th, entered Benveneida. Quitting the latter on the 6th, we marched into Llerena the same afternoon. As we passed the windows of a convent in the suburbs of the city, the fair inmates cheered us through the gratings of their miserable cells, and continued to wave their white handkerchiefs, till every red coat was lost in the distance. The joy of the nuns may have been sincere, but if the tittle-tattle of the neighbouring towns could be credited, the inhabitants of Llerena had very little regard for us.

Towards Toledo

The enemy having shewn an unwillingness to retire from Berlenga, Sir Rowland Hill, at the head of his whole corps, marched from Llerena on the 8th of July to dislodge them. The infantry, preceded by the Spanish cavalry under the Conde-de-Penne-Villamur, moved direct upon Berlenga, but the British cavalry moved by a more circuitous route to the left, with the view of making a dash at the right wing of the French force in front of the town.

Six miles from Llerena, the Spaniards came up with the enemy's advanced piquets, which they attacked and drove in, in rather good style. The ground being favourable for cavalry, the French retired at extended order, followed by their opponents, who skirmished with them very prettily, till the enemy rejoined a portion of their friends on a height in front of Berlenga. The force of the two parties being now more upon an equality, the Spaniards proceeded with greater caution. The infantry however continued to advance at the usual pace, in order to arrive at a given point at the hour fixed for the British cavalry to make the attack. As we approached the height on which the main body of the French cavalry in *front* of Berlenga were posted, the latter retired, crossed a deep ravine, and took post on an opposite ridge. The town of Berlenga, which lay between these two eminences, and a little to our left, was still in the hands of the enemy, but was evacuated immediately by them on seeing their companions on the left retiring across the valley.

To annoy them a little, and retard their retrograde movement till our cavalry should arrive, the artillery were ordered to play upon the two columns, and the infantry to close up in rear of the artillery. On the infantry taking up their ground, the French artillery saluted each battalion in succession,—a mark of attention for which our artillery shewed themselves sufficiently grateful. The effect produced by this mutual interchange of civilities would have been much finer, could we have induced the enemy to make it more general. In this object, however, we were completely foiled by the non-appearance of our cavalry, until the enemy had withdrawn almost beyond the reach of pursuit. Such was the issue of our movement on Berlenga, which in the morning promised so brilliant a result. At the close of the business the troops were thrown into Berlenga, but at sunset we quitted the town, and bivouacked in the vicinity.

Early on the following morning, we began to retrace our steps to Llerena. The day being extremely hot, and not a single drop of water to be had between the two places, a great many of the men sunk upon the ground completely overpowered, some of them to rise no more. During the latter part of the march, my thirst was so great, that when about a quarter of a mile from Llerena, I was forced to lie down, and might have been reposing near the same spot to this day, had not a soldier kindly offered me a mouthful of *mud* and *water*, (the only liquid any of them could procure) which revived me so much, that in course of a few minutes, I was enabled to follow my friends into town.

On the 18th of July, we bade a final *adieu* to Llerena, and retired to Benveneida. Resuming our march at sunset the same evening, we arrived at Zafra at sunrise on the following morning.

An hour before our battalion marched from Benveneida, the wife of a private soldier of the 3rd Company presented her lord and master with two fine chubby boys. On the two being presented to the astonished father, he exclaimed, in accents of the deepest despair, "Gude preserve me, Betty Watt, what can I do wi' them?"

On the day we returned to Zafra an officer received over three inhabited, and four uninhabited houses for the use of his company. The latter had neither doors nor windows, and the floors were covered with nastiness of every description. Notwithstanding this, however, the acting captain retained the best house to himself; and as he would not share it with the other officers, they, as a matter of course, were compelled to occupy the only other one which could accommodate them,—a house large enough to have held the whole company. The other house being very small, six men only found shelter under its roof.

The consequence of this selfish conduct I need not point out, farther than this, that it drew upon the head of the principal actor a degree of odium which he could never remove. From this it is sufficiently obvious, that in the distribution of quarters, officers commanding companies should never permit anything like selfishness or partiality to appear in any part of their conduct. On the contrary, they should invariably hand over to the non-commissioned officers and privates, the houses best calculated for their accommodation, although the honourable, and really humane act, may have the effect of circumscribing their own personal comforts.

In regard to the quartering of troops, I trust the following hint may be of some use to those military gentlemen who have not yet had an opportunity of performing that duty on foreign service.

On receiving over the houses intended for the accommodation of his company, the officer in charge of it should visit the quarters along with a sergeant, who should be made to pace every apartment, and mark on a piece of paper the size of each in square yards, reckoning each pace a yard. On this being done, all that remains for the officer to do, is to sum up the whole, then divide it by, the number of men in the company; the result will shew him at one glance the exact space which each individual is entitled to, whether that may be one square yard or twenty.

On entering the square of Zafra with a few friends, about ten o'clock in the morning of the 28th of July, we beheld with sincere sorrow the Marquis of Almeida flying from one place to another, and with a stentorian voice offering to bet thirty *doubloons* to one that *it was true*. I say sincere sorrow, for *not knowing the cause* of his offering such odds, we really fancied that the noble patriot had gone mad. On getting a little nearer, however, we were informed that a Spaniard, an entire stranger, had waited upon the chief magistrate a short time before, and given him an interesting account of a battle fought near Salamanca, on the 22nd July, between Lord Wellington and Marshal Marmont, in which the latter had been totally defeated. Daily expecting to hear of the retreat of the northern army into Portugal, no one gave credit to the poor man's story but the marquis. Indeed some threw out hints of the man being a spy.

On this being reported to him, he instantly made a voluntary tender of his person to be incarcerated in the common jail till the official dispatches arrived, when he could be punished if found to have deviated from the truth. I need scarcely add, that on the arrival of the official account next morning, he was permitted to return to the banks of the Tormes, having previously received something more substantial than empty thanks for his patriotic conduct in travelling such a distance with no other object in view than to be the first to give the gratifying intelligence of the victory to the British general and his patriotic countrymen in Estremadura.

The French troops in and around Hornachos having been reinforced to an extent, which caused considerable uneasiness to our general for the safety of our cavalry stationed at Villa-Franca, the 1st and 2nd Brigades of Infantry moved from Zafra a little before midnight on the 28th of July, and at eight o'clock next morning encamped close to Villa-Franca. On the march Sir Rowland Hill was so kind as to communicate to us the heart-stirring tidings from Lord Wellington on the banks of the Tormes, which, as may be supposed, were received by officers and men with a universal burst of applause. In the evening the troops were ordered a double allowance of grog, to drink in a full-flowing cup the health of Lord Wellington and his gallant companions.

Everything being quiet at Villa-Franca, we quitted our encampment on the 31st, and moved to Fuente del-Maestre. General L'Allemand having attacked our cavalry in front of Villa-Franca, early next morning our brigade was ordered to move to their assistance with all possible dispatch. We had proceeded about half-way, when we were desired to return; but we had scarcely commenced our retrograde movement, when a third order made us again wheel to the right-about, and proceed according to our original instructions. This marching and counter-marching, under a broiling sun, we cheerfully put up with, knowing it was caused by the movements of the enemy; but we could not so easily prevail upon ourselves to forgive the tardy movements of those who kept us roasting three hours in the streets of Villa-Franca, before they handed over the quarters allotted to the brigade.

Between small, ill-ventilated rooms, an over-heated atmosphere, and empty purses, our situation in Villa-Franca was far from an enviable one. During our stay, many of us were cooped up in apartments, into which no thrifty housewife would have put her pigs, even for a single night. By repeated threats of a morning visit from the enemy, it was deemed advisable to detach five companies of infantry two miles to the front, every evening a little before sunset, to render assistance to the cavalry and infantry piquets, in case of an attack. About eight o'clock one evening, when the right wing of the 92nd Regiment, under Colonel Cameron, happened to be on this duty, a smart *tirailleur* fire, in the direction of Villa-Franca, struck with astonishment the ears of the Highland Colonel.

Convinced that the French had eluded the vigilance of our outposts, and penetrated to the town, he ordered small piquets to be posted around the main body, and dispatched an officer and a few files of men towards Villa-Franca, to obtain intelligence. Night-marching almost every soldier detests,—for night-fighting few have a greater relish,—consequently the feelings of the men were wound up to the highest pitch, the situation in which they found themselves placed being one of those which no soldier admires. An hour and a-half passed away, and there were no tidings of the party sent towards the town. Despairing of seeing it again, a second was about to set out on a similar errand, when the other returned with a message from Sir William Erskine, commanding in Villa-Franca, which at length satisfied us that the ominous sounds which had disturbed our repose, proceeded, not from the muskets of an enemy, but from those of a loyal and joyous people, who had adopted the above mode of testifying their loyalty to their king, and gratitude to the British general, for wresting their *capital* from the iron grasp of a ruthless despot.

At daybreak on the following morning, the enemy, anxious no doubt to ascertain the cause of the firing, attacked our cavalry, and captured three of the heavy brigade. This shews that there is little pleasure to be enjoyed unmixed with a pro portion of the ills or inconveniences of life,—for,

Something that's bitter will arise,
In the midst of all our jollities.

At an early hour on the 28th of August, we took leave of Villa-Franca without the smallest regret, and with the other brigades moved toward Llerena. In the afternoon the 1st Brigade occupied Usagre, and on the following day joined the other brigades in a field near Villa-Garcia. Early on the 30th we quitted the above encampment, but instead of marching directly upon Llerena as we anticipated, we filed to the left, and in the afternoon encamped on a height a short distance from Llera. Next day we entered El-Campilo, remained in it till sunset, then left it and bivouacked in the vicinity. Before daylight, on the 1st of September, we directed our steps towards Zalamea, which, after a very fatiguing march of fourteen hours, under a scorching sun, and over a parched desert, we entered and took possession of considerable stores of grain left behind by the enemy.

Here we met with a very flattering reception from the inhabitants, and really we required it to keep up our spirits; for the want of water was so severely felt by the whole of the pedestrian portion of the procession, that as often as a little pool of thin *mire* fell in our way, hundreds scrambled for even one little cup of the nauseous draught. The following morning we marched to Quintana,—on the 3rd we entered Maguela,—and next forenoon again occupied Don Benito.

On receiving notice that Marshal Soult had raised the siege of Cadiz, the constituted authorities in Don Benito made every preparation to celebrate the gratifying event with *éclat*. For this purpose the new constitution was ordered to be proclaimed on the 7th September, and an illumination for the same evening. Accordingly, the magistrates and principal inhabitants walked in procession to *hustings* erected in the grand square, where, at twelve o'clock, the ceremony was performed, amid deafening shouts of assembled thousands. In the evening the town was *brilliantly illuminated*, every window emitting a light equally refulgent as that produced by a

Little farthing rush-light.

The people, however, seemed quite delighted with the display, and it was *our policy*, no less than *our duty*, to express ourselves pleased with it also.

The retreat of Marshal Soult from Cadiz, in the direction of Valencia, and that of the Count D'Erlon from the banks of the Guadiana to join him, having rendered our stay in Estremadura no longer necessary, we bade *adieu* to Don Benito on the 13th off September, crossed the Guadiana at a ford about a mile from the town, and marched to *Majaides*. Next morning our brigade occupied Villa-Macia, and on the 15th Truxillo. Here a few pieces of brass cannon were found under some wood, in the residence of the noble family of Conquesta, (the descendants of the great Pizarro,) who were at that time in Cadiz.

We took leave of Truxillo on the 18th of September, and in the evening bivouacked on the face of a steep bank in front of Jaraceijo. On the 19th we moved through the pass of Merabete, crossed the Tagus by a pontoon bridge, near to the site of the one which we destroyed four months before, and encamped in the evening a little in front of Almarez.

The 30th being the rear battalion of the column of march on this occasion. Colonel Stewart halted it, as soon as the leading files had arrived at the farther end of the bridge. On forming line, the whole stood fronting the old *tete-du-pont*, and Fort Napoleon, in the capture of which they acted so conspicuous a part. At a signal given to the men by their gallant leader, the whole gave three times three hearty cheers, the band all the time playing "God save the king." The whole battalion appeared quite electrified, and at the close of the ceremony followed their comrades,—the band playing the "Downfall of Paris," and the "British Grenadiers."

Colonel Stewart's conduct on this occasion cannot be too loudly applauded, or too generally imitated. Officers commanding battalions should embrace every opportunity in their power of shewing the soldiers under their command, that although they cannot reward with promotion all those who signalize themselves in battle, they can appreciate their merit and gallantry, and bear both in grateful remembrance; for courage in an army depends very much upon example, and the desire of being distinguished by the superior officers. Indeed, it is scarcely possible for any but those who have been in action, to have any idea of the wonderful effects which are occasionally produced by a kind word or look from a general or officer, at the head of a battalion on the field of battle, or with what ardour a private soldier will run into danger, when he conceives that his conduct is observed by his officers. A little attention from officers, similar to that bestowed on the 50th by their colonel at Almarez, will always be more than repaid by their troops on every occasion, when they are called into action.

On the 20th September, we moved forward to Naval Moral, and encamped. Next morning we occupied Calzada-de-Orepesa, and on the 22nd La-Gartera. A little before midnight on the 25th, we marched from the latter place, and at ten o'clock next morning, entered Talavera-de-la-Reina, amid the noisy acclamations of almost the whole population.

Talavera is immortalized by the victory obtained by Sir Arthur Wellesley over the French army, on the 28th of July 1809. Previous to the French invasion, the city, which stands on the right bank of the Tagus, was one of the most beautiful and flourishing in Spain. But we found all the streets nearest the bridge in ruins, many of the others greatly injured; in short, the whole town, with the exception of a few streets, in a state of complete dilapidation.

The inhabitants talked incessantly of the battle of Talavera, and were perfectly deafening in their praises of Lord Wellington and Sir Rowland Hill In fact, they never pronounced the name of the latter, but in terms of glowing admiration. His desperate defence of the eminence on the left of the British position, which secured the victory, has gained him an imperishable name in Spain. Centuries may pass away, but to the latest ages, the kind people of Talavera will venerate the name of a British soldier.

With very considerable regret we took leave of the warm-hearted Talaverians, and directed our steps towards Toledo. Soon after crossing the Alberche, the road leads into a vineyard, several miles in length, and which on the right and left extends to a considerable distance. The grapes, ripe and delicious, were overhanging the footpaths in such a manner, that we would have required no small portion of the nautical skill of a Commodore Trunnion to pursue our course, without coming in contact with the beautiful clusters which hung around us in most inviting positions. Before midday we arrived at Cybola, where a *cool* reception awaited the *Highlanders*.

When Sir John Hope was detached with a division of the British army towards Madrid, in November 1808, he selected amongst others for that duty, the 71st and 92nd Regiments. From some petty cause or other, the private soldiers of these regiments were not on the most friendly terms. From a year's residence in South America, many of the 71st could speak the Spanish language with considerable fluency, which gave them a decided advantage over their friends in their daily intercourse with the natives. Taking advantage of this circumstance, some of the 71st insinuated on various occasions, and at different places, that the 92nd Regiment was a disgraced corps, and in proof of their assertion, they never failed to point to the *kilt*, which, they affirmed, the king had condemned them to wear as a mark of infamy for misconduct before the enemy. This, like all other tales of scandal, spread like wildfire, and in time reached the ears of the worthy Cybolians.

A corps of cowards being too rare, and by far too curious a sight even in Spain, to be lost for a little personal trouble, the villagers, on hearing of the arrival of the 92nd at Talavera, proceeded some to the latter, others to the high road from it to the capital, to get a peep at the *brave men* whom George III. had sent to assist in driving the usurper from the Peninsula. From that day they had considered the Highlanders as a corps in disgrace, and consequently, when the latter entered their village on the 26th of September, they were looked upon as men totally unworthy of the notice of the meanest inhabitant. But when an explanation took place, the people laughed immoderately at their own credulity, and it was no sooner known in the town, that instead of a mark of disgrace, the kilt had been given to them as a mark of His Majesty's confidence and regard, than the whole country was inundated with the Highlanders, proceeding by invitation of the inhabitants, to partake of the delicious fruits which their richly stored vineyards afforded.

Next morning we proceeded towards Torrijos, where we arrived about one, p.m. During our march we passed five or six considerable towns, at all of which the people received us with the utmost demonstrations of joy. On approaching the gates of Torrijos, Sir Rowland Hill was received by the magistrates in their robes,—they gave him a hearty welcome within their walls, and in honour of the event, ordered the town to be illuminated the same evening. The display here was infinitely superior to that at Don Benito.

The sun found us considerably advanced on the road to Toledo, when, for the first time, he shewed his cheering countenance on the morning of the 29th. About a mile from the gates, the magistrates in their scarlet robes, the governor, the famous guerrilla chief, El-Medico, and a great many of the first nobility and gentry residing in the city, congratulated Sir Rowland Hill on the favourable state of affairs, and gave him a most cordial welcome within the walls of their ancient city. As we proceeded from the gates towards the grand square, the cheers of welcome which assailed us from every door, every window, and every balcony, were truly electrifying. Joy beamed in every countenance; and amongst numerous loyal ejaculations, "Long live kind George III.!" "Long live Wellington!" "Long live Hill!" and "Long live Ferdinand VII.!" fell from the lips of delighted thousands. In the principal square, the front of every house was literally covered with the symbols of joy used in Spain on similar occasions, *viz*. quilts of every description, sheets, silk flags, and handkerchiefs, and as we were the first British troops that had ever been in Toledo, the city was most brilliantly illuminated in the evening.

Toledo, once the capital of Spain, stands upon a rock, three sides of which are washed by the Tagus, which, murmuring sullenly as it rolls over its rugged bed, adds considerably to the romantic scenery around. The streets are narrow, but well paved, and kept tolerably clean. The precautions adopted by the inhabitants to exclude the rays of the sun from the interior of their dwellings, are so effectual, that on a clear summer day, a stranger seated in the most spacious room, would be apt to fancy the hour twelve midnight, when it was only twelve midday.

Toledo was at one time famous for its manufacture of sword-blades; but the mode of making them being known only to the manufacturer, no real *Toledo* blade can now be had but at a prodigiously high price. So excellent was the material of which the blades were manufactured, and so careful was the maker of his reputation, that if the least notch appeared on the edge of a blade after undergoing the operations of tempering, and striking repeatedly on a sharp iron instrument, it was instantly thrown aside as a piece of old iron.

Early on the 30th, we crossed the Tagus by a stone bridge, almost under the walls of the city, marched four leagues, and encamped in a rich valley between the ruinous village of Villa-Major and the river. On the 1st of October we occupied Aranjuez.

Sometime previous to our leaving Toledo on the 30th, various itinerant spirit-merchants hovered on our flanks, and to the annoyance of every person in the brigade, kept bawling the name and quality of the commodity they had for sale. Anxious to obtain a ready sale for their wares, the spirited gentlemen were frequently not over scrupulous in soliciting the favours of their foreign friends. On approaching to where Colonel Cameron of the 92nd regiment was standing giving orders to his battalion, one of the merchants, with a very large bottle under his arm, roared out, "*Aquerdente, Senhores, Aquerdente*," and was just on the point of repeating the dose in the colonel's ears, when the latter gave the "*big belly'd bottle*" such a whack, that in an instant it was flying through the air in a thousand pieces.

On perceiving the fate of his best friend, the poor itinerant bounded forward like an antelope, and after throwing down a dozen or two in his progress, fled with the speed of lightning, lest his head should share the fate of his bottle, and his brains, like his brandy, be made to sprinkle the pavement of Toledo, by the talismanic wand of the Highland chief.

The Tormes

Aranjuez, though not a pretty town, is prettily situated in a beautiful valley, watered by the Tagus, which, entering it on the east, winds through it towards Toledo, receiving in its course various tributaries, the most considerable of which is the Jacamah, which joins the Tagus a little below the town. Honoured, previous to the French invasion, with the presence of the Court for a few months every season, Aranjuez really possesses a greater degree of neatness and regularity in its streets and buildings, than is any other where to be met with in the Peninsula. The principal streets are broad, and at regular distances cut at right angles by others of less importance. In this respect it very much resembles the New Town of Edinburgh,—but here the resemblance ceases, for when compared with the princely residences in the Modern Athens, the buildings in Aranjuez are but houses in miniature.

The principal building of course is the royal residence, which stands at a little distance from the lower part of the town, and close to the left bank of the Tagus. It is a commodious, and rather handsome structure, but at the time we were there it had a very sombre appearance, the palace being empty, and everything around it being in a state of the greatest confusion.

A day or two after we arrived at Aranjuez, a few of us proceeded to the palace to get a peep at its furniture and interior embellishments. On demanding admission, we were refused, and had just turned on our heels to return the way we went, when we espied Sir Rowland Hill, with his staff, bearing down upon the palace on a similar errand. Having *tacked* ourselves to the skirts of Sir Rowland's coat, we obtained admittance, and had the honour of accompanying him through every corner of the palace. Sir Rowland being accompanied by one of the servants residing in the palace, we were shewn some curiosities, and received a few particulars regarding the conduct of some of its former inmates, worthy of being kept in remembrance.

On arriving at the queen's bedroom, we were all struck with astonishment at the mean and wretched appearance of the apartment, which the guide observing, he immediately began to explain the causes which led her majesty to select it in preference to many others more worthy of royalty, but had not proceeded beyond two or three sentences, before Sir Rowland Hill shewed himself so disgusted with the recital, that he darted from the apartment, apparently anxious to escape as speedily; as possible from so tainted and pestiferous an atmosphere: and to those who know anything of that amiable general's private character, this will not excite surprise, for through life, he has not been less distinguished for his great moral worth and piety, than for his unconquerable courage in the field of battle.

Every Sunday, when stationary, the whole of the division invariably attended divine service, and in order to mark his respect for the sacred ordinances of religion. Sir Rowland's orders were, that every officer should appear in his best uniform. The troops were always formed in square, and the large drum of one of the battalions served the clergyman as a desk. One Sunday afternoon during our stay in Almendralejo, a very young clergyman, newly arrived from England, volunteered to officiate for our chaplain. On going up to the drum, the young aspirant for clerical fame appeared completely from home. Being quite at a loss to know to what use he should apply it, he surveyed it for some time with a scrutinizing eye; and then, as if fully satisfied that it could only have been placed in the square for him to stand upon, he, at one leap, posted himself on the drum-head, to the utter astonishment of the whole division, no member of which before that day had ever seen a similar feat attempted.

When the first ebullition of surprise had subsided, a titter ran along the inside of the square like a running fire. Sir Rowland Hill preserved his gravity with difficulty, and General Chowne was forced to turn his back. In momentary expectation of seeing the minister return to old mother earth in rather an awkward manner, General Howard stepped forward, and in his usual mild and gentlemanly way, said, "Sir, I think you had better come down, I am afraid the drum will not bear you;" but whether the young chaplain was so captivated with his new situation, or found greater difficulty in resuming his original position than the general anticipated, I know not, but neither hand nor foot moved he. Perceiving by this how matters stood, assistance was instantly procured, when the minister descended in safety, but more than satisfied that every man *should look before he leaps*.

It being evident that Soult and Jourdan would regulate their movements by the issue of Lord Wellington's operations before Burgos, most anxiously did we look for the official details of the capture of that fortress. Day after day, however, passed away, and still the glad tidings did not arrive. This state of affairs in the north began at length to create an unpleasant impression in our quarter, for Soult's advanced guard, which was known to have left Valencia on the 12th, approached our cantonments on the 22nd of October. To oppose this army of 50,000 tried soldiers. Sir Rowland Hill had a British, Spanish, and Portuguese force of from 35,000 to 40,000 men. On the 23rd, the 2nd division crossed the Tagus at Aranjuez, and marched, the 1st brigade to Colmanar-de-Orejo, and the others to several villages up the right bank of the river, between Fuente-Duenna, and Aranjuez.

On hearing that a body of the enemy's troops were moving upon Duenna, our brigade was ordered from Colmanar to that place on the 25th, to defend the passage of the Tagus in that neighbourhood. On our arrival we found the Spanish corps of Generals Elio and Freyre in bivouac close to the village On the 27th, the enemy appeared on a height opposite to Duenna, whence they pushed forward a strong reconnoitring party towards the bridges. To prevent them finding out the state of the bridge, the 60th Rifle Company lined the bank of the Tagus, and kept up a smart fire on their advanced guard of cavalry, but the shots being rather long, very little execution was done. In about an hour they retired altogether out of our view.

The day being unusually fine, some men of the brigade were enjoying themselves in the limpid stream, when the enemy descended the heights to reconnoitre the bridge. Warned of the rapid approach of the enemy, our men quitted the water, and remained on the left bank till the enemy were quite close to them. Before leaping into the river to return to their own side of it, one of them placed himself in a nameless attitude, which roused the ire of the Gallic soldiers to such a pitch, that one of them, foaming with rage, galloped forward almost to the verge of the river, and deliberately levelled his carabine at the unprotected person of the poor fellow who was still in the water. This cowardly act called forth such a spontaneous and deafening shout of indignation from every mouth in our brigade, that the arm of the assassin was paralyzed. The hand which grasped the weapon from which the messenger of death was to be sped, dropped as if by magic by his side, and then, covered with confusion, and heartily ashamed of his conduct, he wheeled his horse to the right-about, and rode off at full speed.

Marshal Soult's plans being now pretty fully developed, Sir Rowland Hill used every effort in his power to counteract them. The allied force was ordered to concentrate in a position on the right bank of the Jacamah, near to its junction with the Tagus. All the corps of observation were withdrawn from their advanced positions on the Tagus. The first brigade quitted Fuente-Duenna at ten o'clock, p.m. on the 27th October, marched the whole of that night, and next day, till one, p.m. when the three regiments were ordered to occupy the village of Villa-Conijos. The same evening at seven o'clock, we resumed our arms, crossed the Jacamah about midnight by the Puente-Largo, and at four o'clock in the morning of the 29th, took up the ground allotted to us in the position before alluded to.

Sir Rowland Hill having ordered two arches of the Puente-Largo to be destroyed, the engineers were busily employed in making the necessary preparations to carry these orders into execution when we crossed the Jacamah. By some accident, the head of one of the seventy-first officer's horses came in contact with one end of the large drum of that regiment, just as the leading files of the corps were passing over the spot where the artificers were at work. The night being extremely dark, the horse was so frightened, that it plunged and reared at a frightful rate, to the great annoyance and terror of those around it. In a moment the hollow sound produced by the collision, was converted by the soldiers into an explosion of the mine under their feet, and the prancing of the horse could be nothing but the stone and lime passing from beneath them, into the abyss below.

As but a very few were aware of the real cause of the noise, the panic soon spread through the rear of the column, throughout which confusion reigned triumphant for a minute or two, the whole expecting every moment a watery grave. So great was the panic, that I was fairly lifted off my feet and carried several paces to the rear without touching the ground. Had the enemy been at our heels, the issue of this trifling incident might have been dreadful.

Confidently expecting a visit from Soult, we stood to arms a little before daybreak, every brigade on the ground it was to occupy in the event of an attack. Conceiving a battle inevitable, we were not a little delighted to find ourselves at sunrise, in a position which made considerable amends for our deficiency in point of numbers. Soult no doubt took a similar view of it, for instead of attacking us, his battalions at daylight were either cooking at Aranjuez, in motion towards

Toledo, or endeavouring to pass over the Tagus above the town. Seeing that no immediate offensive movement was intended, we cooked, in order to be prepared for whatever might occur. Before we had finished, however, Sir Rowland Hill received instructions to retire, in order to form a junction with the northern army which had been forced to retire from Burgos.

Accordingly the second division broke up the same afternoon from its position on the Jacamah, and retreated to Val-de-Mora. Next morning we passed close under the walls of the capital, three miles from which, on the road to the Escurial, we encamped. During our march, the rain poured in torrents, nor did it terminate with our fatiguing march, but continued with unabated violence till sunset. By this time the soldiers were rendered almost unfit for duty, having no tents to shelter them from the storm. On the 31st we retired to the Escurial; seven battalions were quartered in the palace, the rest in the town. Though the residence of a long race of kings was here assigned us as a resting-place for the night, I know that not a few of my friends would, with cheerfulness, have resigned their apartments in that magnificent habitation of royalty, for the rustic comforts of a shepherd's cottage.

On the 1st of November we retired to the foot of the Guadarama pass, and next morning ascended it, and reached the summit after a three hour's zigzag march. Here we had a most extensive and captivating view of the country in every direction, save the north. Descending the western slope at a much quicker pace than we had ascended the eastern one, we arrived at Villa-Custine about sunset, and bivouacked. On the 3rd, 4th, and 5th, we continued our retrograde movement, and on the 6th, occupied a position a league in front of Penaranda. On the 7th, we passed through the town of Alba-de-Tormes, crossed the Tormes by a long bridge close by the town, and encamped on a sloping ridge about half-a-mile from the river.

A little before sunset on the 8th, the first brigade received orders to recross the Tormes, and occupy Alba-de-Tormes, and if attacked, to defend it to the last extremity. The brigade consisting of the 50th, 71st, and 92nd Regiments, was supported in this movement by General Hamilton's division; of Portuguese. On the 9th General Hamilton made every preparation for a vigorous defence. An old castle which commanded the approach to the bridge was repaired, and garrisoned with 150 men. The old Moorish wall which surrounded the town being in a state of complete dilapidation, was placed in a better state of repair, it being the only protection our men possessed, against an enemy in possession of the heights, which completely commanded every part of the town. The latter was divided into three districts, and a district given to each British regiment. The streets and various buildings were barricaded, and that portion of each battalion which was not required to line the walls, were kept in reserve in the square.

The piquets of a body of British cavalry, under General Long, were driven in on the 9th, and early on the 10th, the main body was compelled to retire to the left bank of the Tormes. Soon after, the enemy appeared upon the heights above the town, and continued to increase till two o'clock, when everything being ready, they opened their fire upon the town from twenty pieces of cannon, and pushed forward their light troops close to the walls. During the cannonade, which continued for three hours without intermission, the French infantry, consisting of 8000 men, were repeatedly formed to carry the place by assault.

But notwithstanding the dreadful showers of shot and shell which plunged and danced in the streets in every direction,—the bold and determined manner in which the soldiers performed their duty, and the intrepidity and firmness of officers commanding regiments, completely deterred them from making the attempt. The utmost efforts of the French Marshal were directed against Alba for three successive hours; when finding he made no impression on the little garrison, he withdrew his artillery, and did not again renew the attack. His infantry, however, remained in position on the heights, and by keeping up a spirited fire on the garrison, caused General de-Costa's brigade of Portuguese infantry, which was thrown into the town on the evening of the 10th, a considerable loss, during that night and following morning. Our loss was considerable.

From the 10th to the 14th, the first brigade remained in Alba-de-Tormes, during which time the enemy manoeuvred along the banks of the Tormes, as if desirous of crossing and bringing matters to an issue. Every preparation was made to give him warm reception, but his great superiority of force enabled him to throw his principal strength against our right flank, and at length *turn* us out of a position from which he dared not attempt to *drive* us.

The enemy having crossed the Tormes, a considerable distance above Alba on the 14th November, all the troops in Alba and neighbourhood were recalled and placed in position on the far-famed Arepiles. Soon after our retreat the bridge over the Tormes was destroyed, and a few hundred Spaniards were thrown into the castle of Alba. Everything now wore a serious aspect. The British, or rather allied army, consisting of about 60,000 men, was concentrating its disjointed parts on the Arepiles, while the French Marshal, with his eighty or ninety thousand was pressing forward towards the same point, but more with the view, it was generally supposed, of making us retire from the position, than with any serious intention of attacking us in it, unless a very favourable opportunity should have offered; for the fate of Marmont and his fine army had sunk too deep into the breasts of both of the marshals, as well as their master, to be soon forgotten.

On the eve of such an event as that which almost every person considered inevitable, the army had but little to keep their spirits at that pitch, below which no troops should be carried into action. The weather was worse than we had ever found it at the same season of the year. Our men were without tents, their clothing was worn bare, money they had none; provisions were scarce, and the beef which was given to the troops, was but too frequently little better than carrion. The only thing which tended to keep their spirits at all buoyant was the hope of giving their opponents another hearty drubbing. In rather a cheerful mood, therefore, the soldiers resigned themselves to rest on the evening of the 14th, fondly anticipating a successful termination to their labours on the following day.

The whole of the army stood to arms at an early hour on the 15th, and prepared for action. From day-light the troops remained some hours in great suspense, momentarily expecting the signal to rush to the combat. All recollection of past sufferings had apparently vanished, and none appeared to think of anything but victory or death. In the midst of all this anxiety and martial ardour, the distressing intelligence, that part of the army was making a retrograde movement, caused gloom and dismay to reign, where cheerfulness and confidence reigned before. Every one, however, was satisfied that nothing but the most pressing necessity had compelled their chief to retire from before his antagonist, and therefore his mandate was promptly obeyed. In a short time the whole of the troops were on their march towards Ciudad-Rodrigo, pursued by the enemy. The allied army continued its retreat on the 16th, 17th, 18th, and 19th. On the two former days the enemy continued to annoy us, but he gave over the pursuit on the 18th, during which a considerable portion of the army crossed the Ageuda at Ciudad-Rodrigo. On the 19th, the Second Division crossed about three leagues above that fortress, and in the afternoon occupied Robledo.

The allied army continuing to retire into Portugal, was soon after thrown into cantonments along the frontiers. The second division, however, did not follow the footsteps of the others, but remained n Spain. On the 28th of November we quitted Robledo, and moved to Payo, thence across the Sierra-de-Gate, on the 29th to Pyrelles. On the 30th we occupied Cases-de Don-Gomez, and on the 1st of December, Coria.

The Performance of the Army

Language is totally inadequate to convey even faint idea of the fatigue and privations which a considerable portion of the allied army suffered in the ill-fated retreat. From the 6th to the 19th November, our brigade suffered much. The baggage being in the rear, neither officers nor soldiers had anything to shelter them from the inclemency or the weather. Money we had none, being eight and nine months in arrears of pay. The men's linen were reduced to less than one shirt each, and their uniforms were literally composed of shreds an patches. I know nothing to which I can so aptly compare their jackets as particoloured bed-covers for there were not fifty in my own regiment but what had been repaired with cloth of every colour under the sun. The appearance of our poor fellows was, as may be conceived, far from prepossessing when on parade.

But hideous as was the spectacle when viewed at a distance, it became ten times more so when close to the eye. In the former case the patches only were observable; in the latter, hundreds of Burns'"crawling fairlies" were seen pacing the exterior of the patches, in numerous bands, and although a war of extermination was waged against them daily from sunrise to sunset, yet they were not finally rooted out, till we had been in cantonments two or three weeks. Placed in the fields without tents to shelter them from the midnight blast, without a change of linen, or money either to purchase that luxury, or to add to their scanty stock of provisions, was it possible for them to be so long exposed, night and day, to the pelting of the pitiless storm, *without suffering severe privations*? Let those who doubt the fact make a trial on the first opportunity, and be convinced.

That staff-officers are not the proper persons, however, to judge correctly of this, will be readily conceded by every person who may read the following facts:—Soon after our arrival in Coria, the Marquis of Wellington addressed a letter to the superior officers of the army, in which he called upon them to pay attention to the discipline of the troops under their command, which he, affirmed, had fallen off in the previous campaign, to a greater degree than any army with which he had ever served, *or of which he had ever read*. "Yet this army," continued the noble and gallant general, "has met with no disasters, *it has suffered no privations*, which but a trifling attention on the part of the officers could not have prevented, and for which there existed no reason whatever in the nature of the service; *nor has it suffered any hardships* excepting those resulting from the necessity of being exposed to the inclemencies of the weather, at a moment when they were most severe.

It must be obvious, however, to every officer, that from the moment the troops commenced their retreat from Burgos on the one hand, and from Madrid on the other, the officers lost all command over their men. Irregularities and outrages of all descriptions were committed with impunity, and losses have been sustained which ought never to have occurred." All this was attributed by the Marquis of Wellington, not to any want of ability of the superior officers;—not to the want of tents, baggage money, or to a *partial failure of the objects of this campaign*, but to the *habitual inattention of the captains and subalterns of the army to their duty*, as prescribed by the standing regulations of the service, and by the orders of the army; though he did not question their zeal, still less their gallantry and spirit.

That discipline was permitted to relax to a criminal degree in some regiments, I readily admit But I cannot allow that the misconduct of one two, three, or even a dozen of battalions could ever form anything like a good apology for the commander of the forces in Spain, bestowing upon the others a sweeping vote of censure for offences which they knew they had never committed. It would be folly in me even to guess at the probable object which the noble and gallant writer had in view, when he seated himself to pen the unfortunate letter of the 28th of November; but I am confident that if its promulgation had been deferred but a few days longer, it would never have seen the light. Instead of huddling the innocent and the guilty together, the marquis would have brought the guilty to punishment, and besprinkled with praise in place of censure, those who had done their duty under every change of situation and circumstances.

Since, however, this course was not followed, I conceive myself called upon even at the eleventh hour, to affirm thus publicly and unhesitatingly, that every officer in the regiment to which I belonged, performed their several duties with credit to themselves, and advantage to the service. And I as fearlessly assert, that *throughout the whole of the retreat, the non-commissioned officers and privates obeyed the orders of their officers*, with the same cheerfulness and alacrity for which they have ever been distinguished. Their spirits were, no doubt, frequently greatly depressed with hunger, cold, and fatigue; yet into their manly bosoms the fell-fiend despair never found a passage. Although covered with rags and vermin, yet they never ceased to be animated with the same ardent patriotism—the same love of their country, and the same thirst for glory, which they had exhibited on so many previous occasions. Under all their hardships and discomforts, their hearts remained truly British. They braved every danger with the most heroic firmness, and submitted to their fate without allowing a murmur to escape their lips.

Before taking leave of this subject, I beg to make a few remarks on regimental instruction, to the almost total absence of which, at that period, I conceive all the irregularities so grievously complained of by our leader, may fairly be attributable.

From the earliest ages, military men have been of opinion, that it is during a period of profound tranquillity only, that the military establishments of an empire can be thoroughly examined, and so improved in all its parts, that its army can take the field at a moment's notice, *ready* and *able* to repel an invader, avenge an insult, or afford protection to a friend, when threatened with the vengeance of a more powerful adversary. Instead of improving, however, many nations renowned for their knowledge in the art of war, have totally neglected their military institutions in time of peace, and as a very natural consequence, frequently drawn upon themselves invasion, defeat, and ruin.

The Romans, for example, were often guilty of this flagrant error, and as often punished for this act of treason to themselves. What but a culpable relaxation in regimental discipline and instruction, during that period of comparative inactivity, in which the Romans remained from the close of the first, to the commencement of the second Punic War, led to all the misfortunes which befell their armies, from the entrance of Hannibal into Italy, down to the battle of Cannæ? As, therefore, what has once happened in this world of ours, may do so again, may not dangers similar to those which threatened the Roman Empire with destruction, also pay us a visit, if we do not adopt the necessary measures to counteract the baneful influence, which a period of similar inactivity may ultimately exercise over all our military establishments?

The British army never can be sufficiently grateful for the many and valuable improvements introduced into our military system, by His Royal Highness the late Duke of York. For more than thirty years, that illustrious prince laboured incessantly to improve the discipline, increase the comforts, and raise the character of the British army in the eyes of surrounding nations, and almost every person knows that by diligence, perseverance, and the most assiduous attention to the duties of his office, he at length succeeded in raising its character to a point of excellence, unequalled for discipline, bravery, and moral worth, by any other army under the canopy of heaven. But as to revise, improve, and consolidate the various parts of the military establishment of even a third rate power, is a task too arduous for any one man to accomplish, how much more difficult must a similar undertaking be in Britain, whose warriors are at this moment to be found in considerable force in every part of the habitable globe? It being impossible, therefore, for the Duke of York to accomplish everything called for in the way of correction and improvement, it ought not to excite surprise, that our military institutions should still claim the attention and serious consideration of the gallant and much esteemed nobleman, who now presides over the military affairs of the United Kingdom.

The discipline of a battalion being invariably more or less perfect, in exact proportion as the officers are more or less qualified to convey military instruction to those over whom they are placed, it should be the grand object of general officers and colonels commanding battalions, to have all the officers under their command thoroughly instructed in every branch of duty which they can be called upon to perform at home or abroad. This appears to me the more necessary from this circumstance, that a great proportion of the junior officers hold erroneous opinions regarding those military qualifications; many of them conceiving that if they can perform a portion of their minor public and regimental routine duties with some appearance of accuracy, any farther attempt at improvement in military science is an *unnecessary waste of their time*, which, perhaps after all, is spent in an idle round of frivolous amusements. By obstinately clinging to those opinions, numerous officers not only permit year after year to roll over their heads without making one attempt to explore the rich mines of military wealth, contained in the various books of instruction, but as a natural consequence of such egregious folly, plod their way through, perhaps, a long military life, more like walking automatons than officers, and then slip into retirement as utterly ignorant of the great leading principles of regimental discipline, as they were on the day they first entered the service.

Besides being a source of great uneasiness to themselves, the inattention of officers to their studies must invariably lessen the general efficiency of their respective battalions. With a few lessons in the facings, wheelings, and manual and platoon exercises, any officer may perform the *formal* portion of his regimental duties; but no officer can ever arrive at anything like a proficiency in drill, or become thoroughly acquainted with his public or regimental duties, until he has treasured up in his memory, every rule and section of the book of rules and regulations for the formation and exercise of the army. To accomplish this most desirable object, a little application is all that is necessary, provided the pupil is assisted in his studies by a tutor qualified to convey military instruction in a clear and forcible manner. But if he is permitted to grope his way through the mazes of that volume without a guide to direct him in the proper path, it is a hundred to one, but he will be found at the expiry of five, ten, or twenty years, to have proceeded but a very short way from whence he started;—totally unacquainted with the ground over which he has travelled, and altogether unable to proceed one step farther.

I may perhaps be told that it is a part of the adjutant's duty to instruct the young officer. I admit the fact; but in doing so must add, that if the adjutant discharges as he ought all the other duties which more immediately belong to his situation, he will have but very little time to bestow on the instruction of officers. From a personal knowledge of the duties of that officer, I am so satisfied he cannot give that attention to the instruction of the young officers which the good of the service requires, that I have no hesitation in saying, that this part of an adjutant's duty should be removed from his shoulders to those of the junior major and senior lieutenant of each regiment.

The duties of a lieutenant-colonel commandant are so numerous and important, that to burden him with others, which some of the junior officers could equally well perform, would, in effect, be to render him incapable of performing any one of them with credit to himself, or advantage to his battalion. And as the senior major has frequently to assume f the command of the battalion in the temporary' absence of the lieutenant-colonel, it would be equally imprudent, I conceive, to select him for this duty. But as the duties of the junior major are neither many or important, I would delegate to him the entire superintendence of all drills having for their object the instruction of the juniors, or the farther improvement of those of longer standing, in every branch of duty which they can be jailed upon to perform at home or abroad. And as the major, in the discharge of this honourable and important duty, would be afforded numerous opportunities of bringing his military acquirements under the eyes of his superiors, it is obvious that he could not be appointed to a situation better calculated to bring him into notice in that quarter, towards which the eyes of all those who look forward to rank, and honours are continually bent.

I would further suggest, that the senior lieutenant in each battalion should be appointed the major's assistant, with the temporary rank of captain, and allowed the pay of an adjutant. Should he senior lieutenant appear to the commanding-officer to be unfit for the situation, an indulgence of a few months might be granted, to enable him o qualify himself for it. But should he, at the expiration of the given period, be still deficient in the necessary qualifications, the lieutenant next in rank should be appointed; failing him, the third, and so on, until one of them is found competent to discharge as he ought the multifarious duties of the office.

In regard to those lieutenants who may from *inattention* be found unqualified six months after the promulgation of any order on this subject, perhaps it might be prudent to transmit their names to the Horse-Guards, in order that they might be made to attend to their duties, or retire from the service, and make room for others more desirous of serving their country. At all events, a hint from that quarter that promotion would be stopped; if improvement did not take place after a farther limited period, would operate powerfully and favourably on the minds of the juniors, and by stimulating them to immediate exertion, and consequent improvement, render a future recurrence to harsh measures altogether unnecessary; for what officer of spirit would not sacrifice rest, comfort *even life itself*, rather than return to the bosom of his family with anything approaching to a stair upon his character?

In order to facilitate the instruction of the young officers, I am of opinion that a company, consisting of forty privates, and a proportion of non-commissioned officers, should be formed in every battalion and the command of it given to the "Captain lieutenant." The men should be selected in equal portions from every company, and none but the very best men admitted into it. This would prove a stimulus to good conduct, which, if carefully fostered, might be productive of much real good to the service. And farther, from the high state of discipline, &c. in which the "Company of Instruction" would invariably appear on parade, the commanding-officer would be enabled at all times to hold it up to the permanent companies of his battalion, as a pattern worthy of imitation in everything touching duty, cleanliness, or intelligence.

The Second Division

On joining his regiment, the first thing to which the attention of the tyro is directed, is the regimental standing orders. These every officer should be able to repeat from memory, in order that none might have it in their power, first to commit a breach of them, and subsequently to plead ignorance of them as an apology for his offence.

On giving the regimental standing orders a snug berth in his memory, the first part of the book of Rules and Regulations for the formation and exercise of His Majesty's forces, should be placed in his hand, *the whole of which he should commit to memory*, before he is handed over to the drill-sergeant, to be instructed in the positions, facings, &c. Were this strictly enforced on all occasions, the pupil's progress would be greatly accelerated, and the lessons of his instructor rendered much more beneficial. Having acquired a competent knowledge of part first, the pupil will then proceed to part second, which he will in a similar manner commit to memory, and afterwards proceed with the company drill.

On being reported fully qualified to join the battalion, the pupil should, previously to so doing, be able to repeat the whole of part third, and as soon thereafter as possible he should be made to commit to memory the remainder of the volume. It might be considered rather unbecoming the rank and years of a considerable majority of the officers at present in the British army, to call upon them to repeat the Rules and Regulations, but I do think that it would do no harm to call upon them for a certificate, upon honour, that they have committed the whole of the volume to memory. The discretionary power hitherto given to officers, which leaves them at liberty either to make themselves acquainted with the Rules, &c. or not, as they please, should unquestionably be withdrawn.

Military instruction should invariably be communicated to a pupil, whether officer or soldier, in an easy, agreeable, and rather captivating manner, so as to give him a relish for the service. For a few lessons given in a clear and perspicuous manner, and aided by a few examples from the Rules and Regulations, will forward the studies of the recruit much more than a long period of harassing and incessant drill. Too much of the latter thaws the zeal, and lessens the inclination of the pupil to please. His tasks become irksome,—disgust with the service succeeds,—which, in a little time, is followed by a deep-rooted aversion to everything in the shape of military duty or study.

It being extremely desirable that the young officer should be qualified to perform the duties of a subaltern, and a portion of those devolving upon a captain, before he falls in with his company on the general parade; the attention of a pupil might with advantage be directed to the following regimental duties, during his progress through parts first and second of the Rules and Regulations. In regard to those duties, I may remark, that however trifling and insignificant some of them may appear, regimental officers may rest assured that they will always find it a dangerous experiment to allow any of them to remain unperformed, or to be performed by *proxy*. For as the whole range of regimental duty lies so immediately under the eyes of the non-commissioned officers and privates, any deviation from the prescribed regimental rules or regulations, is instantly observed, noted, and may, when least expected, rise up against them, and oppose a barrier to farther promotion.

The duty devolving on the regimental subaltern of the day, is by many looked upon as one of form, not of utility. This is a complete delusion; for the comfort, the health of every man in the service, depends in a great measure upon the manner in which this duty is performed. In order, therefore, that the young officer may have a correct idea of this duty, previous to his being placed on the adjutant's roster, the captain-lieutenant should frequently accompany his young friend in a tour through the barrack-rooms early in the morning, and point out to him how the bedding should be folded up. These visits should be resumed at the hour of breakfast and dinner, when he would have an opportunity of observing the state of cleanliness in which the floors and walls of the different rooms ought to be kept,—the manner in which the men take their places at the breakfast and dinner tables,—the respect paid to the visiting-officer,—and the description of *diet* allowed to each individual.

As the subaltern of the day has also to inspect the beef and bread issued to the men, the captain-lieutenant should accompany his pupil to the place of delivery, and there shew him the quality which the contractors are bound to furnish of each. This would enable him to judge correctly between the contractors and the soldiers, and to approve or reject such provisions as may be delivered to the battalion, with the utmost impartiality. In the performance of this, as well as all his other duties, the subaltern of the day should invariably bestow praise where it is merited; for one *kind word* spoken to the attentive soldier, in the *presence* of those of a different character, has frequently more effect upon the conduct of the *latter*, than a *thousand of abuse*.

The next duty which the pupil should attend is guard-mounting. To the eye of an experienced officer, nothing can possibly convey a more despicable opinion of a corps, than to see its officers go through the ceremony of guard-mounting in a slovenly or un-officer-like manner. Indeed the character and discipline of a corps are very frequently estimated by the manner in which the garrison-duties are performed by the various members. So often is this the case, that too much attention cannot be bestowed by the captain-lieutenant, in perfecting his friends in this particular branch of duty.

As soon as a pupil is so far advanced with his drill as to be qualified to assume the command of a section, the company of instruction should be daily formed into various bodies representing guards, and under the command of such officers as may be at drill, put through all the various movements prescribed for that interesting ceremony. By adopting this course, the young officer would be so thoroughly instructed in this duty, previous to joining his company on the public parade, that he could exhibit before the first Martinet in the world with *éclat*.

One of the most important duties which a regimental officer has to discharge, is that which devolves upon him as a member of a court-martial. In order to qualify a young officer to take his seat as a member, he is generally made to attend all courts-martial held in his battalion, for at least six or twelve months after he joins it, and at the expiration of one or other of these periods, is ordered to be placed on the roster as qualified for that duty. To enforce the attendance of the pupil is all very proper; but to suppose that the bare attendance of an officer at courts-martial, for either of these periods, can qualify a thoughtless stripling to give a satisfactory vote on questions involving in their issue, the health, comfort, character, and it may be the very existence of a fellow-creature, is the grossest folly imaginable. Is it not more probable that his inexperience may lead him to invert the order of punishment, by giving to the greater criminal the lesser punishment, and *vice versa*?

Unless a pupil receives considerable assistance in this part of his studies during his probationary drills, he never can form anything like a correct opinion on any case that may come before him; but on any occasion where the smallest difference in the crime may appear from those which preceded it, he will invariably be seen floundering like a fish out of water, quite unable to determine whether the culprit, on being found guilty, should get one lash or three hundred, or one day's solitary confinement, or thirty.

Now, as this appears to be a state of affairs which should not be longer tolerated, I would propose, that, accompanied by the captain-lieutenant, the pupil should make frequent visits to the orderly- room, ransack the pages of the regimental court-martial book, and cull from them such information as may be deemed necessary to render him an important and efficient member.

By adopting this course, the pupil would at once perceive the nature of those crimes which a regimental court-martial can take cognizance of. By attentively perusing the evidence produced on each trial, for and against the prisoner, in aggravation or mitigation of his crime, and then the finding and sentence of the court, he would very soon be able to form a tolerably correct estimate of the nature and degree of punishment, awarded by regimental courts-martial for almost every description of crime.

From the orderly-room the captain-lieutenant should accompany the pupil to a few courts-martial, and there point out to him the military law in regard to the precedence of members, the mode of constituting the court, and conducting the proceedings, and any other information which he may conceive necessary to elucidate the duties devolving upon the members of every court-martial. And as members frequently decline the honour of writing the proceedings of a court-martial, from a natural diffidence, or want of confidence in their own abilities, every young officer, on taking his seat as a member, should be made to write the proceedings of every court-martial held in his corps, till the captain-lieutenant shall report him capable of doing so, without any assistance from him.

Previous to joining his company on the general parade, the young officer should be fully competent to inspect the arms, accoutrements, and clothing of the soldiers. For this purpose a complete stand of arms, a set of accoutrements, and a suit of clothing, should constantly remain in the keeping of the captain-lieutenant, by whom they should be shewn to the pupil, and the use of everything fully explained, as well as the state of repair and cleanliness in which each article ought at all times to be kept. Every part of the musket should be dissected, and the name and use of everything, down to the most minute portion of stock, lock, and barrel, should be communicated to the inexperienced, by the instructor.

It is highly desirable that the troops at home should have their outpost duties frequently brought into view, and in a manner similar to that in which they may have to discharge them in face of an enemy. For as the largest armies are frequently under the necessity of committing their safety and honour to the keeping of very small fractional parts of themselves, it is indispensibly necessary that every officer should be thoroughly instructed in the outpost duty, before he is entrusted with the command of an out-lying piquet in a position of danger. But it may be asked, how is this to be accomplished, seeing that no part of the troops are ever employed on this duty at home? I answer,—by attending to the hints given in the following pages.

Until an officer has acquired a thorough knowledge of ground, in a military point of view, it is quite impossible for him to become so intimately acquainted with his outpost duties as he ought to be; From various books he may receive information on the subject, but nothing beyond a little theory; and every officer knows that theory is but the assistant of practice. In theory, it is the simplest thing imaginable to march a piquet to a given piece of ground, to post the sentinels, fell trees, and raise various kinds of works to strengthen the post. But let any officer, without some previous instruction, attempt to accomplish these things, and he will find everything widely different. The officer, whose guide and instructor is theory, moves at all times hesitatingly,—is irresolute in all his movements,—and when posted, knows not whether he is right or wrong. An experienced officer, on the contrary, marches his piquet to the post assigned it with confidence,—perceives at one glance all the favourable and unfavourable points of the ground around him,—plants his sentries in an instant, and adopts such measures as are necessary for the security of the whole. Let us, therefore, by a little home practice, in addition to theory, endeavour to acquire such a knowledge of this duty, as on the day of trial will render us the trust-worthy guardians of those who may be compelled to place their repose, their safety, and their honour in our hands.

The major and captain-lieutenant should once or twice every

week, proceed with parties of officers into the country, in order to make a military survey of it for several miles around the headquarters of their corps. When advancing, the major and his assistant should point out to their friends, the strong or weak points of every prominent piece of ground in a defensive point of view,—the most eligible situations for defensive posts,—for raising redoubts or breastworks,—the number of troops requisite to defend each post,—the strong and weak parts of each,—the best mode of strengthening the latter; and places best calculated for out-piquets.

On counter-marching, the column of course will assume an offensive attitude. The appearance of the ground will be totally changed. The defensive posts established on the advance, will now fall to be attacked or turned. The major will consequently have to shew his party how this is to be accomplished, and after describing the various modes by which the object might be gained, he will point out those which he may conceive deserving of a preference. If there should happen to be any houses or villages on the road, the major should give the officers some idea of the number of troops that could be quartered in each house or village, in case of emergency. In fine, every information relative to out-post duty, should be fully and distinctly communicated.

As soon as the officers can take a view of the country with a military eye, piquets of exercise, accompanied by the major, should be dispatched into the country two or three times a-week,—remain out all day, and return to their quarters in the evening. Until all the officers shall have been at least twice on this duty, those going on piquet will require the major's assistance in the posting of their piquets and sentries, in doing which, he must shew them by actual experiment that a sentry posted *one yard* too much to one side or the other, may be productive of the most disastrous consequences to themselves, and every one in their rear.

And, it is the imperative duty of every officer to be prepared to make a brave and successful defence, or to effect a safe and honourable retreat, one and all of them should be instructed in the best and most expeditious way of felling trees;—arranging them for the defence of their posts, and raising little field-works, or other obstacles for similar purposes. When each officer shall have been twice on piquet, the major should discontinue his trips with them to their posts, but continue to give them such instructions as he may deem necessary on marching off their piquets. During the day he should visit each piquet, make such observations on the dispositions of the officers as may be called for, and where errors have been committed, either in the choice of ground, or in planting their sentries, he must assist his friends in making a more desirable disposition of their forces.

All officers whatever, on every change of quarters should be called upon to give in military reports of the country for several miles round their posts; and as a great proportion of our officers hare had but little experience in drawing up such documents, the major and his assistant should superintend the efforts of the juniors, till they can perform that duty themselves with facility and correctness.

As but a very small proportion of the subaltern officers have had the pleasure of witnessing the daily movements of a large body of troops on service, perhaps the following hints regarding the marching, and quartering of those composing the second division of the allied army in Spain, may not be unacceptable to them, particularly as the duties which officers of all ranks have to perform on these occasions, cannot be reduced to practice at home.

The Second Division consisted of ten British, and three Portuguese battalions of infantry, and when formed in line, stood thus,—

1st Brigade.
50th, 92nd, 71st.

3rd Brigade.
3rd, 57th, 66th, 31st

4th Brigade, Portuguese.
6th Caçadores, 18th, 6th.

2nd Brigade.
28th, 39th, 34th.

In forming a brigade or division, the reader will perceive that the same rule is invariably observed. When a brigade is composed of three battalions, the senior battalion takes post on the right, the next in seniority on the left, and the junior in the centre; but when it consists of four, the third in seniority forms the right centre, and the fourth the left centre of the brigade. The senior is denominated the right battalion, the second in seniority the left, the third the right centre, and the fourth the left centre battalion. When a division consists of three brigades, No. 1, is posted on the right, and is called the right brigade; No. 2, takes the left, and is styled the left brigade, and No. 3, forms the centre, and is denominated the centre brigade. But when the division is composed of four brigades, No. 3, takes post on the left of No. 1, and is called the right centre brigade, and No. 4, being on the right of

No. 2, is named the left centre brigade.

The following order of march was almost invariably observed. When the division moved right in front, the 50th Regiment formed the leading battalion, and was followed by all the others in the order above shown; but when it moved left in front, the order of march was completely reversed. On all occasions the division moved with a rear and advanced guard, and when the proximity of the enemy rendered it necessary, with skirmishers on each flank.

When the division was to occupy cantonments.; the quarter-master-general of the division, the majors of brigade, quarter-masters of regiments, and a non-commissioned and intelligent private soldier from each company, preceded the march of the column, that the quarters might be properly told of previous to its arrival. After selecting suitable residences for the staff-officers of the division, the quarter-master-general divided the remainder into as many parts as there were brigades, and handed a part over to each major of brigade. The latter, on setting apart houses for the brigade staff, divided the rest, and delivered over to the quarter-masters' of regiments, quarters according to the strength of their respective battalions. The quarter-masters, after providing suitable accommodation for their regimental staff, divided the remainder, and handed the proper proportions over to officers commanding companies, who, after providing for themselves, and the other officers in their respective companies, handed the other houses over to the non-commissioned officers and privates.

When the division was to encamp, the same parties as before named accompanied the quarter-master-general to the ground which it was to occupy. When the division was to remain a few days in camp, the various battalions were formed in open column of companies at wheeling distance, and when in line facing towards the enemy. When the space was confined, or we were to remain but one night on the ground, the companies were occasionally drawn up at half or quarter-distance. The men's kitchens and other conveniences were always in rear of the encampment. The company officers pitched their tents about thirty or forty paces in rear of the arms. The senior major, sixty paces in rear of the right wing; the junior major at a similar distance from the left; and the lieutenant-colonel still farther to the rear, and immediately opposite to the centre of the battalion.

Each battalion furnished a subaltern officer to take charge of its own baggage on the march. Each brigade, a captain who took charge of all the baggage of the brigade, and a field-officer was appointed to look after the whole. When the division moved right in front, the baggage animals of the lieutenant-general commanding the division led the way. and were followed by those of his personal and division staff;—then moved the baggage of the general or other officer in command of the leading brigade, and his personal staff. After the latter, followed that of the lieutenant-colonel commanding the leading battalion;—then that of the regimental staff, followed by the baggage of the grenadier officers, and the officers of the other companies in regular succession. The baggage of the other regiments followed in similar order. When the division moved left in front, the order of march, as far as regarded *company baggage* was reversed, but that of all the other officers moved as above described. The baggage of one corps was never permitted to intermix with that of another. At the close of every day's march, the subaltern made a report to the captain and his own commanding officer; the captain to the field-officer and general commanding the brigade; and the field-officer reported to the lieutenant-general commanding the division.

Before taking leave of this subject, I beg once more to urge on the attention of young officers, the necessity of their applying head and heart to their several books of instruction, if they wish to acquire a competent knowledge of their duties, and be at all times prepared to discharge them in a manner satisfactory to themselves, and beneficial to their country. When we look back and reflect how very few officers of the hundreds of thousands who have served in the British army during the last two or three centuries, have acquired that knowledge of the military art which qualifies an officer to form the plan of a war, we are forced to conclude, either that but few officers ever attain so much knowledge of their profession, or that opportunities have been wanting to develop their abilities in this peculiar department of their art. Now, it will be readily conceded, that there has been no lack of opportunities, consequently, we are led to the opinion, that the want of abilities in some, but he want of application on the part of a much greater number, are the sole causes why so very few officers have risen to anything like eminence in the art of war.

I shall be told, perhaps, that it is not at all necessary that every officer should be qualified to form the plan of a war. In this opinion I perfectly agree: but in doing so I cannot shut my eyes to his fact, that unless all those are able to do so, who aspire to the higher ranks of their profession, they will, on a command of importance being offered them, be under the necessity of declining it, or of accepting the trust, in the full knowledge of their own incompetency to discharge its duties. To avoid the necessity of adopting either of those unpleasant alternatives, particularly the latter, which might put to hazard their own reputation and the interests of their country, nothing more is required from those officers who really intend to make the military art their sole business through life, than diligence and assiduity in the prosecution of their military studies.

Personal experience has very generally been considered the officer's best instructor; yet as it is a very rare occurrence for a general to have an opportunity of attacking an enemy twice under exactly similar circumstances, and as the hundredth part of those accidents and changes of position which invariably take place in battles and sieges, cannot possibly come within the observation of one man, every officer who wishes to discharge his duties with ability, *must of necessity add to his own the experience of others*. This can only be accomplished by scanning the page of history, and making himself acquainted with the memorable actions of the most illustrious warriors of every age and country,—a study, in the prosecution of which, the young aspirant will discover the rocks on which so many officers have shipwrecked their fame and fortunes, and how the more successful commanders manoeuvred, when they raised for themselves monuments of fame which will endure to the end of time.

The Storming of Bejer

We had not been long in Coria, when a considerable number of our men found a residence in hospital, and not a few of our oldest and most experienced officers a premature grave. Amongst the latter, were Lieutenant-General Sir William Erskine, commanding the cavalry of Sir Rowland Hill's corps; Colonel Wilson, 39th Regiment, and Colonel Stewart, 50th Regiment; the former commanding the Second, and the latter the First Brigade of the Second Division.

The French being also without tents, were equally tired of the campaign, and in want of repose. Their clothing being much like our own, they, on retiring into quarters, looked around for something to shelter their bodies from the inclemencies of a Spanish winter. At Bejer, a town fifteen leagues from Salamanca, and about an equal distance from Coria, there was at that time a large quantity of woollen cloth in possession of a manufacturer, who had calculated on a very different issue to the campaign. This the French fixed their eyes upon, and to seize upon it, an expedition under General Foy, was prepared at Salamanca.

On receiving notice of the enemy's intentions, Sir Rowland Hill ordered the 71st Regiment and 6th Caçadores to advance from Monte-Hermosa, and an adjoining village, to the aid of the inhabitants of Bejer, and the 30th and 92nd were pushed forward from Coria to Monte-Hermosa. These movements convincing the enemy that the rich prize would not be tamely given up, they thought it prudent to retire, and try whether a little undisturbed repose might not lull us into a criminal security.

Monte-Hermosa was exclusively occupied by farmers and their dependants. The streets being extremely filthy, and in the most wretched repair, we found it most unpleasant to be out after sunset. Altogether it was an uncomfortable quarter; the weather being wet and extremely cold, the windows without glass, and the apartments without fire, I declare I never knew what it was to be warm, save when in bed, or sometimes after dinner.

In the second week of February, General Foy made another dash at Bejer, but Sir Rowland Hill having received timely notice of his intentions, ordered the 71st and 6th Caçadores to move from Banos to Bejer, the 50th to Banos, and 92nd to follow as a reserve. When the 71st and Caçadores occupied Bejer on the 12th of February, Foy was only a few miles from it; but on hearing of their arrival, he again retired. To secure the place against any future attack, the 50th and 6th Caçadores were thrown into Bejer as a permanent garrison, the 71st occupied the villages of Puerto-de-Banos, and Candeleiria, and the 92nd Regiment the town of Banos a few miles in rear. The 60th Rifle Company were quartered in Herbas.

A few days after this attempt had been so timeously frustrated, the hills of Bejer and Banos again rung with the dreadful note of preparation. Thinking to carry it by surprise, Foy advanced again at the head of 3000 picked troops, and with so much secrecy, that he was within a short distance of the piquets, before Lieutenant-Colonel Harrison of the 50th Regiment, then commanding the garrison, received notice of his approach. So unexpected indeed was the attack, that one of the outlying piquets was nearly surrounded before the officer in charge of it knew that the enemy was nearer to them than Salamanca.

In a few minutes after driving in the piquets, Foy was before the gates of Bejer anticipating an easy victory. But unfortunately for Foy and his followers, the several entrances were guarded by detachments of the old 50th, over whose lifeless trunks it behoved them to march before they could accomplish their object. The attack was made with all the characteristic bravery of Frenchmen, and was repulsed with that unflinching courage so peculiar to that excellent corps. Foy's great numerical superiority gave him decided advantages, but this had an effect on the spirits of the troops, directly the reverse of that which might have been anticipated, for as the danger increased, so did the courage of the troops, till Foy, perceiving that his reiterated attempts to penetrate into the town, were not to be attended with any other result than a defeat, withdrew before his adversaries could turn it into a disgraceful one. Part of the garrison followed the fugitives, and inflicted on them a severe punishment for their effrontery in attempting to intrude themselves into Bejer society without permission. Foy's loss amounted to upwards of a hundred killed and wounded, and amongst the latter, was an *aide-de-camp* on the Staff of the General.

On receipt of the first notice of Foy's approach, Colonel Cameron, 92nd Regiment, then in command of the First Brigade, ordered four companies of the 71st Regiment to move from Puerto-de-Banos to Bejer, and the 92nd to advance to a position in front of the pass of Banos, in order to be in readiness to move to wherever their services might be required. The former exerted themselves to be up in time, but were too late to take part in the action. They, however, had the pleasing satisfaction of witnessing the flight of their foes, and the victorious march of their friends from Bejer's bloodstained gates.

Banos stands in a narrow valley surrounded with rugged mountains, some of which rise in precipitous masses from the banks of two little rivulets, one of which winds past the town on the west, and the other, after dividing the village into nearly two equal parts, joins the first at the lower extremity of the town, and then meanders through the valley, till its waters are lost in a more notable stream. The northern division is situated in the Province of Leon; the southern in Estremadura. The inhabitants of this town have ever been distinguished for their industry, and loyalty to their sovereign, for which they have sometimes paid rather dearly.

One day, soon after we entered Banos, one of our officers rather unguardedly inquired at his landlady, if the inhabitants of Banos were *hearty in the good cause*. On the question being put, the lady with an air of great importance, arose, walked to a window which overlooked the ruins of some houses which had been burned down by the French, and then pointing to them, said, "Sir, to these I refer you for an answer."

The French on one occasion carried off the wife of one of the most respectable inhabitants in Banos, on the pretence that her husband was a patriot, and did not restore her until the latter paid them several hundred dollars. On the cash being paid, the lady returned to her home in a state of mind bordering on insanity; and at the time we took leave of Banos, she still furnished a living and melancholy monument of the miseries which the ambition of one man had drawn down upon the inhabitants of the Peninsula.

The life of a private soldier, when on service similar to that in which the British troops were engaged in the Peninsula, is but too often one of such vicissitude, hardship, and privation, that to see the poor fellows occasionally placed in situations where they can enjoy something approaching to the comforts of a domestic hearth, far from the din of war, must, I conceive, yield to others, as it never failed to do to me, a degree of pleasure far beyond the power of language to express. In one of those situations, our merry blades rather unexpectedly found themselves on entering Banos, where in every house the nut-brown knee, and weather-beaten countenance, met with nothing but smiles, and the most marked attention.

And what is still more astonishing, the longer we remained amongst them, the more friendly did the town's-people become, till at length the soldiers and the inhabitants of each house messed together as one family,—the former furnishing beef, bread, &c. and the latter pease, beans, pork, oil, garlic, and other vegetables. To show how much attached the inhabitants were to the men, I may mention the following fact:—When Sir Rowland Hill passed through the town, a day or two after the Highlanders had left Banos, a deputation, composed of the principal inhabitants, waited on him, to return him thanks for the protection he had afforded them against the enemy. Before the deputation departed, the general inquired if they had any complaints to prefer against the regiment that had just left them; to which the head of the deputation instantly replied,—"Sir Rowland Hill, had you been here when the Highlanders marched out of our village, our tears would have answered your question."

Now, to what can we attribute the friendly reception which the 92nd met with at Banos, and the subsequent kindness which they experienced in that rural town, but to that kindred spirit which seems to possess the breast of every mountaineer throughout the world? In all ages, and in every clime, the mountaineer has invariably been found to possess in an eminent degree that heroic courage which nothing could shake,—no dangers appal. To enumerate those countries so distinguished in historical record for having given birth to a hardy and intrepid soldiery, appears superfluous; for where is the man who has not personally perused, or heard read over the details of those battles, the issues of which have furnished the world with decisive proof, that in every country famed for its rocks, its hills, and its torrents, spirits, daring and adventurous as the heroes of romance, have ever been as numerous as its male population? Scotland, for example, the land of the mountain and flood, whose snow-cap't hills formed an impervious barrier to the victorious legions of the Queen of the world, has, from the first invasion of her soil by a foreign foe, continued to send forth a race of warriors unrivalled for deeds of arms on the field of strife.

But why should I particularize, for in every quarter the mountaineer has ever been distinguished for his rusticity, hospitality, and bravery. In Asia, almost the only opposition offered to Alexander's career of conquest, was from the natives inhabiting the mountainous regions of that extensive continent. In Spain,—in Switzerland,—and in the Tyrol, feats of arms have been performed not less worthy the attention of the historian, than those of Leonidas and his followers at Thermopylæ. And I conceive this no small encomium; for while the sun shall continue to perform his diurnal journey, so long will the battle of Thermopylæ be handed down from one generation to another, as one of the most splendid sacrifices ever offered up at the altar of liberty. Till the end of time the name of Leonidas will be pronounced with veneration by the sons of liberty in whatever generation they may live, or in whatever clime their lot may be cast.

The conduct of the Spartan king and his three hundred incomparable warriors, at the straits of Thermopylae, has furnished the world with the most incontestable proofs we could desire, that a handful of men, born and reared in the lap of liberty, will never listen to proposals which tend to abridge their freedom, even when backed, as on that occasion, with millions of armed slaves. For slaves, who know nothing but a blind obedience to the will and capricious humours of their tyrannical masters, fight not for glory,—for honour,—or liberty. No; these words have no place in the slave's vocabulary. Freemen alone know the true meaning of them, and knowing it, look upon everything else as nothing in the balance. In the hour of danger, freemen despise everything but what redounds to their country's good; and when duty imposes upon them the dreadful alternative, lay down their lives with as much pleasure as the poor slave feels reluctance in parting with his.

In the latter end of April, a military execution of a most afflicting description, took place in a field about half-a-mile from Banos. The crime for which the unfortunate young man was condemned to die, was desertion to the enemy, and attempting to stab the non-commissioned officer who apprehended him. A little before the hour of execution, the regiment was drawn up so as to form three sides of a square, the other side, as is usual on similar occasions, was left open as the place of execution. Our chaplain being absent, the schoolmaster sergeant accompanied the poor lad to the fatal spot, and all the way from the village read portions of Scripture.

On their arrival at the point assigned them, the criminal joined very audibly in singing a few verses of a psalm, and then, after spending a few minutes in prayer, the fatal cap was drawn over his eyes, and the provost-marshal with his party advanced from the rear of the column to carry the sentence into effect. At this awfully affecting part of the scene, the whole regiment, officers and men, knelt down, and on behalf of him who then stood on the verge of a never-ending eternity, offered up humble supplications to the throne of mercy. In a few moments thereafter the party fired, and in an instant the world closed upon the culprit forever.

Previous to entering upon a new campaign, it was deemed advisable to give all those men who had enlisted in 1806, an opportunity of renewing their engagements, either for a limited or unlimited period. Men not above thirty-five years of age were allowed to enlist for life, and received sixteen guineas. Those above thirty-five for seven years only, and received eleven guineas of bounty. As the great proportion of them had imbibed the notion that they would not survive even the shortest period of service, those who could claim the indulgence very generally accepted the highest bounty, in order to indulge in a few Bacchanalian campaigns, before the Gallic cock should have an opportunity of crowing over their graves.

John Bull has frequently been accused of possessing a prodigious appetite for blood, aye, for human blood, and that give him plenty of it he will part with a little cash, in the shape of taxes, as pleasantly as any man in the world. I shall not say that he is guilty of the crime laid to his charge; but I do assert that he must have viewed our inactivity in 1813, as something bordering on picking his pocket; for loud and sore grumbled John. So much so, indeed, that many thought he would put a Gordian knot on his purse-strings, if our *generalissimo* did not immediately transmit him an assurance that his troops should be instantly put in motion, and neither permitted to eat, drink, or sleep, until they had placed their mouths close to those of the enemy's cannon, to the imminent hazard of their heads, but to the great delight and amusement of John.

The cause of our inactivity may be summed up in a few words. At the close of the campaign of 1812, our cavalry and artillery were very inefficient, from the great loss of horses in action and from fatigue. Many battalions of infantry were miserably clothed,—their accoutrements considerably damaged,—and their camp equipment was in a most wretched state. From various causes their numbers had been also considerably reduced; besides he deaths, many went into hospital in November, who were not fit for service until the beginning of May.

Our military chest required to be relined, our stores of provisions and ammunition replenished, and our camp equipment renewed. Under these circumstances, what could Lord Wellington do but exercise his patience, till men, horses, money, and military stores could be transported to him from England? Such were the causes of our inactivity. These, however, being all removed in the second week of May, the Marquis of Wellington prepared to take the field, at the head of as fine a little army as could be desired.

Crossing the Ebro

The various parts of the grand military machine being prepared, an order from the great master to have the whole put together, and in readiness to move by the middle of May, at length appeared. The crisis now approached which was either to bind Spain in eternal chains, or rescue her from the grasp of her powerful neighbour. All eyes in Spain and in England were consequently directed towards the scene of active operations, and with a never-ceasing anxiety, followed the movements of Lord Wellington throughout the whole of the following campaign.

On the 15th of May, Sir Thomas Graham crossed the Douro, near Miranda-del-Douro, with the left wing of the allied army, ascended the right bank to the Esla, which he crossed, and then advanced upon Zamora, from which, at his approach, the enemy retired towards Toro.

The Second Division assembled in a plain a few miles in front of Bejer, on the 20th of May. On the 23rd we were reviewed by Sir Rowland Hill. Lieutenant-General, the Honourable William Stewart, appeared at our head, for the first time, on this occasion. On the following morning we advanced to Robeira, next day to Mattella, and on the 26th we continued our route towards Salamanca, then in possession of a small corps of the enemy under General Villate.

Lord Wellington having formed a junction with Sir Rowland Hill, advanced with a portion of the cavalry to a height on the left bank of the Tormes, immediately opposite to Salamanca, and, after reconnoitring the enemy, ordered the cavalry and some horse-artillery to cross the river, some by the bridge of Salamanca, and the rest by a ford a little above it, and attack Villate, who was just leaving the city. The order was obeyed with cheerfulness, and success crowned the efforts of the assailants. After a pretty smart affair, the French were defeated, with the loss of 300 killed, wounded, and prisoners. Of the latter there were 140.

The infantry having subsequently crossed the Tormes, and encamped in a plain about half-a-mile above Salamanca, our encampment was visited in the afternoon by a great many respectable people from the city. The ladies exhibited a considerable portion of curiosity on the occasion, many of them pulling aside the folds of our tents, without the smallest ceremony, to have a full view of "*Los Angleses*." At first we were a good deal put about by the conduct of our fair friends, for at the time, we were attired in anything but drawing-room costume.

Early in the morning of the 27th, commanding-officers were requested to have their battalions in as high order as they possibly could, in order to pass the Marquis of Wellington in review on the march. About seven o'clock the head of the column moved from the encampment towards Salamanca, the walls of which we kept on our left hand, till we arrived at the northern gate, when, touching the road leading to Toro, we made a quarter-wheel to the right, and proceeded towards the latter.

On a height, about four or five miles from Salamanca, the marquis took post with his numerous staff. Every battalion, as it approached the reviewing-general, halted a few moments to dress the companies, and then moved past in ordinary time. The morning being extremely beautiful,—not a cloud to be seen,—the appearance of the troops was truly magnificent. As each corps passed, the marquis paid them some flattering compliment; and as the last company saluted, he turned round and said, "Sir Rowland, I will take the gloss off your corps this campaign." How far the marquis kept his promise the sequel will shew. Continuing our route, we arrived at Orbada in the afternoon, and encamped.

The regiments composing the second division having been so widely detached during the winter, and spring months, that brigade drill could not be enforced, without subjecting various corps to manifest inconvenience, officers in command of brigades embraced the opportunity which a few day's rest at Orbada afforded them, of putting the troops through a few field manoeuvres almost every morning. Some of them afterwards promoted games for the amusement of their officers and soldiers, and did not hesitate to take part in the sports of the day.

Every officer of proper feeling must always be anxious to acquire and enjoy a high reputation amongst his brother officers. The love of praise, when an officer endeavours to obtain it by the performance of some meritorious exploit, is highly commendable; for it has frequently led soldiers to the performance of heroic exploits, when all other motives have been found insufficient to carry them through the hazardous enterprise. But if an officer attempts to obtain praise by a very different method,—that of *courting popularity with the men*, his efforts to secure a good name can no longer be commendable, but derogatory to his character. To be familiar with the men is to lose all command over them,—to be harsh to them, the issue will be nearly the same. But to be kind to them, without being familiar,—to attend to their comforts, and inquire into their grievances,—to shew them by his every act that he has their welfare sincerely at heart,—are the only true modes by which an officer can honourably obtain that popularity to which alone le should ever aspire.

We broke up from our encampment at Orbada on the 3rd of June, and that evening reposed on the left bank of the Quarena. Here two hundred French prisoners passed us on their way to England, the whole being the lawful capture of the hussar brigade, and Don Julian Sanchez. Two arches of the bridge of Toro having been destroyed in 1812, these, by great exertion, were repaired with wood by daylight on the 4th, but so temporarily, that on passing over it that forenoon, not more than one man could pass at a time. The boards were so elastic, that but for General Stewart who remained on the north side of the broken arches till all the infantry had passed, I would inevitably have fallen into the river and been drowned. On perceiving me reeling to the left side, and quite close to the edge of the temporary erection, the general sprang forward and caught my hand just as I found myself on the eve of tumbling head foremost into the river. The staff and baggage animals found their way to the right bank by a ford a little above the bridge; some of the smallest kinds were swimming. After the whole of the division had crossed, we moved forward five miles on the road to Valladolid and encamped.

Resuming our march next morning, we advanced five leagues and encamped. Here we could neither get *wood* nor *long grass*, nor any kind of substitute for them to boil our kettles. We were consequently compelled to apply to the chief magistrate of a town adjoining our camp, to hand over to us for a suitable compensation, two or three houses to supply us with fuel. On the 6th, we moved first upon Valladolid, but when within a few miles of it, we brought up our right shoulders, and marched to Cigales. Resuming the pursuit of the flying host on the 7th, we advanced to Duennas, and encamped. Here we were presented with a most appalling spectacle, the dead bodies of two French soldiers lying on a dunghill, not placed there by the Spaniards, but by their own friends, and what is more revolting, one of them *before he was dead*. The dunghill was immediately under the window of a house which they used as an hospital. Conduct such as this is quite unpardonable.

On the 8th we advanced to Torquemada. During the night the wind blew a hurricane, and the rain poured down upon us plenteously. Next day and the one following, we plodded our way towards Burgos up to the knees in mud; and after crossing the Arlanzon, on the afternoon of the 10th, encamped on a height about a league from its left bank. On the 11th we moved forward one league to Los-Valbasas and encamped, and on the following day we drew five leagues nearer to Burgos, where we expected to have warm work.

Just as our division had taken up its ground for the night, as we thought, the sound of artillery in our front called us to arms. In a few minutes we were on the road to the scene of action, but had not advanced above a mile, when we were stopped at a little deep stream, the bridge over which the enemy had destroyed. On this obstacle being surmounted, we crossed, and after advancing two miles farther, halted; and in half-an-hour thereafter, were ordered to return to the same ground on which we had originally pitched our tents. We accordingly retraced our steps, both wet and weary. This unseasonable little affair between our light troops, horse artillery, and the enemy's rearguard, ended in favour of the former, who succeeded in driving back the latter with the loss of some killed and wounded, and one piece of artillery.

At five o'clock in the morning of the 13th of June, Joseph Bonaparte, in a fit of temporary insanity unquestionably, blew up the castle of Burgos. This unexpected act of the enemy afforded a key to his future intentions, for it intimated as plainly as language could have done, that he had no intention of giving us battle south of the Ebro. The destruction of this fortress was the first fruits of the British general's admirable plan of operations. Seeing that it was Joseph Bonaparte's intention to defend the passage of the Douro. Lord Wellington caused Sir Thomas Graham to cross the Douro, as before noticed, and subsequently to hang on the enemy's right flank, in order to turn him out of every position he might occupy. The first part of his operations being attended with success, the hero of Barossa continued to manoeuvre in a similar manner all the way to the Ebro, which he crossed on the 14th at Arenas, and, by turning the enemy out of their position in the line of the Ebro, opened a passage for the centre division on the 15th, and Sir Rowland Hill's corps on the day following.

Descending into the vale of the Ebro, the road leads first down a deep ravine, then in a zigzag form down the face of the mountain, which is high and rugged. From the summit of the latter, the bands of the different battalions played some favourite airs all the way down, the rocks on each side re-echoing the shrill sounds of the trumpet the sweeter notes of the clarion, and the wild murmuring sounds of the bagpipe, with very beautiful effect. Bonaparte having decreed all the country north of the Ebro to be annexed to his dear France the band of each battalion on crossing the bridge, struck up the "Downfall of Paris," which, added to the cheers of the soldiers, made the hills and the valleys ring, till from a thousand places, the latter re-echoed the glad acclamations of the happy band of British soldiers.

After crossing the Ebro, we threaded our way up the left bank, the road on each side being bounded by the river on the left, and a rugged and inaccessible mountain on the right. In several places, the road has not only been cut out of the rock, but the rock actually overhangs the road, and part of the water in more places than one. To retire from such strong ground without making some shew of defending the line of the Ebro, was rather astonishing. However, we were not at all displeased with them for doing so. Having kept close to the river for two or three miles, we turned to the right, and after a farther march of a league, halted, and encamped.

On the 17th we proceeded towards Vittoria, and after a movement of three leagues, encamped in a plain, in which we discovered a few of our companions in a distant corner, busily engaged like ourselves in preparing some scalding soup. On the 18th and 19th we continued moving in the direction of Vittoria, and, on the evening of the latter, encamped on a height which overlooks Miranda-del-Ebro.

On the 18th the light division came in contact with a body of the enemy in charge of stores, which they attacked, and handled roughly. The same division was engaged in a similar employment on the day following. On the 20th the whole closed up to within three or four leagues of Vittoria, in front of which Joseph had taken up a position on the preceding day, with the intention of giving us battle.

Vittoria

A little after daybreak on the 21st, the troops were ordered to be in readiness to march at a moment's notice; but whether we were to be engaged in pursuing or combating the enemy, no one could tell. Appearances, however, were in favour of the latter; for, instead of marching at the expiration of the usual period allowed to intervene between the sounding of the warning-horn and the advance, we remained two hours in camp, waiting instructions, before we could move to perform our part in the grand drama of the day. About five o'clock, however, all suspense was at an end.—To arms, resounded through the camp. In a few minutes every man was at his post, and in a few more we were on the road to Puebla, where we arrived about eight.

On leaving our encampment, the rain, which till then had fallen in gentle showers, entirely ceased, and soon after the sun burst from behind the gloomy curtain, to spread his cheering rays over fields yet unstained with blood,—over rivers, whose streams, meandering through Zadora's vale, were yet undisturbed by the strife of man,—to cheer the sons of freedom on their march to the field of honour, hundreds of whom were destined, long before he had finished his daily course, to take their departure for that bourne from whence no traveller returns.

On quitting our camp we were still in ignorance is to the nature of the service in which we were to be employed, but on our arrival at Puebla the secret was of necessity communicated to us, for he enemy held the heights immediately above us, and we were then not more than three miles from the main body of their army. On this important act becoming currently known, a smile of satisfaction played on the cheeks of the soldiers, and during the time the officers were employed in inspecting the arms, some of the old veterans encouraged the juniors, by relating their deeds of former days; others calculated the probable numbers of the foe; a third party—how long the battle would continue; and the whole made themselves sure of glorious victory.

The high road from Madrid to Vittoria, which runs through Puebla, and then up the left bank of the Zadora, takes a sharp turn to the right, two miles in front of the village. Here it leaves the river at some distance on the left, and after passing through the town of Sabujana-de-Alava, leads almost straight towards Vittoria. Pursuing this route, it was a little in front of the bend in the road that we first beheld the dense dark masses of the enemy, arrayed in order of battle, and the advanced bodies of our own and the French cavalry not more than two or three hundred paces from each other.

The scene which now presented itself to our view was animated and grand beyond description On the right bank of the Zadora, and on the face of a pretty high rugged hill, thousands of our companions were moving from their stations, and preparing to join us in the grand struggle. On our right Morillo and his Spaniards were climbing the face of Puebla's heights, and in our rear, battalion after battalion was closing up, to be ready to execute the commands of their leader. In our front the sight was imposing. Turning our eyes to the right, we beheld the left of the French army posted on the summit of the heights of Puebla, supported by strong body of infantry, and some pieces of artillery, a considerable portion of which was stationed in and around a clump of trees, near to the base of the hill, and about a mile and a-half in rear of their most advanced detachment on the height.

Immediately before us stood the village of Sabujana-de-Alava, in which, and on a height a little to its right, the centre divisions of the French army were posted. This height, which partly commanded the high road, as well as a great part of the river and valley of the Zadora, was literally covered with infantry, and at least one hundred pieces of artillery. In a thick wood, a little farther to their right, Joseph had thrown a considerable body of infantry to protect the passage of the Zadora, and keep up an unbroken line of communication between the right centre divisions and the extreme right of his army, which extended along the river to a point rather beyond Vittoria. It is a singular fact, that instead of damping the spirits of our soldiers, the latter appeared more and more delighted, as the French battalions successively appeared from behind their numerous artillery.

One heart and one soul appeared to animate the whole. All seemed to wish for the commencement of the engagement, not so much from a desire to brave death in the many thousand shapes in which the soldier sees the grim king on the field of strife, but because they had been afraid that the enemy might retire; and as a battle appeared inevitable, might ultimately occupy a position presenting greater obstacles to an attack, than any which they could discover on the plains of Vittoria. With this feeling, therefore, and the fixed resolution to conquer or die, the right wing of the allied army moved forward in silence to begin the tremendous conflict.

At a quarter before ten o'clock, the sound of musketry, on the heights of Puebla, announced to 150,000 warriors, that that conflict had commenced which was to send many of their number to sleep with their fathers. As in almost every action fought in a mountainous district, this one was ushered in with the usual—pop,—then pop-pop,—afterwards pop-pop- pop-pop, and so on, till these ominous sounds ended in general volleys, accompanied with the British cheer, or French *Vive' l'Empereur*, as the tide of success for the time influenced the feelings of the parties. General Morillo, with the 5th Spanish Army, being on the right, was the first to lead the way. His troops having acted for some time in conjunction with the corps under Sir Rowland Hill, were considered superior to almost every other body of Spaniards under the immediate command of Lord Wellington. Indeed, when commanded by Morillo in person, they were looked upon as nearly equal to the second description of Portuguese infantry.

On this occasion they shewed themselves possessed of many valuable qualities, but then these were neutralised by the want of confidence in their officers; for with the exception of the chief himself, and a few more of the superior officers, the men really had no confidence in them. Upon the whole, however, they attacked with spirit, and drove back the enemy in pretty good style. But the superiority in point of ground, and latterly it numbers, would have given the French a decided advantage over their opponents, had not the 71st British Regiment, and Light Companies of the Second Division arrived on the heights soon after the action began, to support our allies. This seasonable reinforcement enabled Morillo to continue his offensive operations, till every post which the enemy occupied on the heights at the commencement was taken from them. In this little brush Morillo was wounded, the French commandant was made prisoner, and the brave Cadogan received his mortal wound.

The heights of Puebla were no sooner in our peeping, than the French Marshal perceived the value of the prize of which his bungling conduct had deprived him. To regain the *key of his position*, therefore, his efforts were for two hours afterwards almost exclusively directed.

This led to the following interesting operations:—

The enemy's intentions were no sooner discovered, than fresh troops were dispatched to the assistance of the Spaniards and British light infantry on the heights. The 50th and 92nd Regiments were the first to proceed on that duty, and had almost gained the summit of the mountain, when they were ordered to retrace their steps. But they had not descended more than half-way, when a third order stopped the retrograde movement, and separated the battalions; the former receiving instructions to proceed to its original destination on the heights, and the latter to move across the face of the hill, and drive back a body of about 4000 French infantry, which had been pushed forward to form an advanced link in the chain of communication between the troops stationed within and around the clump of planting, and those to be employed in the recapture of the heights, about 7000 in number.

The separation of the 50th and 92nd Regiments was not much relished by the soldiers of either corps, but there being no alternative, part they did. The former clambered up the face of the hill, till arriving at the summit, they wheeled to the left, and proceeded along the ridge about half a-mile, till they arrived at the brink of a deep ravine, which ran quite across the hill, a little above, and to the left of the column which the 92nd were about to attack. Here the Spaniards lay along the face of the mountain, and with the 71st on their right, were engaged in a *tirailleur* fire with the enemy. On taking leave of the 50th, the 92nd Regiment descended the hill a few hundred yards, and then, after wheeling a quarter-circle to their right, directed their march towards their opponents, who were posted on a ridge several hundred yards distant, in our progress to which we moved through fields of wheat, considerably taller than any of our men, and over ditches so thickly lined with thorns and briars, that the blood ran trickling down many of the soldier's legs, long before we arrived at the base of the eminence.

On crossing the last ditch at the foot of the hill, the battalion loaded, then advanced in line, slowly, and with a firm pace, every moment expecting a glimpse of the enemy, from whom they looked for a volley, by way of a friendly welcome to the summit of the mossy ridge. With breathless anxiety we pursued our course; not a whisper was heard—all was still as death—save when our colonel, riding along the line, addressed his followers, some in English, others in Gaelic, calling upon them to be firm, resolute, and steady, and on no account to throw away their fire till they had an object in view. He also urged them to be silent till the order to charge was given, when the whole were to join in the good old British cheer, till they came in contact with the enemy, or the latter had fled, when they were again to resume their former silence. Full of hope, joy beamed on every countenance, till on arriving within a short distance of where the foe were originally posted, we beheld our antagonists formed on another height, some distance in rear of the one they had occupied, to which they had rather precipitately retired during our advance.

To hazard an opinion as to what would have been the result of the conflict had the enemy not retired, may be considered superfluous. But I may say, that as there were no more troops belonging to either nation, who could have been brought into play for nearly a quarter of an hour, the two parties, left to settle their own quarrel, would no doubt have considered themselves fairly pitted against each other, in order that the prowess of Frenchmen and Scotsmen might be put to a proper test, in the face of 150,000 of their respective countrymen and their allies, and that as the issue was to settle the claims of each party, it is but natural to suppose that a severe and bloody action would have taken place.

General, the Honourable William Stewart, commanding the second division, arrived just as we had gained the top of the ridge. Finding the enemy had retired, he ordered us to form column at quarter-distance, and then ordered two Spanish pieces of artillery to a rising ground on our right, to cannonade the enemy at the clump of planting formerly mentioned. This drew upon us the fire of a French battery on the left of the wood, which caused us the loss of a sergeant, corporal, and some privates. During the cannonade. General Stewart, addressing Colonel Cameron, said, "Poor Cadogan, I regret to hear, is mortally wounded. The French are pushing strong columns towards our right,—they must be opposed."

Then waving his hand, so as to describe a half-circle in his front, the general continued, "In front, Colonel, it is all sunshine—all sunshine:—it is on the heights of Puebla the battle must be fought. Being now the senior officer in the first brigade, you will instantly proceed thither with your battalion,—assume the command on the heights,—yield it to none without a written order from Sir Rowland Hill or myself,—and defend your position while you have a man remaining." Then taking a pencil from his pocket, he wrote an order to the above effect—the shot and shell flying about his ears all the time.

To receive this order, Colonel Cameron left an officer with General Stewart, and with his corps proceeded towards the scene of action on the heights, where, as the sequel will shew, both were much wanted.

Sometime previous to this movement being made, Sir Rowland Hill had attacked the French advanced posts in front of Sabujana-de-Alava, for the double purpose of preventing them sending more troops to the heights, and taking possession of the village, should an opportunity offer. The Second and Third Brigades of the Second Division were accordingly ordered on this service, and conducted themselves with their usual gallantry. They advanced with great firmness and bravery, but being opposed to men who knew what was required of soldiers on the field of battle, their first efforts were not crowned with that success which their conduct merited.

However, this did not in the least degree depress their spirits. Again they advanced and gained ground, but were once more forced to retire. During these, and many other attacks which followed, it was truly interesting to witness the cool bravery displayed by the assailants, who, after every successive repulse, advanced to the very muzzles of their opponent's pieces before they gave their fire. As the wave, when foiled in its attempt to force itself over the boundary which nature has set for it, recedes but to return with increased force, so were the assaults of our friends renewed, till by the most praiseworthy perseverance and heroic bravery, they finally carried their point, and established themselves in the village of Sabujana-de-Alava. It would be an act of injustice, however, were I to omit to state, that the vanquished also did everything in their power to ensure a different result. More devoted bravery than that which was exhibited at this point, by both parties, is but seldom seen on a field of battle.

A considerable time before the village fell into our hands, the 92nd Regiment had arrived on the heights, and taken part in the operations in that quarter. Ascending the hill in an oblique direction, the 92nd first touched the summit of it at a point about half a-mile in rear of the post occupied by the 50th Regiment. Immediately in front of the latter, a deep ravine ran quite across the mountain, the western side of which was in possession of the 71st and 50th regiments, and the opposite bank in that of the enemy. The western slope was extremely abrupt, and from the bottom of the ravine, really of difficult access. In possession of such a position, in the face of an enemy greatly superior in numbers, common prudence would have dictated that the best policy was to remain on the defensive.

Unfortunately, however, Lieutenant-Colonel R———, was not of that opinion. Being the senior officer on the heights after the fall of Cadogan, he, contrary to the advice of the field- officers of the 71st Regiment, ordered that corps to cross the ravine, and attack a portion of the enemy's troops occupying a position on the northern slope of the hill. With sad presages of the consequences, the gallant Light Bobs set out on their perilous excursion. Perceiving their intention, the enemy formed two bodies of infantry, in order to kill, wound, or capture the whole of the assailants. These corps were kept out of view of the British: and as the latter moved round the northern, the former kept moving round the southern slope, till being nearly in rear of the 71st, they sprung upon them like tigers, pouring on them volleys of musketry, which made many, both officers and men, bite the dust. To extricate them from this perilous situation, it required the full exercise of all the good military qualities which the whole body of the 71st were known to possess.

From the number of killed and wounded, it was afterwards evident that in their unrivalled exertions to escape from the fangs of their opponents, the 71st had not been sparing of their powder. But what could they achieve against such odds? To rejoin the 50th was the utmost they could hope for. To that point, therefore, they directed their steps. To the same point the French troops were marching, and had partially turned the left of the 71st, when the 92nd arrived to take part in the struggle. On procuring a firm footing on the heights, the 92nd halted for a minute, till the rear closed up, and then in open column of companies right in front, was hurried along at nearly a double-quick pace, till it arrived within two hundred yards of the 50th.

Time being precious, we were ordered to form line on the right centre company without halting. As soon as the four leading companies had filed so far to their right, that the right centre one could move forward at the double-quick step, Colonel Cameron placing himself on the left of that company, called to the piper to play the Gathering of the Camerons, and then addressing the officer who led that company, said, "Now, push forward in double-quick time, and give it to them sweetly." During the advance, a dread silence reigned through the ranks, the men's thoughts being employed in the business on which they were to be engaged. Animated by the presence of their chief, and the warlike sounds of their favourite bagpipe, the men advanced with a front firm as the rocks of their native mountains, to meet the foe flushed with a temporary success over their countrymen.

The reunion of the two regiments, the 50th and 92nd, caused the most lively sensation. As the latter approached the right of the former, the whole of the 50th, officers and men, joined in three hearty cheers. On arriving at the verge of the western bank of the ravine, up which the French troops were scrambling, the Highlanders, on perceiving the latter, first poured down upon them a shower of shot, then re-echoed the cheers of their friends on the left, and, with the rapidity of lightning, despatched a second volley into the thickest of the enemy's ranks, which had the effect of making them fly precipitately down the brow of the ravine,—the living on their feet, and the dead in the manner of round logs of wood. This rapid movement secured a safe retreat to the 71st Regiment, which now slowly retired to a position on our right.

This unfortunate attempt to regain possession of the heights, did not deter the enemy from making another trial. The *beaten* troops were moved round the northern shoulder of the hill, on the eastern bank of the ravine, and a fresh body of infantry, in total ignorance of the dangers they had to encounter, carried round the *southern,* to assault us in the same position from before which their companions had so recently been driven. In about half an hour the head of the French column began to descend the opposite eminence, to check which, a few light troops kept up a smart fire of small arms; but the others, arranged along the brink of the ravine in a sitting posture, were ordered to slope their muskets to the rear, and to remain in this position till the enemy had arrived within twenty or thirty paces of them, when the whole were to stand up, and bestow upon the assailants as many pepper-corns as they could conveniently spare.

These orders were admirably obeyed. Not a whisper was heard—scarcely a shot was fired—during the interval between the crossing of the ravine by the enemy, and their arrival near the summit of the bank. As before, however, silence was broken on our lads resuming their standing position, and giving the foe their first fire. The scene which followed was equally animated as that which preceded it. After a smart rencounter, in which the 50th, 71st, and 92nd Regiments took part, the French, as before, were driven back with considerable loss.

The fugitives, as on the former occasion, were withdrawn round the northern side of the hill, and: a third column of attack formed on the southern side, to make another dash at us, in order to obtain possession of that position which they should never have lost. In this

his last effort, the enemy was far from exhibiting the same spirit as in the two former ones, although he made a much greater display of his numerical force. In order to intimidate us, masses of infantry crowned the height, but none of them moved forward to support the troops advanced towards us, whose efforts were feeble and altogether unworthy of themselves. This was attributed to the situation of their affairs in the centre, which a short time before had begun to take an active part in the business of the day.

Sir Rowland Hill being in possession of Sabujana-de-Alava, the 3rd, 4th, 7th, and Light Divisions crossed the Zadora between twelve and one o'clock at various points, a little in front of the enemy and attacked their centre, and right centre columns with much gallantry—Sir Rowland Hill doing himself the honour of waiting on the French left centre divisions in a similar manner, accompanied with the troops under his personal command. From this period, down to four o'clock, events of the most important and interesting description were every moment taking place along the whole of Zadora's vale, from where the Hero of Salamanca issued his mandate to his followers,—to that spot which the Hero of Barossa was deluging with blood, in order to cut off the communication of the enemy with France by the principal and direct road to St Jean-de-Luz.

But who will attempt to describe these events, as viewed by us from the bloodstained heights of Puebla? I confess myself unable to do so as they ought. Let any man fancy himself standing on the summit of a high hill, looking down on a plain covered with 150,000 men, from 10,000 to 15,000 horse, and from 300 to 400 pieces of artillery vomiting fire and death in every direction, and thousands of the infantry pointing their deadly weapons at each other, the space between the belligerents barely permitting them doing so without crossing the muzzles of their pieces,—and he will have some faint idea of what passed on the plains of Vittoria, and be able to paint in imagination a few of those extraordinary scenes to which we were witnesses.

The admirable manner in which the troops employed against the enemy's centre moved forward to the assault, was the theme of general admiration among all ranks on the heights. Joseph Bonaparte and his major-general, Marshal Jourdan, had been at great pains to strengthen this part of their position, aware that if they were driven from it the battle was lost. Every little eminence literally bristled with cannon, behind which 40,000 infantry at least were drawn up in dense masses, ready to pounce upon all who should attempt to attack them. The

French troops being formed within a very narrow space, the service in that quarter during the early part of the action was extremely hot.

Notwithstanding the cool and determined conduct of our companions in their first rencounter, it was not at all surprising that the thundering of the cannon, and cheers of the combatants, should in a little time produce feelings, which none but those who were on the heights can at all describe. Although we never had the smallest doubt as to the issue of the battle, yet I confess that it was with equal pride and pleasure that we beheld from the heights a wavering in some of the enemy's battalions, about half an hour after the engagement began in the centre. Yes, it was with pleasure, for so close and murderous was the conflict in that quarter, that had not the enemy given way, thousands more of our countrymen must have fallen under the terrific fire of their opponents,—it being well known that French infantry will sustain a discharge of musketry for a long time with unflinching courage.

We were, therefore, not at all disappointed to perceive that our small arms made sometimes but a feeble impression on their ranks. For, in the first place, it convinced the soldiers that they were opposed to troops against whom they would require to use all the physical, as well as moral courage which they possessed; and the officers that something besides powder and shot would have to be employed before the French infantry could be forced from their stronghold. For some time, therefore, volley succeeded volley, and the discharges from the artillery rolled in a terrific manner along the vale, without producing any result beyond that of winding up the spirits of our men to the highest pitch to which the bravery of men can be screwed. One of the finest qualities which British soldiers possess, is, that on all occasions their courage invariably rises in proportion to the exertions required of them, a quality which was never more nobly exhibited than on the plains of Vittoria.

On going into action, almost every soldier resolves to be in possession of the laurel leaf, or a grave, before it is done. On this occasion they were unanimous. Never was there a finer field offered them to shew their unanimity than Vittoria, and never did they exhibit it to greater advantage. Proud of his followers, and unwilling to throw away any more of their precious lives than was absolutely necessary, Lord Wellington gave orders to make use of a weapon, at all times irresistible in the hands of British troops. The bayonet, brought to its proper position, was therefore directed to bend its course towards the hitherto immoveable columns of the enemy. Firmly the latter awaited the coming storm, apparently resolved to brave the furious onset. "*Vive l'Empereur*," ran along the line with the rapidity of lightning; but in wishing long life to their sovereign, the soldiers were not unmindful of their own, and consequently, as soon as the hostile lines approached close enough to make use of the steel, the enemy uniformly gave way.

From the first partial breaking of the French line in the centre, the scene of active operations took a wider range. The enemy driven from their vantage ground, and perceiving their principal communication with France seriously endangered, at once resolved to make every hedge a rampart, and every ditch or rivulet a river, and to defend them to the last extremity, to give time to their baggage and their artillery to draw off towards Pampeluna. Arranging themselves, therefore, behind the various ditches and hedges which intersected the fields in every direction, they compelled the British troops to extend their lines also, in order to oppose a front equal to that of the enemy. Interesting as were the first operations when viewed from the heights of Puebla, those which succeeded were much more so.

The salvos of artillery in deed were neither so frequent nor so appalling, but the volleys of musketry were more numerous, and that beautiful mode of firing, called "running fire," was practised on a scale of greater magnitude than had ever before been witnessed by any British officer. How often, during the awful struggle, did I witness the British soldiers walk up to the brink of a ditch, behind which their opponents were arrayed, and in the most cool and determined manner, cross their pieces with the latter before they gave their fire. On those occasions the conflict invariably assumed a sanguinary aspect, for the ditches being generally too deep for our men to pass in face of an enemy, the French always remained on the opposite side, and kept up a smart fire of musketry, till our artillery or cavalry could be brought forward to dislodge them. In this manner the battle raged in the centre from one o'clock till four, by which time the French had been pushed back almost to Vittoria, where all was confusion and dismay, and from whence Joseph and Jourdan were flying to secure their personal safety.

From Lord Wellington's mode of proceeding on the right and in the centre, it was evident that he relied not a little on the faithful execution of that part of the operations entrusted to Sir Thomas Graham, for the success of his enterprise. When the hour passed at which the latter was to attack, (one o'clock) Lord Wellington appeared uneasy, and I believe despatched more than one courier to ascertain the real cause of Sir Thomas Graham's non-appearance. Be this as it may, It was not long after the hour when Sir Thomas brought his men into action, and began that struggle, the issue of which destroyed all the hopes of the enemy, and turned a simple defeat into one of the most complete routes recorded in history.

The French infantry on the heights seeing that all was lost in the centre and on the right, began to execute a retrograde movement between four and five o'clock. On their intentions being discovered, the first brigade, 50th, 71st and 92nd Regiments, and two Portuguese brigades, which had arrived on the hill sometime before, gave chace to the fugitives, but so superior were the enemy at this game, that in an hour and a-half we entirely lost sight of them, although we ran almost all the way. On mentioning this circumstance to a French officer one day, he said, "I will back my countrymen against all the soldiers in the world in a race of that kind."

Continuing the pursuit, we passed Vittoria, and at eleven o'clock, p.m. bivouacked in a field a league and a-half in front of it. By this time the night was so dark, that it was with difficulty we could discover the person immediately before us. Notwithstanding this, however, the troops who had been opposed to each other in the centre and on the left during the day, seemed unwilling to relinquish the honourable avocation of killing and maiming one another, for the deadly strife continued in those quarters till eleven o'clock in the evening.

The price paid for this splendid victory was, from four to five thousand British and Portuguese killed and wounded. The loss of the French was never accurately ascertained, but was estimated at from ten to fifteen thousand killed, wounded, and prisoners. All their cannon, save two pieces, and all their baggage, money, ammunition, and provisions fell into our hands.

Battle Vignettes

The British general who pointed out the road to victory on the 21st of June, has by many been denominated a military quack, who never gained a battle but by sheer blundering. This assertion, no less ridiculous than false, I shall not notice farther than to remark, that the Emperor of the French must at one time have entertained a similar opinion of our unrivalled general's military talents, otherwise how can we account for him appointing a general to the chief command in Spain, who was totally unfit for the station he occupied at Vittoria. On perusing the details of the battle what opinion will military men of later times entertain of Marshal Jourdan's abilities as a general when they discover that he posted a few light troops only on the heights of Puebla, when they should have been crowned with a force sufficiently numerous to have held them against all mortal flesh? What opinion will they have of his military qualifications, when they read, that he permitted his right wing to be driven from his principal and direct line of communication into France, when to have preserved which, next to beating his antagonist, should have been his principal object.

What will they think of the Hero of Gemappe, when they perceive that he not only allowed his wings to be turned, but thrown back upon his centre, and his whole army ultimately forced back upon an outlet, not broader than was necessary to secure the retreat of one of his divisions, on such an emergency? Why, that he was a person perfectly incompetent to command an army of sixty or seventy thousand Frenchmen against such an adversary: for by the first error he placed the key of his position in our hands,—by the second, he barred the door of the principal outlet from the field against himself,—and by the effects produced by these, his army was huddled together, and in a short time became such an ungovernable mass, that he had latterly no other alternative than to abandon his artillery, stores, &c. in order to preserve his cavalry and infantry from entire destruction.

In the company which I had the honour to command in 1813, there was a man named Walsh, whose character was so tainted, that not a soldier in the company would associate with him. Whether designedly, or through neglect, I will not pretend to determine, but on inspecting his arms at Puebla, I found his bayonet bent like a sickle. Enraged at his conduct, I reprimanded him sharply; but instead of expressing regret for the offence, Walsh turned his head as I was moving off, and most unfeelingly said, "What am I to do with the bayonet, Sir? if we charge today I will not be able to thrust it into any *Frenchman's guts.*" This ruffianly speech caused a thrill of horror to run through the company like a shock of electricity.

On our march from Puebla towards the scene of action, Walsh's whole conversation was nothing but a connected chain of blasphemous sentences. Oath succeeded oath, with such frightful rapidity, that his companions at length became horror-struck. In this state of mind he went into action on the lower part of the position, where the shot and the shell plunged around him without producing any visible amendment. The regiment proceeded to the heights, Walsh all the way pursuing a similar course, venting curses on all and everything around, above, and below. When we had arrived within about two hundred yards of the 50th, and *before anyone had heard the sound of a ball at that point*, the unfortunate wretch, in the very act of uttering a dreadful torrent of blasphemy, fell a lifeless corpse, his head having been perforated by a musket ball. Walsh's sudden and striking exit from this to another world, furnished conversation to his companions during the remainder of the day. His death was viewed by them as a striking manifestation of the divine wrath for his numerous and heinous offences against the Author of his being.

Between the second and third attacks on the heights of Puebla, the pay-sergeant of the company, accompanied by a corporal and private, requested my permission to bring Walsh's knapsack from the rear, and dispose of its contents by auction, for behoof of his family. Highly approving of this admirable display of feeling on the part of the company, I waited on Colonel Cameron, and solicited permission for the sergeant to go and take the necessaries from the dead man's back. Quite delighted with the idea, the colonel readily gave his sanction. In a few minutes the auction began; the biddings went on with life, till the whole was disposed of. By this praiseworthy act thirty-one shillings were added to the balance due to the deceased, and remitted to the widow. Two officers of the 50th, who were standing beside me during the sale, declared, with tears in their eyes, that it was one of the most singular and beautiful exhibitions they had ever witnessed. Singular it undoubtedly was; for in the annals of warfare it was perhaps the only *public auction* ever attempted midst the roaring of artillery and volleys of musketry.

A young lad belonging to the Sixth Company committed a singular act of cowardice at Vittoria. On ascending the heights, he, under some frivolous pretence, fell out, but *forgot* to rejoin his comrades. In a few days thereafter, notice arrived from an hospital in the rear, that he had received such a bad wound in the hand that amputation had been performed at the wrist. On investigating into the matter, it turned out, that in order to avoid the *chance of being hit* in action, he had actually inflicted a wound on himself which might have proved mortal. Thus, to avoid the *possibility* of dying the death of the brave, he imprinted the stamp of the coward on his person, and suspended round his neck a load of ignominy and dishonour which can only be hid in the grave.

When inspecting the arms of the first company, a young lad who had never been in action before, stepped up to the captain of it, and informed him he was so unwell that he would be obliged to fall out. On inquiring the nature of the complaint, Captain C. received for answer, "*A sair wame, Sir.*" Conceiving that all was not right, Captain C. was induced to walk with him to Colonel Cameron, who, on taking the *sick* man by the shoulder, and causing him to face the heights of Puebla, pointed to some French sentries on their summit and then inquired if he saw them. Replying in the affirmative, the colonel then said, "Well, my man, those fellows you see on the top of the hill are the best *doctors* in the world for complaints like yours,' and raising his voice he continued. "and by —— if I live you shall consult them this day!"

Covered with shame, poor B. rejoined his companions, moved forward with them in very depressed spirits, but during the action was one of the keenest spirits in the fray, and ever after his captain had more difficulty in restraining his courage than he had in rousing it into action at Vittoria. This little incident shews most unequivocally, that in going into action for a first time, young soldiers should invariably be incorporated with old ones. For had this youth been allowed to retire, under the feigned plea of sickness, he would have remained a coward ever after.

A French colonel, commanding a portion of their light troops on the heights of Puebla, finding the ground unfavourable for equestrian exercise, sent his charger to the rear a little before the action began. Being a very corpulent man, his running pace was that of a duck, which of all others is the worst calculated to carry a person out of the clutches of a *light bob*. Seeing there was no possibility of making his escape, the colonel wheeled round, and surrendered himself a prisoner. Perceiving him covered with a profuse perspiration, our lads were ill-mannered enough to indulge in a hearty laugh at his expense. Seeing he was the butt of the group, the worthy representative of Sir John Falstaff very good humouredly remarked to an officer of the 92nd Regiment on surrendering his sword, "O God! O God! what a fool was I to part with my horse. For the want of it now I have become your merryman."

Colonel Cadogan, of the 71st, who fell on the heights of Puebla, was leading a charge of his light troops when he was hit. The colonel had turned round to cheer on his followers, and had just repeated, "Well done, well done, brave Highlanders!" when the intrepid leader, mortally wounded, fell from his horse into the arms of a kindred spirit. Captain Seton, commanding the light company 92nd Highlanders, son of the late Sir William Seton of Pitmidden, Aberdeenshire.

Yes, tho' too soon attaining glory's goal,
To us his bright career too short was given;
Yet, in a glorious cause, his phoenix soul
Rose on the flames of victory to heaven.

Maya

In the afternoon of the 22nd, the Second Division moved from its bivouac in front of Vittoria, passed through Salvateira, and towards the "wee short hour ayont the twal," encamped in a wood a few miles in front of it. During the march we were every moment presented with numerous evidences, animate and inanimate, of the total wreck of King Joseph's royal fortunes. Around, and on every side of us, lay men and horses, dead and dying, waggons of all descriptions, some overturned and emptied of their contents, others on their wheels, and filled with letters unopened and unheeded, although written to please the taste of everyone in the army, being addressed to officers and soldiers of all ranks, from Jourdan down to the youngest drum-boy, on subjects grave, gay, and voluptuous. On passing a tremendous pile of letters, I presented a handful of them for acceptance to the Marquis of Almeida; but after a long tirade against Bonaparte, he politely declared that he would not *soil his fingers with them*. The Marquis' hatred to the French was only equalled by that of Prince Blucher.

On passing Salvateira, our men were repeatedly invited by a dragoon, dressed in the uniform of a hussar, to join him in a full-flowing can, and he would "pay the piper." Our lads having expressed some doubts as to their new friend's ability to perform his promise, the latter instantly pulled from his boot a doubloon, and holding it up, told the sceptics that his boots were filled with similar pieces. How the cash came into the possession of the hussar it is for him to say; but I think we may infer that he obtained it without running any great hazard of losing a life, which, as a soldier, was worth nothing.

From the earliest period to the present, the armies of every nation have contained men who, unless narrowly looked after in action, are more apt to make war against the *effects* than the *persons* of their enemies. To people of this stamp no leniency should at any time be shown, for in whatever light we may view a military plunderer, he must invariably appear to us dressed in the despicable garb of a traitor to his friends, his sovereign, and his country.

If soldiers would reflect on the ignominy which attaches to the name of a plunderer, and permit themselves to contrast his character with that of a soldier who retires from the service covered with honour, no man, possessing the feelings of a *real soldier*, would for a moment hesitate what course to pursue. The soldier who has discharged his duties faithfully and honourably, plods his way towards home with a breast swelling high with native pride, and when relating to a group of admiring relations and friends around the domestic hearth, his hairbreadth 'scapes by flood and field, receives their congratulations on his safe return, and hears their murmurs of applause, without the smallest blush on his cheek, being conscious that he has done his duty, and that none can upbraid him with one dishonourable act.

Widely different indeed must the situation of the military plunderer be on arriving at his native place. There the bitter cup of self-conviction will invariably rise to his lips, and choak his utterance as often as he attempts to impose upon his friends with tales of war, in which he wishes them to believe he acted an honourable part. There he will spend a life of unceasing misery and extreme wretchedness; for although he may be removed far from any of those companions whose evidence could rise up in public against him, still the never-dying conscience will hourly remind him of the humiliating fact, that he had forfeited all pretensions to the designation of a soldier. Soldiers, therefore, would do well to bear these facts in constant remembrance, and unmindful of everything *save their honour*, conduct themselves at all times, and under all circumstances, in such a manner, that, on retiring from the busy scenes of a military life, they may have it in their power to say,

The wars are o'er, and I'm returned,
My hands unstained with plunder.

Sir Thomas Graham having been ordered to advance towards the French frontier, by the high road leading from Vittoria to Irun, came up with a French corps at Tolosa, which he attacked and defeated with considerable loss. After this rencounter, he continued his route, drove the enemy across the Bidassoa, and invested San Sebastian.

It being nearly four o'clock in the morning of the 23rd before our baggage arrived in camp, we had just thrown aside our wet clothes, and gone to rest, when those pests of every soldier's nocturnal repose—the bugles—again called us to arms. Although our sleep was short, yet a rather comfortable, but hurried repast, enabled us to strut away as gay as larks. But our gaiety unfortunately was short-lived, for in half-an-hour the rain again descended in torrents, and for five hours pelted us severely. Had we been moving, the rain would have given us little trouble. But by some unexplained mistake we were kept nearly five hours under arms, half-a-mile from where we started when we ought to have been under cover of our canvass. Such mistakes should never escape censure, for the health of an army is of paramount importance to a general, and it must be injured by a few hours unnecessary exposure to a deluge of rain. Resuming our march, we drew two leagues nearer to Pampluna and encamped.

The Marquis of Wellington having pushed forward with the Third, Fourth, and Light Divisions towards Pampluna, the Second and Sixth Divisions, and General Hamilton's division of Portuguese followed their friends at an early hour on the 24th. In the afternoon we were visited by a tremendous thunder storm. The lightning appeared before, behind, and on every side of us, in every shape which the electric fluid can be exhibited to the eye of man. The lightning flashed, and the thunder in terrific peals rolled over our heads in a manner so grand, yet appalling, that language is insufficient to convey to those who did not witness it, even a faint idea of the awfully sublime spectacle.

At times the thunder growled for a few moments in a threatening manner, and then burst so suddenly upon our ears, that it was no uncommon thing to see numbers bending their heads, while the artillery of heaven was expending its wrath. About the time that the storm was at its height. Lieutenant Masterman of the 34th Regiment was killed by the lightning, as was the mule on which he was mounted. Nine men of the same corps were also knocked down, but the most of them were but slightly injured. His watch was melted, and his sword belt was cut into as neat little square pieces, as the most expert tradesman could have performed a similar operation with a knife or scissors.

We continued our movement upon Pampluna on the 25th, 26th, and 27th, without meeting with anything worthy of notice, save the smoking ruins of a few houses which the enemy had burned in their retreat, and *one* of the *two* pieces of artillery which Joseph Bonaparte carried with him from the fatal field of Vittoria, and which had been dismounted by some of the artillery brigades attached to the leading divisions two days before. In the evening of the 27th, we encamped in the vicinity of Pampluna.

As Sir Rowland Hill approached Pampluna, the Marquis of Wellington gradually withdrew a portion of the other divisions from before that fortress, and with the Spanish corps of General Mina, proceeded on the 27th to attempt the capture of General Clausel, who being too late to take part in the Battle of Vittoria, was endeavouring to effect his escape into France, by a road to the eastward of Pampluna. Informed of the Marquis' intentions, Clausel wheeled to the right, and directed his march upon Saragosa. There being no visible prospect of bringing the enemy to action, the Marquis returned to Pampluna, and resigned the pursuit of the fugitives into the hands of the indefatigable guerrilla chief.

The French army was so much in want of provisions when it arrived under the walls of Pampluna, that Joseph was compelled to draw largely on the stores of the garrison to satisfy the cravings of his half-starved followers. This was a most egregious blunder on Jourdan's part, for it deprived the Governor of the means of prolonging the defence of the place beyond a very limited period.

On quitting Pampluna, the French army retired towards their own country in two columns, the principal part of it by the pass of Roncesvalles, the other by that of Maya. Conceiving that Jourdan would attempt to fortify the heights at both of those places, Lord Wellington pushed forward the third and fourth divisions, Second Brigade of the Second Division, and some Spanish and Portuguese troops towards the former; and the remaining brigades of the Second Division, and a brigade of General Hamilton's Portuguese division were ordered to proceed against the enemy at Maya.

Accordingly, about seven o'clock in the morning of the 2nd of July, the First, Third, and Fourth brigades of the Second Division, one brigade Portuguese infantry, a few pieces of artillery and some cavalry, moved from their encampment in front of Pampluna, and in the afternoon encamped near La-Zarza. Next morning we plodded our way under torrents of rain, to a bleak mountain a little !in front of the village of Lanz and encamped. Early on the 4th we again moved forward, and about one o'clock arrived at Almandos, after a disagreeable tramp across the dreary pass of Lanz. A little in rear of the village, our columns closed up preparatory to an attack upon the enemy's position at Barrueta, three miles farther in advance.

About two o'clock, the first brigade led by General Stewart in person, entered Almandos, and on arriving at the centre of it, made a sharp turn to the right, filed through several fields by a narrow footpath, descended the left bank of a deep ravine, crossed a small stream, and then scrambled up the right bank, for as the whole face of it was covered with round trundling stones, the operation was; rather a difficult one. We at length, however, gained the summit, and on taking a view of the obstacles we had surmounted, we were not a little surprised that the enemy should have permitted us to obtain a footing in that quarter, without making an attempt to confine our operations within a more limited sphere.

A few hundred men judiciously posted, might have accomplished this, at least, for some little time. On perceiving us fairly established on the left of the enemy's chain of advanced posts. Sir Rowland Hill gave orders for the other brigades to move through Almandos, thence along the high road towards Barrueta, and attack the French posts in front of that town. On being attacked, the latter retired across a ravine which runs in front of the village, and joined their main body, the left of which rested on the summit of a high and very steep mountain, the centre occupied the village of Barrueta, and the right extended to the Bidassoa, the right bank of which they occupied with a few light troops. On retiring behind the ravine, the enemy lined the right bank, the Portuguese the left. Between them a smart fire of musketry was kept up with considerable animation for some time, during which the 50th Regiment made an effort to carry the village.

The latter went up to their antagonists in their usual gallant style, but the French brought forward a very superior force, and drove them back. To support the 50th in this operation, the left wing of the 92nd was pushed towards the village, and the right wing and 71st Regiment kept in reserve. The services of the 92nd left wing, however, were not required, for before they reached the scene of action, the 50th had received orders to retire. Sir Rowland Hill not deeming it prudent to bring on a more general affair that evening.

The enemy being in the same position, the troops cooked early next morning, and on the arrival of the Marquis of Wellington about noon, resumed their arms, and moved against the enemy. Forming the right of our little army, the first brigade was ordered to ascend a high, steep, and extremely slippery mountain on our right, in order to throw itself in rear of the enemy's left wing. The operation was a fatiguing one; but on arriving at the summit of the hill, a peep of the French territory, and of the ocean, which the soldiers aptly enough called the high road to England, banished in an instant every trace of fatigue, as the spontaneous and, deafening cheers of our poor fellows sufficiently testified.

Previous to this, the left column of the enemy paid but little attention to our demonstration against their extreme left, but the boisterous expression of feeling just alluded to, which the enemy had attributed to a cause very different from the real one, made them bestir themselves. Conceiving it to be General Gazan's intention to give us battle, we detached our light companies towards his left flank, and supported the movement with the rest of the brigade. The enemy's centre and right wing were attacked about the same time by our friends in the centre, and in a short time forced to retire from Barrueta. Gazan seeing his left wing turned, and his right wing and centre about to be driven from their stronghold behind the village, gave orders to those immediately opposed to us, to follow the example of their friends, and retire towards Elizonda.

There being but one road by which the enemy could retire, and that one too narrow for the rapid, retreat of 7000 men, part of the French troops moved through cornfields between the road and the Bidassoa, and two or three battalions were thrown across the river, whither they were pursued by some Portuguese infantry. From the time Gazan began to retreat, he never attempted to make a stand, but occasionally turned round, and after peppering us for a few minutes from behind a wall, hedge, or from the windows of a house, again took to his heels.

Some of our light troops on those occasions conceiving it imprudent to attack the enemy in their strongholds, flanked them by moving into the fields, so that the former were always ready to pour a few volleys of musketry on the latter, the moment they retired from their temporary forts. In this manner the retreat and pursuit were conducted till both parties arrived at Elizonda. To prevent a surprise, the enemy had previously run a wall round the town, from behind which, they annoyed our light troops as they closed upon them. The French being forced at length to yield possession of the southern entrance, we walked n, pursued the fugitives through the various streets midst the loud acclamations of the inhabitants, who, before the enemy had finally relinquished their hold of the northern gate, were ringing a merry peal in honour of their deliverance. This spontaneous effusion of loyalty was so grating to the ears of the French soldiers, that, on taking leave of the town, they swore to be revenged on it the first time they returned.

On being driven from his position in the valley of Bastan, General

Gazan retired with the main body of his corps to a high ridge at the head of be valley, and with his left foot in France, and his fight foot in Spain, prepared to give us another meeting before he relinquished his hold of the last position he could now lay claim to in Spain. This position was reconnoitred by the Marquis of Wellington on the 6th, and again on the morning of the 7th. At the close of the last reconnoissance preparations were made for an immediate attack with the view of ridding this part of the Peninsula of the presence of the invaders.

The right of General Gazan's corps occupied a high and very steep mountain, called the Rock of Maya. His centre columns were posted on two heights considerably lower than the other, and about a mile, and mile and half distant; and the left rested on another height still farther to the left. In front of the left centre there was a ridge which ran all the way to the village of Maya,—nearly two miles. On this ridge the enemy had placed some light troops, and again, a mile in front of Maya another body to watch our motions.

The second brigade of the second division being encamped on the right bank of the Bidassoa, was pitched upon to attack the rock, while the other brigades should endeavour to drive the enemy from the other points of their position. Accordingly the former got under arms about 11 o'clock, a. m. on the 7th of July, and ascended a mountain on their left, over which a narrow footpath led to the rock five miles distant. When the second brigade marched from its ground the sky was clear, but fortunately for our friends, a dense fog crowned the conical summit of the rock, just as they were about to cross an adjoining eminence, so much lower than the other, that but for this the enemy would have been able to form a correct estimate of the numerical strength of the attacking column.

With the able assistance of this potent ally, the Second Brigade approached the enemy undiscovered, till they had arrived within a very short distance of the summit of the rock. They were no sooner perceived, however, than their opponents poured down on them showers of bullets; but the action, though severe, was very short, for, making use of the bayonet, the Second Brigade soon rid the summit of the mountain of the presence of the enemy.

In order to deceive the French general in regard to our real intentions, the other brigades remained quiet in their camp for nearly two hours after their companions had quitted theirs. By this little manoeuvre the French were lulled into a fatal security, for, until they saw us fairly under arms, they fancied themselves reposing in perfect safety.

On moving from our camp a little in front of Elizonda, we directed our steps towards Errazu, behind which the most advanced of the enemy's troops were stationed. As we approached them, they retired towards the village of Maya. At first they retired slowly, but the firing on the rock caused them latterly to accelerate their motion. The same cause made us imitate them, in order that we might be at hand to render our friends assistance should Gazan attempt to regain by force his lost possession.

The First Brigade, followed by Colonel Ashworth's Portuguese, advanced rapidly up the valley, passed Maya at a trot, and then, with the 6th Caçadores on our left, moved towards the enemy, with whom our light companies soon came in contact. The firing at this point was kept up with considerable vivacity for some time, but with little loss to either party. Pending these operations of the light troops, the 6th Caçadores had advanced close to the enemy scattered over the northern slept of the rock, with the intention of preventing us communicating directly with the second brigade A smart running fire was the consequence of this collision, which lasted with little intermission till night. Having succeeded in driving back the enemy, and establishing themselves in this post, the 50th Regiment was ordered to a height upon their right, close and immediately opposite to the enemy's right columns.

These various movements a length brought a considerable number of the combatants into close quarters. The shots at first were as usual rather long, but as the afternoon advanced they became shorter, till the 50th and the enemy were more than once on the point of crossing bayonets. Being rather hard pressed, the 92nd Regiment moved to their assistance, but the "old half hundred" had in its usual off hand manner repelled the assault previous to the arrival of their Highland brethren.

General Gazan heartily ashamed of having so tamely yielded up the possession of a post which he should have held while he had a man remaining, made many desperate attempts to regain it, but in all of them he was beat back with considerable loss. During the whole of the operations on the rock, nothing could exceed the conduct of the Second brigade, 28th, 34th, and 39th Regiments, all of whom had made up their minds to give their bodies to the eagles that hovered over their heads, rather than permit the enemy to lodge on the summit of the mountain that night. The 71st Light Infantry rendered us good and efficient service on our right, till night's sable mantle wrapt every earthly object in impenetrable darkness.

The fog being extremely dense, the night dark, and the French little more than two hundred yards from our advanced posts, we lay under arms the whole of the night. So very dark was it indeed, at on the skirmishers being called in, many of them did not really know which way to move to rejoin their battalions. In front, and on our left flank, numbers were, for hours after the action had ceased, bawling, some Francais, others Portuguese. So completely were the poor devils at fault regarding the situations of their respective friends, that two French soldiers actually passed one of our piquets, and were made prisoners before they discovered their mistake.

At daybreak on the following day, General Gazan made another attempt to regain the key of his position, but failing as before, he kept up a loose irregular firing till about seven o'clock, when, seeing he could make no impression in that quarter, he took advantage of the fog to retire with his corps into his own territory. Colonel Ashworth followed him some distance, and skirmished with his rearguard till evening.

When General Gazan retired from the heights of Maya, General Stewart proceeded to look out for suitable ground for our brigade. In doing so, he spent fully two hours, there being no convenient spot but what had previously been occupied by the enemy. Before the general returned from his tour of inspection, a number had begun to grumble at the delay in placing us in camp. In this number was Captain H———s, of the 92nd Regiment, who would not give credit to the stories in circulation, relative to the not very praiseworthy habits of the French soldiery. Seeing that the captain was not to be convinced, one of his brother-officers said to him in mere jest, "H———s, perhaps at this moment some of the gallopers may have already taken a fancy to you;" and then bending forward as if to examine whether such was not the case, he, to his own surprise, was able to convince the captain of the fact by ocular demonstration. The captain instantly sprung from the ground, and bounded along the heath like a deer for several hundred yards, stopping only twice to try whether an extraordinary shake of his polluted ankle would not assist him in getting rid of such vile intruders.

In the action of the 7th July, three Spanish peasants, inhabitants of Maya, joined our light troops, advanced into the very heat of the conflict, and fought with the most determined bravery, till one of them being killed, and another wounded, the third reluctantly quitted the scene of action to convey his friend back to his native village. Had the armies of Spain been composed of such men as these, the Peninsular contest would have been short indeed.

During the early French revolutionary wars, an opinion prevailed in the British army, that the French used poisoned balls. That this opinion still prevailed at the time of which I write, is evidenced by the fact, that on the evening of the 7th, I heard one of the 50th call out, as he passed us on his way to the rear, "I know I am a dead man, I have been wounded by a poisoned ball."

Conceiving it to be the duty of every officer in charge of a company to record every little anecdote, which can tend to illustrate the character or the men under their command, I cannot forbear to notice an act of coolness on the part of a young lad named M'Ewen, which cannot be too much admired. In the action of the 7th, a musket ball grazed his bonnet a little above the ear. Instead of alarming him, however, M'Ewen very coolly turned round his head to mark the progress of the bullet, and on seeing it bury itself in the earth a few yards in his rear, shook his head, and said, "O ye coaxing rascal."

Until we took possession of the heights of Maya, we really knew but little of the real discomforts of a camp. We had occasionally suffered severely from sleet, rain, and cold stiff gales, but such a thing as a hurricane was a total stranger to us. At Maya, however, our position was so exposed to the four wind's of heaven, that blow from whatever quarter it might, the wind always found us at its mercy. One evening, after we had retired to rest, our encampment was visited by a tremendous storm of wind and rain. The former howled, and the latter battered the slender sides of our tents with such fury, that many of them were blown down.

Every precaution was instantly taken to keep the tent-poles and cords from snapping, but in many cases our efforts proved fruitless, for the wind continuing to increase for some time after, down came one tent, then another, and another, till more than a half of the whole were level with the ground. I had just fallen asleep, and was enjoying a very comfortable nap, when "Cast away, cast away!" from a well-known voice, rung in my ears, and roused me from my slumbers. I instantly started up, and fancying what had happened, pulled the strings of my tent, and gave the cast-away wanderer a hearty welcome. But scarcely had my friend recited his hair-breadth 'scape from suffocation, when appearances boded nothing favourable to the little vessel in which we were. Our servants did all in their power to keep the pole upright, but seeing that to be impossible, I ordered them to haul it down, and then, in company with my brother-sufferer, proceeded on a voyage of discovery.

We proceeded, in the first instance, to the tent of three friends, which being more favourably situated than ours, we hoped would afford us shelter. On arriving there, however, all was desolation. We made two or three other unsuccessful attempts to obtain a temporary shelter from the surly blast; but despairing of finding it, and the night being extremely dark, we finally resolved to seek protection under the brow of the hill, and wait with patience the coming of the morning light. Pursuing our way, without a light or a guide, we had considerable difficulty in reaching a spot, where, protected, we might sit and hear the storm expend its fury over our heads.

At length we got under cover, but had not been half-an-hour in our new berth, when our feet became so benumbed with cold, that we found it necessary to move about to bring them again to their natural heat. Wrapt in our cloaks, and with the rain battering in our faces, we were jogging along towards our arms, when all at once we came upon a tent which had withstood the fury of the storm. We were desired to walk in, and accept of what accommodation the inmates had to spare. We did so, but finding the tent pretty well filled with others similarly situated with our- selves, I left my friend Captain H—— under cover, and after a little more trouble I found out the residence of an old friend, where I remained during the remainder of the storm.

When day dawned, nothing but desolation was to be seen in our camp. Out of fifty tents, few were standing, more than the half of them were complete wrecks, and a number of the others were seriously injured. The men's arms and accoutrements were greatly damaged, and a considerable portion of our ammunition was destroyed.

The Gallant 400

The disastrous issue of the battle of Vittoria, and subsequent retreat of the French army into their own country, having convinced Napoleon that neither his brother Joseph, nor Marshal Jourdan, were qualified to lead the armies of France to victory, he instantly dispatched Marshal Soult from Germany, with unlimited powers, to take the command of the French army on the lower Pyrenees, and oppose the farther progress of the British general in that direction. From the first moment of Soult's appointment being known to us, we anticipated warm work; and he seemed determined that we should not be disappointed. On the 23rd of July he issued an order of the day, intimating that his instructions were "to drive the English from the lofty heights which enabled them proudly to survey their fertile valleys, and chase them across the Ebro."

"Let the accounts of our success," continued Soult, in the true Napoleon style, "be dated from Vittoria, and the birthday of the Emperor celebrated in that city." This, although sheer bombast, was not a little ominous of what was to follow,—broken heads and mutilated limbs.

On the 25th of July, the day which developed to us the mighty plans by which Soult intended to carry the orders of the Emperor into execution, the allied army occupied the following positions, extending from Roncesvalles on the right, to St Sebastian on the left. The third brigade, second division, commanded by General Byng, formed the extreme right, and occupied a strong post, three hundred yards into the French territory, which commanded the high road from St Jean-Pied-de-Port to Roncesvalles, five miles in rear. This brigade was supported by the Fifth Spanish Army, under General Morillo. The Fourth Division was encamped on the heights in front of Roncesvalles, a few miles in rear of the others;—and the Third Division were in position at Olaque, in readiness to move to wherever their services might be most required. A few miles to the left of the fourth, Brigadier-General Campbell's brigade of Portuguese infantry occupied Los Alduides, a French village, to keep open the line of communication between the right wing and centre, under Sir Rowland Hill, in the valley of Bastan.

The left wing, under Sir Thomas Graham, consisting of the First and Fifth Divisions, was engaged in the siege of St Sebastian. On their right, the Spanish corps of Generals Longa and Giron extended from the vicinity of the latter towards the heights of Santa-Barbara, where, and at Puerto-de-Eschelar and Vera, the Seventh and light divisions were posted.

The troops entrusted with the defence of the heights of Maya, and valley of Bastan, were stationed as follows:—The Fourth Brigade, Second Division, occupied the village of Errazu; and a Portuguese brigade, under the Conde de Amarante, a position in the mountains in front of that place. On the summit of the ridge, over which runs the high road from the valley of Bastan into France, the 71st and 92nd regiments were encamped,—the latter two hundred yards to the left of the road, and the former three hundred yards still farther to the left. The 50th regiment were detached about half-a-mile from the right of the 92nd, and lay encamped half-way down the ridge on the Spanish side. Three pieces of Portuguese artillery occupied the space between the road and the 92nd; and the 82nd Regiment, from General Barnes' brigade, Seventh Division, were posted about a mile from the left of the 71st. The Second Brigade, Second Division, were encamped in the valley, a little in front of the town of Maya, having the 34th Regiment advanced towards the summit of the heights on the right of the position, on which that brigade had strong piquets posted; and the Spanish General O'Donnel, the Conde-del-Abisbal, formed the blockade of Pampluna, with a force of from ten to fifteen thousand Spaniards.

A little after 11 o'clock, a. m. on the 25th of July, the enemy, ascending the heights by a mountainous path which leads from the French village of Espalete to the Spanish village of Maya, attacked our piquets on the right with great fury. The latter, on the first appearance of the enemy, were reinforced by the light companies of the second brigade, and subsequently by the 34th, 39th, 50th, and right wing of the 92nd Regiment. The first assault of our old friend Druet, the Count D'Erlon, was sustained by the piquets and light troops with much spirit, but the overwhelming numbers of the enemy rendered all their efforts to retain their ground unavailing.

The 34th Regiment being the nearest corps to the point attacked, were soon on the spot, and attempted to arrest the torrent; but, from a similar cause, were nearly cut off. The 50th arrived at the scene of action at this ticklish period—charged the advanced columns of the enemy, and in conjunction with the 34th and 39th, which had followed the 50th, gave a temporary; check to their career. But the Count D'Erlon, availing himself of his great numerical superiority, charged these corps in front, and detached strong columns round their flanks, in order to surround them. At this critical period the right wing of the 92nd Regiment, nearly 400 strong, entered the field, and took part in the fray.

On their arrival, the Highlanders were a good deal blown, having advanced from the pass about a mile and a-half, at a hurried pace. The situation of their friends, however, was such, that they formed line on coming in sight of the enemy, and were ordered forward by Colonel Cameron, who commanded on the heights at the time, without a moment's repose. The enemy perceiving our intention was to charge them, halted, and thereby afforded the 34th and 50th Regiments an opportunity of retiring, and re-forming their ranks. Enraged at the failure of his attempt to capture those two battalions, the French General turned his fury against the Highlanders, with an intention of annihilating them with showers of musketry. They, however, nothing intimidated, returned the fire of their opponents with admirable effect.

Perceiving that D'Erlon was acting cautiously, Colonel Cameron withdrew the right wing of the 92nd, in order to draw the enemy to a piece of ground where he could charge them. In this he partly succeeded; for the French general, mistaking our voluntary retreat for a constrained one, pushed forward from three to four thousand of his troops, who on advancing towards us, made the air ring with their shouts of *Vive l'Empereur*. Conceiving that the enemy had made up his mind to prove the point of our bayonets, Cameron retired about thirty paces and then ordered his men to halt—front—and prepare to charge. On seeing us halt, the enemy did the same, and instantly opened on us one of the most terrific fires of musketry which we had ever witnessed. At this time the space between the combatants was not more than one hundred and twenty paces, while the numerical force of the enemy was nearly eight to one against us.

From the 92nd, to the French front line, the ground was almost level, but immediately behind the enemy's advanced body, and from the opposite bank of a narrow ravine, rose rather abruptly a considerable eminence, from the face of which the French musketry told with fatal effect on their opponents. This, however, the Highlanders did not return, for conceiving that the French general wished to get quit of them by a general charge, the 92nd directed the whole of their fire against that part of the French force stationed on the brow of the ravine nearest themselves, and which was so coolly and admirably given, that in ten minutes the enemy's dead lay literally in heaps. The slaughter was so appalling indeed, that the utmost efforts of the French officers to make their men advance in front of their slain, failed.

At times they prevailed upon a section or two to follow them,— but whenever they obtained a glimpse of the mangled corpses of their comrades, which everywhere surrounded them, they invariably gave way, and retired from the scene of blood. For more than twenty minutes the Highlanders sustained the unequal conflict, at the expiry of which more than one half of the men had been killed and wounded; and all the officers wounded, and borne from the field, but two lieutenants.

Being one of the two, and the senior in rank, I found myself at once placed in a situation of considerable importance, surrounded with difficulties, and beset with dangers on every hand. The enemy immediately opposed to us was certainly not fewer than 3000,—our numbers had by this time been reduced to something under 200, and a great part of them had no ammunition. Thus situated, and with no friends in sight to render us assistance, it appeared to me that the most prudent course I could adopt, under all the circumstances, would be to retire, particularly as it became every moment more and more evident that the French general's object was either to annihilate us with his fire, or surround us with his endless masses. We retired accordingly, pursued slowly by the enemy, and without the loss of a man, but such as fell by the terrific showers of musketry which they poured on us during the retreat.

On our arrival behind the height on which we had been engaged, we found the 28th in close column, and the right wing of the 71st hastening forward to our relief. The former attacked the enemy's leading columns, but soon after moving down the hill to the right, the Bragge Slashers joined the 34th and 39th Regiments in the valley, and left our rear completely uncovered. Under these circumstances, the 50th and shattered remains of the 92nd right wing retired towards the pass, where General Stewart, who had now arrived from Elizonda, was making the necessary preparations to retard the progress of his opponent.

Detaching the right wing of the 71st, and part of the 50th, to a position in rear. General Stewart, at the head of the left wings of the 71st and 92nd, awaited the enemy. The latter, after a little skirmishing, brought forward a strong body of infantry to overpower all opposition. Seeing that a general affair would be attended with no favourable result at this point, General Stewart, after a few rounds, withdrew the advanced wings, and marching them through the intervals between the 50th and 71st right wing, placed them again in position about two hundred yards in rear of the latter.

The enemy followed, and were warmly received by the 50th and 71st. A smart firing took place, which, as before, ended in the retreat of our friends through the intervals between the left wings of the 71st and 92nd. In this manner, each half of the troops alternately retiring, we retrograded fully a mile, when, being reinforced by the 82nd Regiment, we halted.

At the commencement of the action. Colonel Cameron adopted the necessary precaution of detaching Captain Campbell of his own corps, with 150 men, to the summit of the rock of Maya, it being the key to the whole position. From this formidable post the little garrison rendered us considerable service; for the face of the mountain being everywhere covered with whinstone blocks, Captain Campbell, in imitation of Andrew Hoffer in the Tyrol, hurled them down on the pursuers, and frequently with great effect.

But neither stones, bullets, nor bayonets, checked the progress of the enemy, for the Second Brigade having deviated from the natural and prescribed route, retired across the valley of Bastan, some miles to our right, and left us in numbers from 2000 to 2500 to contend against eight or nine thousand. The consequence of this false movement was such as might have been expected. The enemy seeing the two bodies completely separated, followed up the advantages they had gained over our column, and at length pressed us so warmly, that General Stewart, in order to stop the farther effusion of blood in a hopeless cause, dispatched an order to the troops on the rock to retire. It was then about seven o'clock in the evening.

Fortunately, however, the cheers of the troops at the base of the hill, reached the summit of it before the bearer of the order. These cheers were occasioned by the arrival of General Barnes with the 6th regiment, and some Brunswick infantry, being the remainder of his brigade. A more seasonable reinforcement no troops ever received. On the first appearance of it, our lads were perfectly frantic with joy.

Being seated at the time, they, although greatly fatigued, sprung upon their feet, and then, without *either asking* or *obtaining* permission to advance, rushed down upon the enemy with irresistible force, and drove back his numerous hordes in the finest style imaginable. Taking it for granted that we had been reinforced, D'Erlon retired about a mile. In order to strengthen our position we had received a great addition to our numbers, General Stewart caused the covering sergeants to take ground in the usual regular manner, by which operation he intended to convey to his opponent an idea that he only waited for the light of a new day to renew the combat.

Marshal Soult having attacked at daybreak the same morning the right of our army at Roncesvalles, with an overwhelming force. Generals Cole, Picton, and Byng, after doing everything in their power to repel the attack, were ultimately compelled to yield up their position to the enemy, and draw off towards Pampluna—the relief, or reprovisioning of that strong fortress being the enemy's principal object. To frustrate his designs, it became necessary for Lord Wellington to concentrate a considerable portion of his army in a position in front of Pampluna. For that purpose we retired from Maya the same night, and after a fatiguing night's march, halted next morning at seven o'clock, on a height in front of Barrueta.

Vignettes of the Battle

I believe one of the best judges now In Britain has pronounced the action of the 25th July to be one of the most brilliant achievements performed during the late Peninsular war. Will posterity credit the fact, that 2600 British troops not only retained the key of their position, in despite of the utmost efforts of 11,000 of Bonaparte's best infantry for nine hours, to wrest it from them,—but on receiving a reinforcement of 1000 men only, actually recaptured about a mile of the ground which the enemy had acquired in the early part of the day ? Will posterity believe that 400 British soldiers stretched 1000 Frenchmen dead or maimed on the bed of honour, in less than half-an-hour? I fear not, without something more than a bare assertion; and therefore I take the liberty of relating the substance of a conversation which passed a few days afterwards, between the French general who commanded on that occasion, and a British colonel, who was wounded on the 25th, and from the severity of his wound was obliged to be left behind when we quitted the valley of Bastan.

The Count D'Erlon, whether from a humane or an interested feeling, I know not, waited upon Colonel H——, in passing through the village where the latter was confined to bed, and after condoling with him on the consequences of the action of the 25th of July, said, "Pray, Colonel, how many *Sans Culottes* (Highlanders) have you in your division?"

"One battalion," answered the colonel.

"One regiment of several battalions, I presume. Colonel," retorted D'Erlon.

"No, General, only one battalion I assure you," replied Colonel H——.

The count then in a playful manner, and with a smile of incredulity in his countenance, said, "Come now, Colonel, don't quiz me, do tell me candidly, how many Highlanders you had in action on the right of your position on the 25th?"

On this query being put, Colonel H—— said, with great earnestness, "I give you my honour. General, there was only half a battalion, not exceeding 400 men in all."

On recovering a little from the surprise which this reply created, D'Erlon fixed his eyes on Colonel H——, and after a few moments pause, said with considerable emotion, "Then, Colonel, they were not men, they were devils,—for before that body of troops I lost one thousand killed and wounded."

On calling the roll of the company on our arrival in the bivouac of Barrueta, I found the casualties of the preceding day to be 11 killed, and 35 wounded, a considerable portion of whom died in hospital.

I was much gratified on this occasion by a mark of attention and respect bestowed upon me by the men of my company. We were all without shelter, and our fare was neither rich nor abundant. To shew their regard, however, in a way which they truly thought would be most acceptable to me, the poor fellows, fatigued in body, and distressed in mind as they were, erected a beautiful hut, and made a neat table for me, which on awaking from a long nap I found groaning 'under a load of soup, *bouilli*, beef-steaks, young potatoes, and a bottle of very good brandy. One word more, I conceive, quite unnecessary, to shew the dispositions of the men I had the honour to command in the memorable campaign of 1813.

During the retreat from the right of the position towards the pass of Maya, I received a message from a wounded brother officer, that he wished particularly to see me. The moment he observed me, he held out his hand, and with much feeling said, "O! —— I am most happy to see you have escaped unhurt from that dreadful place. I have two favours to ask of you," he continued, "the first is, to assure Colonel Cameron that I have never ceased to retain a grateful recollection of all he has done for me; and the other is, that you will see this purse conveyed to my relations." Here his voice failed, and a tear started in his eye. On recovering a little, he, quite aware that his wound was mortal, again grasped my hand, then raised his eyes, and after fixing them steadfastly on me for some moments, said, with a smile of resignation on his countenance, "I fear I detain you, ——,farewell, my friend, forever farewell, and may God Almighty for ever bless you."

In the action between the right wing of the 92nd Regiment, and the French on the right, an officer of the latter, rendered himself rather a conspicuous object to us, by his repeated and gallant attempts to induce his men to charge our little band. I never felt so much for any individual as for that truly brave man. Seeing that none of his followers would move in front, he advanced alone about fifteen paces before them, struck his sword into the ground, and then crossing his arms upon his breast, stood facing us several minutes without moving hands or feet,—our men all the time doing everything in their power to bring him down. Their efforts, however, were fruitless, till one Archibald M'Lean stepped to the front, and kneeling down, took deliberate aim, and killed him. To have shot this officer under any other circumstances but those in which the 92nd were placed, would have been considered by us as an act of deliberate cruelty. But when the respective numbers of the combatants on that occasion are kept in view, every impartial man will admit, that the death of the French officer was indispensibly necessary to ensure our safety.

The following little anecdote speaks more powerfully in favour of national corps, than volumes written on the subject could possibly do. The power of national music over the minds of soldiers in the field, was never more conspicuously displayed, than towards the conclusion of the action of the 25th July. Thinking that his friends would feel grateful to him for one or two of his favourite military airs, the piper-major of the 92nd Regiment "Set his drone in order," and made the hills and the valleys ring with the "Gathering of the Camerons." The effects were instantaneous. Every man was on his legs in a moment, and anxiously looking to General Stewart, who was then a few paces in their rear, wounded in the leg, for an order to advance.

He, however, instead of gratifying the men, warned them of the fatal consequences that might follow a movement in advance at that particular moment, and desired the piper not to play again till ordered. In ten minutes, Cameron, unmindful of the general's injunctions, repeated the dose, which produced exactly similar effects. Enraged at the piper's disobedience. General Stewart again stopped him, and forbade him at the peril of his life to play until ordered. On the arrival of General Barnes, soon after with the remainder of his brigade, Cameron the piper, conceiving that in common courtesy he was bound to welcome his friends to share our dangers, struck up the "Haughs of Cromdale," in his very best style. At the sound of that well-known national air, the Highlanders rushed down upon their numerous foes with the most undaunted bravery, who, panic-struck at their audacity, wheeled to the right about, and fairly ran, hotly pursued by the whole corps.

In the action between the 92nd right wing and the French on the

25th of July, William Bisket, a private soldier in the company under my charge, was wounded in the thigh, and forced to retire. Leaning upon his musket, he quitted the scene of action, the blood all the way flowing copiously from the wound. When about two hundred yards from us, he halted to take a farewell view of his comrades.

On perceiving them still supporting the sanguinary conflict with undiminished ardour, he rejoined them. Before falling into his place in the ranks, I advised him to retire, and inquired what motive could have induced him to return without having his wound even bandaged. Being a quiet and very worthy character, he replied coolly, "To have another shot at the rascals. Sir, before I leave you." The gallant fellow fired once, and was in the act of doing so a second time, when an- other ball passed through the bone of his arm, above the elbow, and compelled him finally to retire from the field, regretted by his admiring comrades.

Captain A. A. of the 71st Light Infantry, being on out-piquet at the pass of Maya when the French attacked our position, on the 25th July, was among the first to observe their advanced columns forming in rear of the heights. Having communicated this circumstance to Colonel Cameron, who commanded at the pass, he, in company with some other officers proceeded to Captain A's. post, to satisfy himself whether the captain's suspicions were well or ill founded. After looking at the French for a few moments through a glass, one of the young officers remarked, that what Captain A. supposed to be French troops, was nothing more than a few bullocks. As this remark went to impugn the vision of the gallant captain's little grey optics, he very indignantly retorted in the true Hibernian accent,

"By J——, my young friend, if they are bullocks, let me assure you, that they *have bayonets on their horns.*" Few had greater reason to remember the correctness of the captain's remark than the individual who provoked it, for in the action that followed, he was severely wounded by one of Captain A. A——g's bullocks, as all Frenchmen were afterwards denominated by us.

La Zarza

The cool and admirable manner in which General Stewart took up his ground at the close of the action on the 25th of July, caused D'Erlon to believe that we had been strongly reinforced, and only waited for a new day to renew the combat. So confident was the count of this, that he lay the whole of the 26th on the heights of Maya, without making one offensive movement. About two o'clock, p. m. on the 27th, his advanced columns appeared a little in front of Elizonda, and on being joined by those in the rear, prepared to attack us. But our presence being required in another part of the country, we declined the honour intended us, and retired from Barrueta encampment. The Sixth and Seventh Divisions having preceded us on the road to Pampluna, our progress, after passing Almandos, was considerably retarded by their baggage. About sunset we began to ascend the pass of Lanz; but in consequence of the obstacle just mentioned, and the darkness of the night, we were compelled to halt on the summit of one of the lower heights.

At daybreak we resumed our march,—passed through the village of Lanz, and about midday halted near La Zarza. Thinking ourselves secure of a resting-place for the night, those whose chins required a little trimming set about that operation, and the butchers in due time sent us our allowance of tough beef, which was no sooner divided than popped into our kettles. Everything was proceeding as favourably as could be wished—the beef was walloping in the camp-kettles, and the razors running as quickly over our faces as the stiff and lengthy stubble would permit them,—when, lo! the horn again sounded, not the note of preparation, but to fall in and be instantly off. In a moment the ground was covered with soup and butcher-meat, and half- shaved soldiers stood laughing at each other in every direction. The scene altogether was most ludicrous. In less than ten minutes we were on the road to Pampluna, a few miles in front of which the allied army, and the enemy under Marshal Soult, were engaged in the work of mutual destruction.

In the confident hope of forcing a passage to Pampluna, before a sufficient number of the allied forces could be collected in that quarter to prevent him, Marshal Soult attacked the third and fourth divisions in their position at Huarte, at an early hour on the 28th. But these troops, assisted by some Spanish battalions, and a brigade of Portuguese infantry, repelled the enemy's first assault with great gallantry. By dint of numbers, however, the French were at length enabled to outflank the Fourth Division on the left, and were proceeding to follow up their advantages, when the Sixth Division very opportunely arrived, and threw their force into the scale against the enemy. But although the arrival of this division must have satisfied the marshal that he could no longer hope to penetrate to Pampluna, he nevertheless continued his attacks long after every prospect of success had vanished. In them all he was most signally defeated, and at length driven from the various heights with terrible slaughter.

Being too late to take any part in the battle of the 28th, we halted a few miles in front of Pampluna, and bivouacked on the slope of a steep hill. Next morning we advanced about a mile, and bivouacked on the right of the road leading from Pampluna to La Zarza. Having received information that Soult, despairing of success, had dispatched his cavalry and artillery into France on the 29th, the Marquis Wellington, conceiving his opponent would soon follow with his infantry, attacked the left and centre of the French army at daybreak on the 30th, and after a very sharp action of four or five hours duration, defeated him with great loss. Seeing his left wing turned, and his retreat into France seriously endangered, Soult reinforced his right wing, and between ten and eleven o'clock, a. m. filed a large body of infantry towards the left of our corps, with the intention of making Sir Rowland Hill retire from his advanced position, and permit the French columns to withdraw quietly into their own country. Sir Rowland, however, with his few battalions, prepared to repel the assaults of Soult's masses, amounting to upwards of 20,000 men.

As soon as it became obvious that Soult intended to attack us, the first brigade moved across the high-road, to line the brow of an elevated ridge on its left, and facing the plain on which the enemy was forming his columns of attack. The Second Brigade was ordered to support the First, and Two Brigades of Portuguese Infantry occupied a height on the right of the road. The Eighth and Light Companies of the 92nd formed a guard to Sir Rowland Hill, who took post on a height to the left of the road.

The enemy's preparations being completed, they pushed a strong body of infantry along the base of the hill on which we were posted, with the view of ascending it at a distant point, turning our left, and forcing us to retire. To counteract this design, the first brigade made a corresponding movement along the summit of the ridge, which being everywhere covered with large trees, and long brush-wood, was not observed by our opponents. The latter showing a disposition to make an attempt on a part of the ridge of easier access than the other parts of it, the 50th halted to frustrate their designs. The 71st formed in extended order from the left of the 50th, to skirmish with the enemy should they endeavour to force their way to its summit.

The 92nd was formed into two divisions, the right formed a kind of moveable column, to support those who most required their services, and the left was pushed along the summit of the hill, to watch the motions of the enemy on the left. Having the command of the right company of this column, I was desired by the adjutant-general of the division, to move down alone from the right of the company about 130 yards, and on the first appearance of the enemy on my right, to give notice to the officer in command. I had advanced a considerable distance without being incommoded with the movements of the French, when all at once their approach was announced by a rustling noise about thirty yards distant on my right. I instantly gave the alarm—but before my men joined me, three of the enemy's light infantry fired at, but missed me. These we attacked briskly, and drove back with great loss.

After this we continued to skirmish with the enemy at extended order, until one of their grenadier battalions issued from a wood on our left, and with drums beating, and loud shouts of *Vive l'Empereur*, advanced to the charge. Calling in our skirmishers, we prepared to receive them in the warmest manner we could. The French were from five to six hundred strong—we had only four companies, not two hundred in all. Notwithstanding this disparity of force, however, our commandant, Captain Seton, conceiving it most politic to meet the foe half-way, stepped in front of his little corps, and with his bonnet in the left hand, and his sword in the other, said with great coolness and animation, "Ninety-second, follow me!" then after proceeding about twenty paces, he fell into the rear as usual on such occasions, and gave the word,—"Charge."

Our lads moved forward with great spirit to measure bayonets with their opponents, and what the issue of such a conflict would have been it were idle even to guess. But from such an unequal trial of strength we were most unexpectedly relieved by the 34th Regiment, who coming in sight of us just as we were moving forward, gave three hearty cheers, and joined us in our offensive movement against the enemy. Being still greatly inferior to the enemy in numbers, they seemed, for a little, quite determined to wait our assault; but somehow, when we had arrived within thirty or forty paces of them, they wheeled about and retired, hotly pursued by the two little corps. Their loss was considerable. Their commanding-officer, a fine young man, with two or three decorations at his breast, fell mortally wounded.

We were not allowed to enjoy our triumph very long, however, for the enemy, reinforced, again advanced against us. We returned their fire for some time with considerable effect, but receiving at length such an accession to his force as enabled him to outflank us on the left, we were reluctantly compelled to retire from the ridge we occupied, to another, and almost unassailable one, a mile in rear.

The other regiments of the second brigade, and Portuguese troops, were also hotly engaged; but during the time we were at work on the first position, the latter were not within our view. On retiring from that post, however, we had them completely under our eyes, and it must be admitted that some of the Portuguese battalions behaved uncommonly well. Attacked by greatly superior numbers, they were forced to retire fighting, to the summit of a height nearly two miles in rear of their original position; but being there reinforced by a brigade of their countrymen, they in turn became the assailants, and drove the French down the ridge at the point of the bayonet. This closed the serious operations of the day, but a loose irregular fire was kept up between the enemy and the Portuguese, till after sunset. The enemy's loss in this day's action was great; ours also was considerable. My little band was reduced from thirty-six to twenty-four, five being killed and seven wounded.

An order having been issued early in the morning of the 30th, for all men who could not keep up with their battalions to be sent to the baggage, I selected three of the company to proceed as directed. Two of them went with *apparent* goodwill, but the other respectfully told me that he would much rather die than leave us. The fate of these three men being rather striking, may furnish the curious with a subject for conversation.

In the action of the 25th July, William Dougald, the one who would not leave us, was hit three times with spent balls in the course of five minutes. These wounds, though not much minded at the time, became so inflamed by subsequent exertion, that on the 30th he was scarcely able to drag his right leg after him. I shall never forget the exertions he made to keep up with his companions, and the admirable manner in which he performed his duty in action, till stretched a lifeless corpse on the heights of La Zarza.

John Brookes, one of the two who quitted the company agreeable to order, was also struck on the 25th of July by a musket-ball, which hitting him on the throat, was miraculously turned aside by his stock, without doing him any apparent injury. But the parts soon became inflamed, and by the 30th, any words he uttered were quite unintelligible. The brave fellow having obeyed my orders with apparent alacrity, I was much surprised, on going into action, to observe him only a few paces in the rear, on his way to rejoin us. Having no time to take notice of Brookes' disobedience of a positive order, he proceeded with the company, and conducted himself with his usual spirit and gallantry, till another musket-ball struck him on the same place on which he was hit on the 25th July, passed through his neck, and killed him on the spot.

The other, Hugh Johnston, my servant, quitted us in company with Brookes, and rejoined his companions along with him. Soon after going into action a ball lodged in his groin, and he was borne a little way to the rear, the blood all the way flowing profusely from the wound. Our subsequent movement on that day placed him in the enemy's hands, where he remained all night without medical aid. On the retreat of the enemy next morning I despatched three men to carry him into La Zarza. Finding him greatly exhausted, they offered him a little spirits and water, on receiving which he lifted up his head, and having faintly said, "O! I would like to see him," reclined his head on the breast of one of his companions, and, with a smile on his countenance, bade *adieu* to all earthly things. Such was the premature fate of as good a soldier, and faithful servant, as ever graced the ranks of the British army.

On retiring from the ridge on which we had been so long engaged on the 30th, the—Portuguese regiment of infantry was ordered to cover our retreat. From some cause, however, best known to themselves, the whole, save about 150, took the shortest road to a place of safety, and left the others and their colonel, a fine young Highlander, to cover the retreat of their allies in any manner they could. In the valley between that ridge and the one to which we retired, there were some houses which should have been held by the Portuguese, but in consequence of their conduct, were soon taken possession of by the enemy. Enraged to see this post lost by the bad behaviour of his men, the colonel galloped up to the standard-bearer, snatched the standard out of his hands, and after attempting to rally a part of his troops, flew like lightning towards the enemy, till he arrived within a hundred yards of the houses, when he waved the standard round his head, and continued to do so for a considerable time, amidst showers of the enemy's shot.

The gallant colonel having both an uncle and a brother in our regiment, it was with great difficulty we could keep our men from breaking away from us, to render their countryman that aid which the Portuguese refused to give him. Our orders being peremptory, we durst not move, but we had the pleasure soon after of congratulating the young warrior on his admirable display of some of the finest military qualities of a soldier, and on his many hair-breadth 'scapes, his cloak and body-clothes being pierced in several places by musket-balls.

None but those who have had an opportunity of witnessing it, can have any idea how very little soldiers in general think of the danger which frequently surround them while on active service. The officers of the first brigade were reclining under the cooling shade of a wide-spreading tree on the 29th of July, and cracking their jokes, as if each had received a fifty years renewal of his earthly existence, when an officer of the 50th Regiment, who had been stationed at Lisbon, passed them in a very comfortable state of equipment. On his dismounting to report his arrival to the commanding-officer,—Colonel Fitzgerald of the 60th, then commanding the light companies of the second division, rose and cried, "Come, is any one inclined for a bet?" His query being answered in the affirmative,—"I will bet twenty dollars to one," rejoined the colonel, "that the officer just arrived in our bivouac is either killed or a prisoner with the enemy in twenty-four hours." The bet was taken,—the officer, horse and all, was in the hands of the French before the expiry of the period named by Fitzgerald, but the bet was never paid, for the latter was only a few hours later in following the other into the Gallic dominions.

This reminds me of another bet, which fully corroborates what I have asserted in the first sentence of the preceding paragraph. The

28th Regiment being hard pressed on one occasion during the Battle of Barossa, in March 1811, some officers of another corps expressed doubts as to the 28th being able to repel the assault of so superior a body of troops. On hearing this, Major B——, who well knew what the Bragge Slashers could do, galloped forward to the *doubters*, and offered to bet thirty dollars to one, that the 28th would "thrash the rascals soundly." The bet being declined, the major soon after, and on seeing the storm thickening, pulled out his purse, and holding it up, cried, "this purse of gold to a doubloon, the Bragge Slashers lick them yet." The bet being taken, and the 28th having repelled the enemy's attack. Major B—— rode up to the taker of the bet, and very coolly said, "The *doubloon*, if you please. Sir."

On that memorable day, the same gallant individual commanded a body of light infantry, whose inexpressibles were in a most tattered condition. Their hearts, however, appear to have been sound, for they repeatedly urged the major to let them down upon the enemy. This, however, he could not for some time do. But a favourable opportunity at length offering, he turned round to his followers, and in his usual cool and humorous manner, cried with the voice of a Stentor, "Now charge you bare —— blackguards." This singular address was received with uproarious mirth. The charge was successful, and before the little ragged band regained their original ground, it was generally supposed that each individual had acted strictly on the advice given by Norman Stewart of the 92nd to a comrade in Holland, in the year 1799, and "shot a shentleman for himsel'."

About the middle of the action between the right wing of the 92nd Regiment and the enemy, on the 25th of July, my pay-sergeant, tapping me on the shoulder, said he wished to speak to me. On my stepping a pace or two to the rear, and inquiring the purport of his communication, he replied with a tremulous voice, "Oh! Sir, this is terrible work, let me change places with you for a few minutes." Respecting very highly the friendly motive which induced sergeant C—— to offer to place himself *between me and the enemy's bullets*, I merely desired him to attend to his duty in the rear. In five minutes the poor fellow made a similar proposal, by which time dozens of our men lay around us killed and wounded, and the enemy in front literally in heaps. "I respect your motives, sergeant C——, but don't trouble me again on this subject," was my reply.

On resuming his post in rear of the company, C——'s eyes bespoke the severest disappointment, and continued to do so till a musket-ball entered his body a little above the groin, when calling upon me by name, he said, "I am killed." On perceiving him stagger, his brother, a private in the same company, flew to his assistance. Convinced that his wound was mortal, he requested to be laid down in rear of the company, being in great agony. The request, however, had scarcely been made, when a second ball struck the brave and warm-hearted sergeant, and killed him on the spot.

The Pass of Donna Maria

At daybreak on the 31st, the enemy occupied the same ground as on the previous evening, but soon after, they exhibited some degree of restlessness, and about eight o'clock they appeared on the wing. From the thrashing which Soult had received the day before, we knew quite well that he did not mean to become the assailant, consequently we prepared to harass him in his retreat, and to prevent as many of his followers as possible from effecting their escape into their dear France.

When we started in pursuit of the French corps immediately in our front, we were not very sanguine of bringing it to action, but as we proceeded, appearances became more favourable, till at length our light troops came up with their rearguard about midday in a wood, when an interchange of the formalities usual on such occasions took place between them, to the great amusement of the fire-eaters, but to the great grief of those who wished themselves a thousand miles from the seat of war.

The main body of the enemy had by this time gained the pass of Donna Maria. On each side of the road the hill was so covered with large trees and long brush-wood, that their troops were compelled either to keep the high road, which was but narrow, or ascend the eminence after the manner of riflemen, a mode of marching ill calculated for troops accustomed to move in close order. On arriving at the extremity of the wood in which our light troops first came up with the enemy, we found ourselves within three hundred yards of their rearguard, which was crowded together on the road, and making what speed they could to get out of the range of our artillery. This, however, they did not accomplish so quickly as they wished. Having with some difficulty got forward one field-piece and one howitzer, their fire was instantly directed against the confused mass with fatal effect, almost every shot or shell taking effect.

So well directed was the shot, that the very first knocked down a number of men, and threw the whole body into such a state of agitation, that they immediately abandoned the road, and hid themselves amongst the trees and brush-wood. Our artillery being now no longer useful, the infantry were called upon to play their part. The 50th Regiment ascended the hill on the left of the road, to operate against the enemy's right flank. The 71st, at extended order, skirmished with the French along the face of the hill from the right of the 50th to the road; and the 92nd advanced by the high road, and attacked the enemy in front. These corps were supported by the Second and Fourth Brigades, Second Division; and the Seventh Division, under the Earl of Dalhousie, moved towards the enemy's left flank, by a road running parallel to the one on which we were posted. The Brunswick infantry, and *Chasseurs Britannique*, being in the Seventh Division, and their uniforms having no resemblance whatever to that of any portion of the British army, our lads, on first getting a glimpse of them in a wood on the opposite bank of a deep ravine, mistook them for Frenchmen, and peppered them for a few seconds, till the mistake was discovered.

Pushed hard on every hand, the enemy had no alternative but to face about and fight for life and liberty. Their skirmishers being driven in on their main body, from seven to nine thousand strong, the French opened upon us a smart fire of musketry, which, as their danger increased, became more and more animated, until their balls flew over and around us in dreadful quantities. In defiance of their shot, however, our troops advanced with great spirit, to wrest the heights from the enemy. But in this they were foiled, and ultimately forced to retire with very considerable loss. A second attempt was also unsuccessful. But the third, made in conjunction with the second brigade, so completely succeeded, that the enemy were driven from the summit of the pass with great slaughter. Towards the conclusion of the battle, a musket-ball grazed my head, but I never quitted my corps, and was quite well again in a few days.

The troops of the Second Division being much fatigued by the operations of the 30th and 31st, the pursuit of the enemy was entrusted to the Seventh Division, and the former descended the hill arid bivouacked. At the close of this day's engagement I could only muster *thirteen privates, out of the eighty-two non-commissioned officers and privates which I carried into action six days before.*

On the 1st of August we once more entered the valley of Bastan, and in the evening encamped in front of Elizonda. A little after sunset we were visited by a terrific thunder storm. The peals were extremely loud, and the flashes of lightning which preceded them were so vivid, and followed each other in such a rapid succession, that for several hours the whole firmament appeared in one continued blaze. In fact, between the flashes of lightning, the roaring of the thunder, and the dreadful torrents of rain which battered incessantly on our tents, very few of us ever closed our eyes.

On the 2nd of August the allied army resumed possession of every post which it occupied on the 25th of July. In the evening the first brigade marched into Errazu, and next day took possession of its old ground on the heights of Maya, then thickly strewed with the mangled corpses of friends and foes.

In the early part of the campaign of 1813, our attendance on divine worship was very far from being so regular as our worthy chaplain wished. But this he knew was not our fault, but that of our opponents, who on almost every Sunday contrived to withdraw our eyes from the countenance of the minister, and force us to rivet them upon their darling pastimes. Having been often deprived of a congregation, Mr Frith, on visiting our encampment on Saturday the 24th of July, said, on parting with a few of us, "Gentlemen, we shall have divine service tomorrow, God and the *French* willing." With what fearful effect the French again interposed between us and our clergyman on that occasion, has already been shown.

But Mr Frith was not only an amiable and admirable expounder of the sacred text, he was also a gallant soldier. Being up with the leading columns on the 31st July, and seeing the artillery officer at a loss to find a road through some wood which obstructed his progress, Mr F. instantly placed himself at the head of the artillery, and never resigned his post until he planted them on the ground where they were to open upon the flying host. On perceiving the minister in this new character, some of our men felt much inclined to treat themselves to a laugh at his expense. One of them vociferated, "Gude guide us, look at the clergyman leading the artillery;" to which a second having added, "'Am sure *he* has nae business to place himself in danger;" a third, by way of rejoinder, said, "Haud your tongue, ye gowk, he's the very man that should be here—*he's prepared*."

No two generals ever possessed, in a more eminent degree, the confidence and esteem of their troops, than Sir Rowland Hill and Sir William Stewart. The many amiable qualities, and public and private virtues possessed by the former, endeared him to every individual under his command. Spurning the airs which generals sometimes assume, not with the view of rendering their troops more perfect in their field movements, but to annoy and harass those very individuals by whose exertions they are endeavouring to raise themselves to rank and honours. Sir Rowland Hill's sole delight consisted in providing for his troops,—seeing them comfortable, contented, and happy,—easing them at all times of as much fatigue as his duty would permit,—and, when an opportunity offered, in directing with proper effect their warlike energies against the enemy.

Some individual or individuals were kind enough to bestow upon Sir William Stuart the appellation of the enthusiastic madman. I only pray, that in every future war in which my country may be engaged, every officer, from the general of division, to the youngest ensign, may prove himself worthy of being admitted a member of that distinguished body of which the gallant and enthusiastic general was one of the chief ornaments. Sir William Stewart was without doubt an enthusiast in his profession. On service, his military duties engrossed his whole attention. Late and early he was to be seen visiting the outposts,—reconnoitring the approaches towards his posts and encampment, from the advanced posts and encampment of the enemy,—or in making observations, which, in case of an attack from, or upon the enemy, might be of service to him in making the necessary disposition of his troops. And in regard to the comfort, &c. of the men, he trod as nearly as possible in the footsteps of his gallant superior.

Sir William being wounded in the leg on the 25th of July, was reluctantly forced to leave us on the 27th. But on hearing of the battle of the 30th, he caused his leg to be properly bandaged, and with a pillow fastened so as to keep the leg from coming in contact with the stirrup, or the sides of the horse, mounted, and rejoined us a little before we came up with the French on the 31st. The loud and enthusiastic cheers of the soldiers welcomed him back. But their joy was soon turned into mourning,—for in less than three hours a musket-ball passed through the general's arm, a little above the elbow, and compelled him once more to go to the rear. On rejoining the division a few weeks afterwards, a party of the private soldiers of the 92nd, placed themselves near to the road by which Sir William had to pass to their corps,—and on his arrival, one of them stepped forward and said, "Oh, General, ye maun drink wi' us!" to which unexpected request the latter replied, "With all my heart, my man."

On taking the cup in his hand. Sir William expressed himself much gratified by their attention, and in finding them in such good health and spirits,—and then returning it, rode off towards the encampment, where the rest of the regiment, drawn up in front of their tents, received their General and friend with joyous acclamations, every bonnet flying into the air as high as its owner could heave it. The concluding part of the ceremony, though gratifying to the feelings of Sir William, had nearly proved the means of depriving him of one of his personal staff, whose horse having never before been honoured with a Highland welcome, was so unprepared for such a reception, that it wheeled to the right about, and to the great amusement of the spectators, but to the imminent hazard of the rider's neck, galloped down the hill at a winning pace.

When the French attacked the heights of Maya, on the 25th of July, a great proportion of the baggage animals of the 92nd Regiment were five or six miles from the encampment on a foraging excursion. In this number both my company and private mules were included. Some few returned in time to carry away the tents and baggage; others, in making the attempt, were taken by the enemy, but my two, when about half a mile from the camp ground, seeing the French quite close to it, wheeled about, and by the great exertion of the batman escaped, but the fatigue proved too great for my company mule, for it was seized with an inward complaint, and died a few days after.

I provided another mule for the company, and applied for compensation, which I received in the following year. Having lost at the same time all my personal baggage, except a few articles saved by the attention of my servant, who emptied his knapsack of his own property, and filled it with mine; I made out a list of the articles I had lost, affixed to each the price at which I could replace it, and transmitted the state signed by the commanding officer to the secretary of the Board of Claims in London. Along with this I also transmitted a separate note of a few articles of use to the men, which I had paid for on taking over the accounts of the company. Sometime after, I received intimation that I was to be allowed the value of the last mentioned articles, but not a farthing of the value of my own baggage. To be deprived of *any* compensation for articles which I had *actually* lost, I certainly considered a great hardship, and I do so still; for some who did not lose so much (though perhaps their all) received the *full allowance of Forty Pounds.*

The members of the Board, I conceive, must have been influenced in their decision, by the fact, that my private mule was preserved, nothing being more natural than for them to conclude, that as my mule had been saved, so must my personal baggage also. Though their decision, therefore, may have been warranted by the facts before them, yet I think that before they had decided upon my claim under these circumstances, the members of the Board should have applied to the commanding officer, whose signature was affixed to the list of articles, to know whether my mule had been in camp any time from the first appearance of the enemy, to the period we abandoned our all to them. Had they taken this trouble, they would have discovered that *a more just claim for compensation was never laid before them*. Having neglected to do so, however, I am still minus the value of my baggage, and my claim still remains in the office of the Board of Claims, furnishing rather strong testimony against the old maxim, that *Honesty is the best policy*.

Roncesvalles

Early in the morning of the 9th of August, the 2nd Division, on being relieved by the 6th, quitted the heights of Maya, and in the evening encamped within the French territory at Los-Alduides. Next day, after a long and tough pull, we arrived on the summit of one of the tremendous ridges near Roncesvalles, on which our companions were so long engaged on the 25th of July, the rain pelting us with merciless violence the greater part of the way. Water was much wanted, but the fog was so dense that the men were afraid to proceed in search of it, lest they might pop into the enemy's camp in place of their own.

A few men, therefore, from each company, paraded in fatigue clothing, and formed a complete chain of guides at a few paces from each other, till they succeeded in their object at some hundred yards distant. From this wilderness not a house was to be seen, nor a living creature, save ourselves, our baggage animals, and flocks of carnivorous birds hovering over the unburied corpses of friends and foes, which strewed the heights in every direction. Here lay the body of a friend—the tongue, the eyes, and large portions of the flesh torn from various parts of the body. There lay a foe with his bowels strewed around him in every direction. In many parts of the mountain, the birds were seen in the very act of tearing the flesh from the bones of the dead, a spectacle of the most sickening and heartrending description imaginable.

On the 11th, and subsequent days of August, our engineers chalked out various redoubts, block-houses, and breastworks, which when finished, occupied the following commanding points on the position of Roncesvalles.

The road from Pampluna into France, after running through the village of Roncesvalles, ascends about half a mile, then on the summit of the lowest part of the whole range, branches into two roads, that to the right, running with an easy ascent along the Spanish side of a high mountain, till it reaches the summit,—thence two miles down the opposite side, till it crosses the French frontier, when it runs down the top of a ridge towards St Jean Pied-de-Port. The left branch first runs along the side of the mountain, facing the French territory, with an easy ascent for two miles, then descends rapidly into a deep valley, whence it again ascends for a mile and a-half, and then descends again towards Los Alduides.

Our advanced posts were stationed between four and five miles from Roncesvalles, on the road to St Jean Pied-de-Port, the advanced piquet being posted at a point where the road has been cut through a rocky ridge, which runs to the left as far down as the rivulet in the valley, and on the French side the greater part of it is inaccessible. It was here that the gallant Byng and his brigade made such a noble stand against Soult on the 25th of July. On a height immediately in rear of this ridge, we erected a block-house into which the piquets were to throw themselves in case of an attack. On another height, a little in rear of the first, we raised a redoubt, and as it commanded the road, we planted a few pieces of cannon in it. This fort the inlying piquets were to occupy in every case of alarm.

On the highest point of ground, and about half way between the latter and Roncesvalles, there was another redoubt, and a little in rear of it a block-house. The face of the hill looking to France was pretty thickly studded with breast-works, as also was each side of the pass, immediately in front of Roncesvalles. Two miles from the pass, on the road to Los-Alduides, a high, and extremely steep narrow ridge, runs straight towards the French territory. On the highest peak of this ridge, and about a mile and a half from the road, the advanced piquet of the left brigade was posted. In a kind of ravine, half a mile in rear of the latter, there was a captain's piquet, and a little in rear of it, a block-house, into which the captain was to throw himself in case of an attack. At a short distance from the road, and a few hundred yards from the ridge on the left, we raised a pretty strong redoubt, which commanded the road and ground all around it.

From the day we took possession of those heights, down to the final surrender of St Sebastian on the 9th of September, we were kept on the alert, always prepared every morning, an hour before daylight, for whatever might occur, being in daily expectation of another visit from our old friend Soult. Our duties all this time were more annoying than severe, for although our ears were stunned every morning with the sound of artillery, and often with musketry, under our very noses, yet our active warlike operations were confined to one or two hostile demonstrations, and the strengthening of our position in the manner before related.

We were often at a loss during this inactive period how to pass a few of the dull hours, which hung heavily on our hands, for none could with safety leave the camp for more than an hour at a time, and there, our amusements were extremely limited. The *fire-eaters* took delight in watching the progress of our field-works, reconnoitring the enemy's advanced posts, and the roads leading to them. The politicians confined themselves to their tents, and explored the pages of the weekly packet of London and Edinburgh newspapers, which we received at that time pretty regularly. Those to whom the rattle of the dice had greater charms than the sounds of musketry, generally assembled around a tent, or under a large tree, and when the company was numerous, those who could not be accommodated with active employment, laid bets upon the issue of each game. Whist, however, was the favourite game amongst the officers, many of whom, or their heirs, have still depending considerable sums of money on the issue of rubbers begun in 1813.

On the 25th July, a whist party had finished one game, and were nine all of the second, when the bugle called upon them to take part in a game of a very different description. Conceiving that they might steal as much time as would permit their bringing the second game to a close, they actually played it out, and then rushed from the tent, the whole exclaiming, "We will finish the rubber when we return, the game is single to single." The rubber is, however, still in dependence, for the same party never afterwards met. Two of them were wounded the same day; another was taken by the enemy on the 30th, and the fourth who escaped the balls of the enemy in Spain, is the only one of the four now alive.

A newspaper was the most acceptable present which any friend could send to us, during the Peninsular contest. The French officers acknowledged to us frequently, that they were miserably ill-informed of the issues of their most important movements and engagements. Papers they received, but their contents were generally so much at variance with the truth, that it was quite a common saying, "he lies like a *Moniteur*," or "he lies like a bulletin." Even the generals of brigade were often kept in ignorance as to the result of their most important operations. For example, General Foy was so imperfectly informed in regard to the issue of the battle of Vittoria, that he sent a flag of truce by an *aide-de-camp* for the loan of a London newspaper containing the details of that celebrated engagement. The General's request was complied with.

In a few days the paper was returned, along with a few others of Parisian manufacture. This was done by Foy, to shew us that it was his wish to lessen the horrors of war as much as was consistent with that military etiquette so necessary to be observed by every officer entrusted with the command of the advanced posts of an army, in the presence of an enemy.

Having alluded to advanced posts, I may state that to ensure the complete safety of a camp, every outlying piquet should be accompanied by two officers, when the opposing armies are encamped close to each other. Many things frequently conspire to render the private soldier more inclined to resign himself into the arms of sleep, on going on sentry, than to watch with that caution so essentially necessary to the safety of himself and friends. In bad weather, for instance, or after a long and harassing march, it is often difficult to keep the sentries from indulging in a fatal nap, though there are few of them but know that by doing so they may probably entail on the army defeat or disgrace. In such circumstances the duties of an officer are unremitting, and frequently so severe, that he is forced, through exhaustion, to lessen the number of his visits. The consequence of this is, that the sentries are but too apt to indulge in sleep.

If, in addition to a piquet of this kind, an officer has one or more non-commissioned officers piquets under his charge, or if his own sentries should be widely extended, it is totally impossible for one officer to pay that attention to the whole, during the night, which the safety of the main body of the army so imperiously demands of him. Either he must neglect the main body of his piquet, or the detached piquets and sentries. If he visits the sentries, he must leave the main body of his piquet in charge of the sergeant, or delegate the duty of visiting the sentries to the latter. Now, although the non-commissioned officers in general are much inclined to conduct themselves correctly on such occasions, still we must not forget that they have not the same inducements to a zealous and faithful discharge of their duty which their superiors have, and, on that account I should conceive it prudent, to avoid the alternatives previously alluded to, by appointing two officers to every outlying piquet,—for a trifling inattention on the part of the sergeant has been, and may again be productive of most disastrous consequences.

From the surrender of St Sebastian to the capitulation of Pampeluna, on the 31st of October, we felt much more at our ease than we did previous to the first event. For the fall of the former not only lessened Soult's inducements to attack us, but added a considerable number of troops to our effective force in the field. Our amusements were also increased by this event. From that period we occasionally descended to the village of Roncesvalles, and treated ourselves to a comfortable dinner, and a tolerable bottle of country wine. For some time we had excellent *races* once a-week, and a *bullfight* every Thursday. The mounted officers, who were lovers of the chase, had a rich treat afforded them two or three times every week by Sir Rowland Hill, whose pack of hounds was much at the service of the officers of his corps.

About the middle of October, however, our situation became rather uncomfortable. The ground was so saturated with moisture, that wherever we encamped, in a day or two the whole of our encampment was a perfect puddle. Previous to this we had slept on the ground, but we latterly made little bedsteads of the branches of trees, and by raising them about nine inches from the earth, and covering them with a little straw, grass, or fern, we became so very bad, that all the troops on the right of the position were recalled from the heights, save the outlying piquets, and a body of 500 men, called the inlying piquet, to support the others in case of an attack.

On the 27th of October I made one of the party of 500. When we moved from Roncesvalles the morning was fine, the frost was severe, but there was not a breath of wind. In the afternoon the sky overcast,—soon after snow began to fall, and before sunset the wind began to whistle. Everything now portended a storm, and to meet it we made every preparation in our power. Throughout the whole of the night the snow fell, and the wind howled, and at daybreak on the 28th, the snow was drifted to a considerable depth. At ten o'clock, a. m. on the 28th, we were relieved by new bodies of troops, and instantly bade *adieu* and forever to the right of the allied position at Roncesvalles.

In our progress back to our encampment, the snow dealt with us mercifully; but we had scarcely reached our tents when it resumed the tricks of the preceding night, and continued to fall, without the smallest intermission, till one or two o'clock next morning, by which time it was a foot and a half deep in the valley, where not drifted, but on the hills it was in some places twelve feet in depth. Part of the out-lying piquets were covered, and had to be dug out of the snow in a pitiable state: some of them lost the use of their limbs.

In consequence of the quantity of snow which fell on my tent on the night of the 28th, the pole of it snapped in two places about four o'clock, a. m. on the 29th, and, without any warning, down came canvass, pole, and snow on the top of me. My bed being nine inches from the ground, the snow and canvass pinned me so completely to it, that on awaking, I fancied myself bound hand and foot, for neither the one nor the other could I move. Respiring for some time with considerable difficulty, I began seriously to think that some persons were attempting to smother me. But recollecting at length the position of my bed, I made an effort to throw myself from it, which with difficulty I accomplished. Placing my head under the bed, I breathed more freely; and, after a great struggle, I pulled a penknife from my pocket, cut a hole in the canvass, made my escape, and after wandering fully half an hour, I at length got under the protection of a friend, the pillar of whose house was made of sterner stuff than my own.

On the same day the brigade marched into Roncesvalles. General Byng being in possession of a house which was handed over for the officers of the 92nd Regiment, he, in the handsomest manner, not only gave up the greater part of it instantly, but sent us all a kind invitation to dine with bins, which the field-officers, and a few more, accepted.

About the middle of October, General Mina and his guerrillas encamped in our neighbourhood.

Strolling one day in the vicinity of the Spanish encampment, I was accosted by an officer in very good English. I soon discovered that he was a Frenchman, who had spent some time in London. At a subsequent period he entered the service of Napoleon, and served as an officer in a cavalry regiment till December 1812, when he married a Spanish lady, *took leave of his countrymen,* and joined Mina, by whom he was appointed a lieutenant in one of his *French companies,* of which he had one in every battalion. These companies were composed almost exclusively of deserters, and Mina as a mark of regard, *or something else,* assigned to them the *post of honour* in every action. Of this the lieutenant complained bitterly, but without sufficient cause,—for what could Mina do with the deserters, but place them in situations where the eyes of all his corps could be upon them. Had he adopted a different course, he would not have acted with his usual sagacity. For when two nations are at war, and a native of the one betrays his country by deserting to the enemy, the latter, however much they may be gratified with the *treasonable act*, never can have any regard for the *traitor*. For having betrayed his paternal country, it is but natural to infer, that on the very first favourable opportunity he will betray his adopted one.

The lieutenant, however, seemed to me to have taken a diametrically opposite view of the matter, and as it is much to be feared that ninety-nine out of every hundred of deserters apply the same flattering unction to their feelings on taking the rash, the fatal step, officers cannot too often explain to their men the heinous crime of desertion, and endeavour to show them that it is the *treason*, and *not* the *traitor*, which finds favour in the eyes of those to whom the latter tenders his services, on deserting the standard of his native land.

The French cavalry regiment to which this officer was attached, having been cannonaded for some time by the British, in November 1812, with little effect, the French soldiers, who had never before been opposed to British troops, indulged in a hearty laugh at the expense of our artillery officers. By and bye, however, our artillery having got the proper range, sent a *shrapnel* amongst them with fatal effect. The gay and joyous countenances vanished in a moment, for *eleven* men had fallen, and none had discovered whence the messengers of death had sped on their fatal mission. Another shell followed close in the wake of the first, and doing similar execution, threw the whole corps into confusion, and some of them walked their horses slyly away. During this state of excitement, a third shell struck the enemy's column with as fatal effect as its predecessors, when the whole regiment scampered from the field, exclaiming that *the devil had taken command of the British artillery.*

The Last Battle

Before daybreak on the 6th November, a Spanish piquet, posted in a valley about a mile in front of Roncesvalles, was attacked by the enemy, and almost all killed or wounded. Although surprised, the Spaniards defended themselves with bravery, and rendered the success of their opponents rather dearly purchased.

The surrender of Pampeluna having placed a farther effective force of ten thousand men at the disposal of the Marquis of Wellington, and changed the whole aspect of our affairs on the Pyrenees, no time was lost in making the necessary preparations for a successful attack on the enemy's fortified position, extending from St Jean Pied-de-Port on the left, to St Jean-de-Luz on the right. Accordingly the Second, Third, and Fourth Brigades of the Second Division, marched from Roncesvalles on the 6th November for the valley of Bastan.

Our advanced posts having been withdrawn from the right of our position, to the block-house half-way between it and Roncesvalles, the enemy, anxious no doubt to discover what we were doing, pushed forward a strong reconnoitring party on the afternoon of the 7th, and attacked the block-house, in which there was a captain's piquet, composed almost exclusively of men of the 92nd Regiment, and commanded by a Captain Holmes of that corps. On the first alarm the First Brigade got under arms, and marched towards the scene of action. General Mina, who had for some time suspected the retailers of vegetables, &c. from the French side of the heights, of giving the enemy information of our movements, flew into the little market-place, and with a whip made them scamper off at a gallop, squeaking and screaming like as many pigs.

On performing what the Spanish chief thought an act of justice, he mounted his charger, and made the best of his way towards the block-house. Falling in with a few hundreds of his own troops returning from a reconnoitring excursion, he caused them to wheel to the right about, and follow him. These brave fellows, preceded by their leader, and followed by us, ascended the mountain at a rapid pace. On drawing near, the enemy's fire was withdrawn in a great measure from the block-house, and directed upon the Spaniards, although at rather too great a distance to do much execution, and before the latter got very close, the French made off, hotly pursued by them.

About four o'clock, p.m. of the 8th, the First Brigade marched in the direction of Maya, and between twelve and one o'clock next morning, arrived in the village of Los Alduides. The night being extremely dark, the road narrow, and winding occasionally round the corners of frightful precipices, our movements were not unattended with danger. The mule of a brother officer, which was fastened to mine, slipped a foot on rounding one of the sharp turns of the road, and falling over, rolled to the bottom, and was killed on the spot.

At daybreak on the 9th we resumed our arms, and rejoined the other brigades in rear of Maya, about four o'clock in the afternoon. On descending the high ridge which bounds the valley of Bastan on the east, the whole space from Elizonda to the heights of Maya, seemed covered with men, horses, cannon, and baggage. On such an occasion the heart of the bachelor beats light, but—

Ten thousand thousand fleet ideas, such
As never mingled with the vulgar dream,
Crowd fast into the mind's creative eye

of their married brethren, who, far from an amiable wife and darling children, feel those inward pangs which the former never feel, and which, but for hope, sweet hope, would in many instances render them anything but efficient members of a battalion in the field of strife. But

Hope springs eternal in the human breast,
Man never is, but always to be blest.

On finishing our cooking operations, the men stretched their wearied limbs on the cold ground till about nine o'clock in the evening, when they prepared to resume their march. Being in orders for the brigade baggage-guard, my name had scarcely appeared in the orderly books, when my tent was filled to an overflow with officers, some depositing gold, others secrets, and a third party the addresses of friends to whom I was to make known their melancholy death, should they fall in the conflict. The scene altogether was affecting. But previous to leaving our bivouac, I prevailed upon my commanding-officer to relieve me of this duty and appoint another more advanced in years, to whom I delivered up all the secrets, gold, and addresses, and proceeded with my company.

Leaving our resting-place a little after nine o'clock, we crossed before midnight the summit of that memorable ridge, where, far from friends or home, many of our companions had reposed ever since the 25th of July.

O valiant race,
Though overpowered—triumphant, and in death
Unconquered.

From the heights we moved down the top of a ridge which leads thence towards the village of Urdax. The march, though short, was of the most unpleasant description. The night being dark, the ground uneven, and covered with long grass and heather, and the eyes of the whole being more than half-closed in sleep, every moment some of us were tumbling heels over bead, to the imminent danger of our noses, but to the great amusement of those few who kept themselves awake.

The rear of the first brigade was in the act of crossing the small River Nivelle, when at half-past six o'clock, a. m. on the 10th, the artillery of the left wing announced to us that the grand struggle had commenced. A few hundred yards from the left bank of the river, we were ushered into a field, where we found the other brigades of our division preparing to take part in the business of the day. Being by this time dreadfully jaded, our brigade was permitted to take a little repose before being called into active employment.

The left of the enemy's position rested on a height in rear, and considerably to the left of the village of Anhoe, and thence extended along a range of connected little hills, which there runs across the country in front of the towns of St Pe and St Jean-de-Luz to the sea. On their extreme left the French had crowned the heights with two strong redoubts, and occupied them with a considerable body of infantry. A little lower down, on the same ridge, and immediately behind the village of Anhoe, there were three redoubts, each mounting several pieces of cannon of large calibre. Farther to their right, and towards the left centre of their position, the enemy had every little eminence decorated with a field work of some description or other; and from the centre to the extreme right, the whole was very strong, Soult expecting that our principal attack would be made in that direction.

The Third, Fourth, Sixth, and Light Divisions were directed to move against the centre, and right and left centre of the French lines. The First and Fifth were to amuse the enemy on the right, and the Second Division, General Hamilton's division of Portuguese infantry, and Morillo's Spanish corps, were directed to attack the redoubts in rear of Anhoe.

The first operations of the armies were completely hid from our view; but by degrees the tide of war began to roll towards us from the centre, and by ten o'clock the battle had begun to rage with considerable fury along almost every part of the enemy's line. In the centre, our companions had warm work of it for some time; but having, after a desperate struggle, obtained possession of one of the enemy's principal redoubts, in which were nearly six hundred men, the others deemed it more prudent to walk off, after doing all the mischief they could, than yielding without or braving assault.

The grand object of the attack on the centre, the breaking the enemy's chain of fortified posts, being obtained, the troops engaged at that point were ordered to bring up their right and left shoulders;—the sixth division, and General Hamilton's Portuguese their left;—and the Third, Fourth, and Light their right, and attack the inward flanks of the enemy's right and left wings, and in conjunction with the troops on their right and left, endeavour to make them relinquish their hold of the other portions of the position.

Generals Stewart, Clinton, and Hamilton, severally led their divisions to the attack of the enemy behind Anhoe in fine style. Nothing indeed could possibly be more beautiful than the operations of all the three, preceding, and pending the assault of the heights and redoubts. The face of the ridge being in some places a good deal cut up, and in others thickly studded with breastworks, our companions found the ascent more difficult than some of them anticipated. But these obstacles, instead of dispiriting the assailants, rather urged them forward with a firmer and more determined pace, for

> The love of praise, howe'er concealed by art,
> Reigns, more or less, and glows in every heart:
> It aids the dancer's heels—the writer's head.
> And heaps the plain with mountains of the dead.

Having, therefore, after a long and a tough pull, fairly obtained a footing on the higher part of the ridge, they proposed to carry the forts by assault. This part of the operations was particularly interesting, as in the execution of it our troops were to shew to the world whether their military prowess was confined to field operations, unobstructed by stone walls, or whether every description of military work was to them the same. The conflict was severe, but not very long, for the enemy, seeing that the British were determined to bear down all opposition, retired from their strongholds one after another, and at length making a virtue of necessity, finally left the heights, (their own guns giving them a parting salute,) and retired towards Cambo, on the Nive.

The allied forces which moved against the French right wing, were long and sharply engaged in the neighbourhood of St Pe. They at length succeeded, however, in forcing the enemy from the town to some heights above it, from which they annoyed our men very much with a sharp discharge of musketry till it was pretty late in the evening, when

The bugles sang truce for the night cloud had lowered,
And the sentinel stars set their watch in the sky,
And thousands had sunk on the ground overpowered.
The weary to sleep, and the wounded to die.

Pending these operations, a body of Spanish troops crossed the heights of Maya, and attacked the advanced posts of the enemy's left wing with spirit; but pushing their success farther than prudence warranted, they were attacked in turn, and driven into the valley of Bastan, where the French succeeded in capturing some of our light cavalry baggage. How the enemy accomplished this, was a complete puzzle to many. It was related at the time, and very generally credited, that if common prudence or exertion had been used, not a particle of baggage would have fallen into the Lands of the French. On obtaining possession of the person and personal baggage of a British paymaster, the enemy pressed him hard for cash. Conceiving that a few guineas would satisfy his unwelcome visitors, he handed them as many as would have made the whole party more than half-seas-over. These they most kindly accepted, and politely solicited a fresh supply.

In hopes that a few more would rid him of their presence, the paymaster consented to make a farther sacrifice, but instead of satisfying, it only tended to sharpen the appetite of the plunderers for the precious metal. A fresh supply was necessary, and down came a hundred guineas. Surely the fellows will now cry enough, thought the paymaster, but, no! another hundred rung in his ears like the sound of a funeral bell. On tendering the second hundred—I have no more, said the paymaster—we will prove that replied the French. Tapping him on the shoulder, the latter said in a jocular manner, "Come now, just another hundred if you please," and repeated the same thing on receiving every additional hundred, till the paymaster had "dropped," not quite so many guineas as the blind beggar of Bethlehem-Green did on the marriage of his daughter, but considerably more than he could afford to lose, or any government should under similar circumstances be called upon to pay.

In this battle, generally termed the battle of the Nivelle, our loss was 3000 killed and wounded; that of the enemy was estimated at 4000 killed and wounded, and 1500 prisoners. Fifty-one pieces of cannon also fell into our hands.

Soult having withdrawn his right wing from its position in front of St Jean-de-Luz during the night of the 10th, and morning of the 11th, the allied army moved forward on the latter, the left wing towards Bayonne, the right upon Cambo on the Nive. About ten o'clock, a.m. on the 11th, the Second Division quitted the heights from which they had driven the enemy the preceding day, and after a trip of three or four miles halted in a field, where, under a torrent of rain, it remained the whole day without making any attempt to drive the French farther back, although they were but a little way from us all the time. The French, however, retired about sunset; we advanced to an eminence covered with heath, on the left of the principal road from Anhoe to Cambo, and about three miles from the latter. Here we spent a most uncomfortable night, for the brush-wood being so wet that it would not burn, we were deprived of our usual allowance of warm water, either made into soup, or its more refreshing relative, tea.

Sir Rowland Hill being ordered to dislodge the enemy from Cambo, the division got under arms a little before midday on the 12th. The Second and Third Brigades moved first towards the river Nive, but on arriving within a few hundred yards of it, they brought up their left shoulders, and then advanced direct upon Cambo. The first brigade moved obliquely to the right, till it gained the high road, and then pushed along, drove back the enemy's piquets within a short distance of their works, and turning to the right, ascended an eminence which overlooked the town, and the whole of the enemy's defences within range of the artillery. Here Sir Rowland reconnoitered the French, when finding them better prepared for us than was expected, he contented himself with driving back their light troops, and cannonading the garrison. In the evening we retired about a mile, and encamped.

Two worthy paymasters, anxious to see how the heads took leave of the shoulders of their friends, but at such a distance as to preclude every chance of a similar compliment being paid to themselves, very knowingly rode round the rear base of the ridge on which we were posted, conversing on every subject save dead and wounded paymasters. Moving along, therefore, in conscious security, and casting an eye occasionally to the left to see if any friendly sconce was twirling down the face of the hill, Mr A. had just withdrawn his optics from that quarter, and remarked to Mr B. that they had a better berth of it than their friends on the top of the hill, when a large cannon-ball plunged into the earth, under his horse's belly,— on perceiving which,

Away went Gilpin— away went he.

We had not been long in our bivouac, before the rain began to pour on us with its usual severity, and continued to pelt us unmercifully throughout the whole of the night. Our baggage being still in rear, and the wind being high, nothing could be more truly miserable than the situation of the whole brigade at daybreak on the 13th. By arranging ourselves around a few blazing fires, however, we contrived at length to have one side always pretty comfortable. Thus while one-half of our persons was nearly roasted, the other was cold as a piece of ice.

On the arrival of our baggage in the afternoon, we were more comfortable, but the rain ceased not night or day, from the evening of the 12th, to the morning of the 16th, when the enemy retired across the Nive, and destroyed two arches of the bridge to prevent us following them. On taking possession of Cambo, a few hours afterwards, its whole population consisted of a dragoon who had been left behind, an old man and his wife, completely bedridden, and a pig, for the head of which I paid a few days after no less than *four dollars*. The absence of the inhabitants we did not regret, for having left all their bedding behind them, it afforded us a treat such as we had seldom experienced during the previous six months, having been only *thirteen nights* under the roof of a house, out of one hundred and eighty-one days the campaign had continued.

Liberty is so highly prized by, and is so essentially necessary to the well-being of every individual, that we cannot be surprised that men should be tenacious of what they conceive to be their glory and happiness, and in defence of, or to preserve it, sacrifice all, even life itself.

An example of the strength of this feeling, appears in the following occurrence:—

About an hour after we took possession of Cambo, a private soldier of the 66th British Regiment, who was made prisoner by the enemy on the 10th of November, escaped from his jailers, and from a village immediately opposite to Cambo, made direct for the bridge, amid a sharp fire from a long chain of sentries. Finding the bridge destroyed, he seemed to hesitate whether he would return to his prison, or commit himself to the raging waters. A great part of our brigade having by this time lined the bank of the river, provided with ropes, canteen straps, &c. to assist him, cheered on seeing him stop, which no doubt encouraged him to attempt a passage from the right to the left bank of the Nive. In an instant he plunged into the river, which being dreadfully swollen, carried him down at a fearful rate; for a few seconds, appearances were in favour of his gaining the left bank in safety, but after being more than two-third parts of the way across, he sunk, then rose, but sunk again. A second time he appeared on the surface of the foaming deep, but in two or three seconds he again disappeared, and never rose again.

The French having destroyed all the bridges on the Nive, and the river being so far above its usual level, as to render a passage by the fords impracticable, the two armies remained cantoned on the Nive and the Adour, from the 16th November to the 8th of December, without either party attempting to resume the offensive. During all this time we were really on a friendly footing with our opponents. The latter came down to the right bank of the Nive, and conversed with us freely on every subject save politics. They were particularly anxious, however, to obtain information regarding the campaign in Germany, for they candidly admitted that the retreat of Bonaparte towards France, but ill corresponded with the bulletins he had caused to be published at Paris. To enlighten them in the matter, we sent them some London newspapers, for which we received a few *Moniteurs* in return. This we continued to do on the arrival of every succeeding packet from England, until our intercourse was again interrupted by active operations.

War, even when conducted according to the law of civilized nations, is attended with so many evils, that every man possessed of one spark of humanity, will forbear to add to them; and when measures of severity are absolutely necessary to accomplish those things which his duty may require him to perform, they will still be tempered with moderation and humanity, and instantly cease when the object he has in view is obtained. The lustre of military achievements is tarnished by nothing so much as by cruelty, which affords pleasure only to men of the most depraved habits. Acts such as that which I am about to relate, whether to gratify a mean grovelling revenge, or to suit political convenience, cannot fail to expose' the perpetrators to the indignation of every person in whose breast there is to be found one particle of justice or humanity.

An officer of the 92nd Regiment being on piquet at the bridge one evening, hailed the French sentry posted at the opposite side of the chasm made by the enemy when they retired from Cambo, and as he spoke the French language fluently, desired him to say to the officer on piquet, that he wished to have a little chit-chat with him. The latter instantly appeared, but instead of agreeing to the proposal of his opponent, he threatened him with the vengeance of all the men under his command if he did not immediately retire. In vain did Lieutenant H———bs explain the object he had in view. Bellowing and stamping like a madman, the French officer would listen to no explanation—would hear of no apology—the opportunity of lessening the number of his enemy's being too favourable to allow to pass unimproved. Finding that the wrath of the hot-headed mortal would only be appeased by blood, Lieutenant H———bs considered it more prudent to retire than brave the other alternative offered him. He accordingly walked away towards the piquet-house at the end of the bridge, on entering which, a ball struck the door a few inches from his head, fired from a French musket, by order of this disgrace to the military habit.

A few days afterwards I was detached one morning before daybreak up the left bank of the Nive, to watch the motions of our not-to-be-trusted *friends*. Placing myself behind a very large tree, immediately opposite to a village where the enemy had a considerable body of infantry, I fancied myself completely out of their view. Obtaining a glimpse of me, however, before they had dismissed their troops from the alarm-post, the officer commanding the out-lying piquet advanced towards the river, and lifting his cap, pointed to Cambo. Paying no attention to the hint, it was instantly repeated. Having again disregarded it, he, instead of repeating the friendly signal, called down two files of his piquet, and detached as many to his right and left.

These ominous preparations, particularly as my mission had ended, induced me to remove from my hiding-place, and wend my way to Cambo. With my friend's bridge adventure fresh in my recollection, and not knowing but I might be treated in a similar manner, I quitted my retreat cautiously, which my opponent observing, he, to remove all suspicion from my mind, again stepped forward, and after saluting me two or three times in the most gentlemanly manner, rejoined his piquet, evidently pleased with the issue of the affair. The conduct of this officer forms a delightful contrast with that of his brother sub. at the bridge of Cambo, who, of all the French officers then immediately opposed to us, was perhaps the only one who could have been guilty of such a cruel, and truly ungentlemanly act.

Being of opinion that the death of every officer killed with the first battalion, whose proper place at the time was the second battalion at home, would afford his countrymen good grounds for charging him with the crime of *murder*, Colonel Cameron laid it down as an invariable rule, to apply for leave to send home the officers belonging to the second battalion, on their being relieved by the effective members from home. Accordingly, on the arrival of a detachment at Cambo, on the 27th November, the colonel applied, and obtained permission for myself and three other officers to proceed to England.

The latter having arranged with the paymaster early in the forenoon, took leave of Cambo at three o'clock on the 8th of December. But eight o'clock having tolled before that indispensable personage and myself had adjusted our matters, and as an order had been issued some hours before, for a general attack upon the enemy's position along the whole line of the Nive, I waited upon the commanding-officer, and requested permission to accompany him across the river on the following morning. To this application he quickly and sternly replied, "No, Sir, you have done enough;" and as if this refusal was not sufficient, he sent the adjutant to me a few minutes afterwards to intimate, that if I did not leave Cambo immediately, I would incur his displeasure,—and if I attempted to join the regiment in the morning, he would place me under arrest. Although perfectly aware that the colonel's conduct proceeded from a friendly intention, I was nevertheless dreadfully disappointed, for on such an occasion I thought he might have indulged me.

The night being dark, and my knowledge of the road being slender, I ventured for the first time in my life to disobey the orders of my commanding-officer, and join a party of my friends who had assembled to dedicate a cup to him who was on the eve of bidding some of them an eternal farewell. After spending two or three happy hours, we threw ourselves upon our mattresses, to catch a little repose before we should be called upon—my brethren to proceed in search of new dangers and victories, and I in search of home and friends. When I gazed on the gay and joyous countenances of the group, as each individual rose to retire from the festive scene, and reflected on what an important change they severally might undergo before the close of another day, my feelings had nearly overpowered me. To describe them on that occasion words are inadequate. Suffice it to say that they were the feelings of a man taking leave of companions whose friendship he possessed,—friendship contracted in the haunts of peace, and cemented in the field of strife. Not that kind of friendship which grows out of interested motives or designs, but that which makes one man take as much interest in the fate and fortunes of another, as if they were his own.

Having performed the painful task of taking leave of my friends, I bade *adieu* to Cambo about four o'clock in the morning of the 9th of December, and proceeded towards Espalete. I had not proceeded far, however, before I fell in with a column of Portuguese infantry hastening to the place of rendezvous. Ashamed to meet them under such circumstances, I quitted the road, but had scarcely done so, when I popped into a ditch filled with water and clay. In a most uncomfortable state I jogged along till I reached Espalete; where meeting with an old acquaintance in the person of a commissary, I walked with him to his lodgings, and there spent a couple of hours, cracking the shells of a dozen of my friend's eggs, and exchanging the midnight dress for one more comfortable and less offensive to the eye. On arriving at St Pe, we procured a little refreshment in a house which still bore numerous marks of the conflict of the 10th of November, some of the musket-balls being still in the wood of the partitions and windows. The worthy occupants having a son a prisoner of war in Scotland, they begged our acceptance of a few apples to carry with us to the Land of Cakes.

Arriving in St Jean-de-Luz about sunset, we procured a billet upon a fifth-rate tavern. The entertainment was bad, and prices exorbitant. Next morning we quitted St Jean, and proceeded towards Passages, the place of embarkation. On a height on the right bank of the Bidassoa we remained half-an-hour, indulging ourselves with a distant view of the conflict between Sir John Hope's corps and the enemy near Bayonne. Crossing the river soon after, we passed through Irun, and halted for the night at Renteria. On the 11th we arrived in Passages, and next day embarked in the *Britannia* transport for England.

Previous to going on board, we had the pleasure of seeing Colonel Kruse, at the head of the regiments of Frankfort and Nassau, march into Passages to embark. These two corps quitted the standards of the enemy during the action of the 10th near Bayonne. They were very fine looking fellows, and seemed quite delighted with the prospect of returning to their native country.

Early in the morning of the 17th December, our transport, and ten others, under convoy of a gun-brig, sailed from Passages. On clearing the harbour, we cast a wistful eye towards the spot whence we had come, and could not resist repeating, Farewell ye tented fields!—farewell ye plains and towering heights, stained with the blood of the best and dearest of our friends! For our native land we now leave thy shores, where in the bosom of our families we hope to spend a few days in peace and domestic felicity. Gallant companions,—of your heroic deeds we will read with delight, and in the fond expectation of again joining you at an early period to share in your dangers and your glory, we bid you all farewell!

At this time the sky was clear—not a cloud in the horizon, and scarce a ripple on the water. So beautiful indeed, and cheering were the rays of the Sun, that the mighty Leviathans themselves skipped and gambolled for joy. Two of these tremendous marine animals actually remained alongside of us for more than an hour. At sunset the weather was equally promising, but soon after, the clouds,

Dispersed and wild, 'twixt earth and sky
Hung like a shattered canopy!

While

―――― *unheeded from the Bay*
The vessel ploughed her mournful way.

At seven, p. m. the wind became foul, and blew fresh. An hour after,—the lightning flashed, and the thunder rolled,—at first like the long-roll of the muffled drum, but latterly like the salvo's of a numerous artillery. At three o'clock, a. m. on the 18th, the thunder ceased,—but from that hour down to four o'clock in the afternoon of the 20th, when we returned into port, the wind blew a perfect hurricane.

We again put to sea on the 27th of December, and after a very pleasant passage, landed at Plymouth on the 4th of January 1814. On the 6th we proceeded towards London, where we arrived on the evening of the 8th, after a tedious ride. On arriving in London, we quitted the stagecoach in the Haymarket, placed all our trunks in a street coach, under charge of Captain M'R—— of the 79th Regiment, and walked to the Old Slaughter's Coffee-house, St Martin's Lane,—for many years the head-quarters of the officers of our regiment, when duty or curiosity led any of us to visit the metropolis. On the gallant captain's arrival, a trunk of mine was found to be absent without leave, in which were deposited upwards of twenty letters from officers, and two orders for money, besides a number of valuable articles of wearing apparel.

On perceiving my loss, I wished to advertise it as stolen, but Mr Reid of the Old Slaughter's strongly opposed this, and it was finally advertised as lost. The result showed the soundness of Mr Reid's advice, for by ten o'clock on the morning the advertisement appeared in the *Times*, the portmanteau was at the bar *unopened*. In London, gangs of depredators are constantly prowling the streets in search of plunder; and when they obtain it in the way they got hold of my baggage, they generally keep it past them for some time unopened, when, if advertised as lost, and a reward offered, as in my ease, the thief then returns the property like an *honest* man, and receives the reward of his *dishonesty*.

At the end of a week I took leave of the metropolis, and after spending a few days with my friends on the way, I rejoined the second battalion of the regiment in Glasgow, in the end of January.

The Waterloo Campaign, 1815

The few months which I spent with the Second Battalion in Glasgow, were so extremely barren of incident, that I shall pass them over in silence. The regiment quitted the metropolis of the West on the 1st, and occupied the Castle of Edinburgh on the 3rd of August 1814. On the 16th of the same month, I, along with seven officers and 140 men returned to Glasgow, and from thence went to Greenock to embark for the First Battalion in Ireland. On our arrival at the place of embarkation on the 21st, we were not a little astonished to find that the transports had quitted the harbour that morning empty. Three other detachments marched in on the same day, but the whole were ordered to rejoin their second battalions. We remained in Greenock nearly three weeks, to our great personal discomfort, and the manifest injury of our purses. An order at length arrived for us to proceed to Glasgow, whence two of the officers, and all the men, returned to Edinburgh, and the rest joined the First Battalion then quartered in Fermoy. In November I returned to Scotland, where I remained until April 1815, when I joined my old companions, then on the eve of embarking for Belgium.

Being quite unprepared for such an event, the return of the Exile of Elba to France produced varied sensations in the breasts of the members of the British army. Those who, during the previous contest, had ascended the ladder of promotion at a pace little swifter than that of the snail, viewed the prospect of another interminable contest with no very agreeable feelings. Those who had friends who could give them an additional hitch up the ladder, or help them to some snug staff situation, were quite delighted on the occasion. A third class, if their assertions could be credited, were more anxious to have a place assigned them within point blank shot of the enemy's artillery, than one, far removed from the scene of danger. But who for a moment could give credit to such an asseveration? Where is the man, who, having a choice of alternatives, would not rather prefer remaining in a place of security with honour, than rush into one where the chances are decidedly against his escaping without a severe or a mortal wound? Point him out, and he shall very soon be told, that either he possesses the spirit of a demon, or he longs to commit a suicidal crime,—for nothing but an unquenchable thirst after human blood, or a sincere desire to quit this world, could make any man prefer a scene of strife and slaughter, to one of peace and honourable repose.

War, the last remedy for the cure of national complaints, should never be applied until every other has proved ineffectual. It ought never to be undertaken but on just grounds, for those who engage in it from motives of interest or ambition, become accountable for all the crimes that are committed,—the property destroyed,—and the human blood shed during its continuance. Happy would it have been for Napoleon Bonaparte, for France, and for all those countries into which he carried his arms, had he viewed war in this light, and considered it more glorious to employ his military talents in defence of his people, and in securing them all the blessings of a lasting peace, than engaging in hazardous enterprises, from which he never could have expected any greater reward than a portion of that phantom glory, which in all ages has proved the ruin and the death of millions.

A conqueror such as Napoleon, who has acquired military renown by the ruin of empires, and the death of millions, cannot be compared to anything more aptly than a flood, which destroys everything in its course,—or to a beast of prey, which delights in blood and slaughter. Man being naturally active and restless, seldom fails, when not usefully employed, to engage in enterprises which but too often injure himself or others. Of this fact Napoleon furnishes us with ample proof. Whenever he had no immediate prospect of advancing his darling object in France, that instant he cast his eye over Europe—selected an antagonist—picked a quarrel with him—put his armies in motion—and then trampled upon the rights and liberties of every nation through which he marched his troops to the scene of action. His towering ambition aimed at nothing less than universal monarchy; to attain which he waded through rivers of blood. For many years neither rocks, mountains, deserts, seas, nor rivers, could check his desolating course.

These facts being fresh in the recollection of the allied sovereigns, the ex-Emperor's landing in France was no sooner communicated to them at Vienna, than the clang of arms resounded throughout every corner of continental Europe,—the trumpet of war again sounded the dreadful note of preparation, and those warriors, who in the previous campaigns had lent their aid to break the charm of French invincibility, were,—when almost on the threshold of their peaceful habitations,—ordered to retrace their steps, without tasting of any of those sweets which a meeting of friends after a long absence never fails to produce.

Having previously purchased a comfortable sea-stock, and supplied ourselves with whatever was necessary for a long campaign on the continent, we left Cork barracks on the 1st of May, and the same afternoon embarked at Cove. Early on the 3rd we prepared to depart, and were clear of the harbour before midday. Scudding along with a favourable gale, we passed between the Rocks of Scilly and the Land's End on the morning of the 5th, looked into Plymouth on the 6th; Portsmouth on the 7th; passed Dungeness on the 8th, and next day dropped anchor two miles from Ostend. In the afternoon a few of the troops were landed, and the rest on the following morning. In the evening of the 10th we moved along the Ghent canal in long boats, as far as Bruges, where we halted till sunrise on the 11th, when we resumed our voyage, and at eight o'clock in the evening cast anchor at Ghent.

The city of Ghent, or Gand, is situated on the Scheldt, and at an equal distance from Ostend and Brussels, *viz.* from twenty-six to thirty miles. The city possesses a spacious market-place, which on market days is almost completely covered with the booths of itinerant merchants. Its streets are spacious and clean, but are cut in numerous places by canals, which intersect each other so in various parts of the city, that to connect the *islands* on which the town stands, no fewer than *three hundred and twenty-eight bridges* were then necessary. In consequence of this, the city covers an amazing space of ground, nearly double that occupied by the city of Edinburgh, though the population does not amount to half the number of the latter. In every quarter of the town we were treated with great hospitality by the people, who were really angry if we would not consent to live with them.

When Louis XVIII. found himself compelled by the defection of his troops to leave his native country, he retired in the first instance to Ostend, and subsequently to Ghent, where a suitable residence was provided for him by the king of the Netherlands. During our stay in this city we were afforded repeated opportunities of testifying to the exiled monarch, how deeply we sympathized with him on his recent misfortunes. He took a daily airing in a coach and four, and was generally accompanied by a detachment of the *garde-du- corps*. For a few days after we went to Ghent, gentlemen were admitted to the royal presence during dinner; a piece of very ridiculous and troublesome condescension. A guard of British troops went on duty at the temporary palace every day, and the officers dined at one of the tables, where a senior officer of the household troops always presided.

At daybreak on the 27th of May, the 28th, 32nd, 42nd, 44th, 79th, and 92nd Regiments, and 3rd Battalion Rifle Corps, marched from Ghent, under the command of Colonel Cameron, 92nd, to Alost, and next morning continued their route to Brussels. At Alost, a French officer, in the suite of Louis XVIIL, but who had held a commission in the British service for twenty-one years, informed us that he was present when Marshal Ney bedewed the king's hands with tears, on taking leave to bring Bonaparte to Paris in an iron cage. He described the interview as so extremely interesting, that not only His Majesty, but all who witnessed it, were sensibly affected. From that time the Bourbon adherents were pleased to bestow on the gallant marshal, the name which above all others is the most abhorrent to the ear of a Christian—"Judas Ney."

Brussels having been described a thousand times over by pens far abler than mine, I conceive it to be quite unnecessary to enter upon a lengthened eulogy of the fascinating squares, parks, and walks, of that celebrated city, and therefore shall proceed to describe the country sixteen miles to the south of it, as it appeared to me on the memorable 16th, 17th and 18th days of June 1815. Before doing so, however, I shall lay before my readers a state, shewing the distribution of the British and Hanoverian troops on the day preceding the battle of Quatre Bras, and also a few particulars illustrative of our proceedings, and that of our great Leader, from the time that the latter received the first intelligence of Bonaparte's movement across the frontier, down to that hour in which we quitted the capital of Belgium to meet our antagonists on the plains of Quatre-Bras.

Cavalry.

The whole were under the orders of Lieutenant-General The Earl of Oxbridge.

1st Brigade,—Major-General Lord Edward Somerset, The 1st and 2nd Life Guards, Horse Guards (Blue) and 1st Dragoon Guards.

2nd Brigade,—Major-General Sir William Ponsonby, K.C.B.
The 1st, 2nd (Scot's Greys) and 6th Dragoons.

3rd Brigade,—Major-General Sir W. Dornberg, K.C.B
The 1st and 2nd Light Dragoons, King's German Legion and the British 23rd Light Dragoons.

4th Brigade,—Major-General Sir Ormsby Vandeleur, K.C.B.
The 11th, 12th, and 16th Light Dragoons.

5th Brigade,—Major-General Sir Colquhoun Grant, K.C.B.
The 2nd, 7th, and 15th Hussars.

6th Brigade,—Major-General Sir Richard Hussey Vivian, K.C.B.
The 1st, 10th, and 18th Hussars.

7th Brigade,—Col. Baron Sir F. De-Arentscheldt, K.C.B.
The 3rd Hussars and 13th Light Dragoons.

INFANTRY.

1st Brigade,—Major-General Peregrine Maitland,
The 2nd and 3rd Battalions, 1st Foot Guards.

2nd Brigade,—Major-General Sir John Byng, K.C.B.
The 3rd Battalion of the Coldstream, and 2nd Battalion of the 3rd Foot Guards.

3rd Brigade,—Major-General Frederick Adam.
The 1st Battalions of the 52nd and 71st, and 2nd Battalion 95th Rifle Regiment.

4th Brigade,—Colonel H. Mitchell,
The 3rd Battalion 14th, the 23rd and 51st Regiments.

5th Brigade,—Major-General Sir Charles Halket, K.C.B.
The 33rd and 2nd Battalions of the 30th, 69th, and 73rd Regiments.

6th Brigade,—Major-General Johnson,
The 54th, 2nd Battalions of 35th and 59th, and 1st Battalion of the 91st Regiment.

7th Brigade,—Major-General Du Plat,
The 1st, 2nd, 3rd and 4th Battalions King's German Legion.

8th Brigade,—Major General Sir James Kemp, K.C.B.
The 28th, 32nd and 1st Battalions 79th and 95th Regiments.

9th Brigade,—Major-General Sir Denis Pack, K.C.B.

The 3rd Battalion Royals, 2nd Battalion, 44th, the 42nd and 92nd Regiments.

10th Brigade,—Major-General Sir John Lambert.
The 1st Battalions 4th and 27th, the 2nd Battalion, 81st and 40th Regiment.

1st Division,—Major-General George Cook,
The 1st and 2nd Brigades.

2nd Division,—Lieutenant-General Sir Henry Clinton, K.G.C.B.
The 3rd and 7th British Brigades, and 3rd Hanoverian Brigade.

3rd Division,—Lieutenant-General Baron Sir Charles Alten, K.C.B.
The 5th British 1st Hanoverian, and 1st Brigade King's German Legion.

4th Division,—Lieutenant-General Sir Charles Colville, K.G. C.B.
The 4th and 6th British, and 6th Hanoverian Brigade.

5th Division,—Lieutenant-General Sir Thomas Picton, K.G. C.B.
The 8th and 9th British, and 5th Hanoverian Brigade.

1st Corps of Infantry,—General, His Royal Highness the Prince of Orange, K.G.C.B.
The 1st, 3rd and 5th Divisions.

2nd Corps,—Lieutenant-General, Lord Hill, K.G.C.B.
The 2nd and 4th Divisions.

The 10th Brigade being composed of troops just arrived from America, only joined us on the morning of the 18th, and at that date were not, I believe, placed in any division.

ARTILLERY.

Colonel Sir George Wood.

The exact number of guns in the field I cannot positively state, but they were estimated at from 140 to 160.

On the 4th of June, the Duke of Wellington, accompanied by Prince Blucher, reviewed the fifth division in the vicinity of Brussels. The Prince was lavish of his praise; and the Duke seemed quite delighted on perceiving so many of his old Peninsular friends again under his command. On passing the venerable warrior, and his more youthful compeer, my attention was completely abstracted from the business in which we were engaged, and riveted on the countenances of the two heroes, to whom, above all others, Europe was most indebted for her liberty in 1814. But for the noble stand which the Duke of Wellington made in the Peninsula, the Russian Autocrat would never have braved the colossal power of the French Ruler; and had Blucher shewn less spirit and enterprise, the allies would not have arrived before the gates of Paris in March 1814. Such being the facts, was there anything unreasonable in us looking forward to the military talents of the Duke, and the spirit and enterprise of the Prince, producing, in 1815, results similar to those of the previous campaign? I think not: but yet I must confess that our expectations were considerably lowered on a minute examination of the number and quality of the troops composing the hostile armies.

The Emperor of France having recalled to his standard a great proportion of his old soldiery, had many thousands who just returned from prison in Britain, Russia, &c. were not only ready, but, their natural bravery having been whetted, rather than blunted by a residence in a foreign land, were also willing, indeed anxious, to undertake the most hazardous enterprises, if directed against their former antagonists.

To oppose an army of 140,000 or 150,000 men, to whom danger had long been familiar, and spoliation but too long their daily occupation, the two chiefs had under their command a force equally numerous, but not all so efficient in the field. The Prussians were a fine body of men, brave, hardy, and well-disciplined, but not a few of them were militia. The Hanoverians were very young men, and many of the officers were little better than children. The Dutch and the Belgians were fine looking fellows, but some of the latter had fought too long under the tri-colour flag. The British were animated with the best spirit, but their numbers were small, and nearly one-half of them had never been in a field of strife. Therefore, although the armies of the Duke of Wellington and Prince Blucher were equally formidable in point of numerical strength, still they were in many other respects greatly inferior to their opponents.

With this force, however, inferior in physical strength as it was, they had no alternative, but to meet the foe should he venture across the frontier. Circumstances, unfortunately, prevented the British general from having the several divisions of his army cantoned so favourably as he could have wished. This, although occasioned by the difficulty experienced by the commissary in finding forage for such a large body of cavalry and baggage animals, has been made the subject of a very grave charge against the field-marshal, by those who have permitted the necessity of the case to escape their observation. But another and more serious charge has been preferred against the Duke on this occasion, *viz.* attending a ball given by the Duchess of Richmond, when he should have been engaged in making arrangements for the dreadful meeting between himself and his formidable opponent.

Had the latter been preferred by some hair-brained or disappointed person, I should not have considered it necessary to notice it here. But having heard the charge preferred by thousands who actually believed it to be true, and knowing, as I do, the whole to be a malicious fabrication propagated to detract from the honours which the Duke had won on many a bloody field, I trust I may be permitted to state a few facts connected with this subject, which is to be hoped will set the matter at rest in the breasts of those who may do me the honour to look into the pages of this volume.

Everything being prepared on the part of the enemy to open the campaign with *éclat*, Bonaparte quitted Paris on the 12th of June, and on the 14th issued a proclamation to the soldiers, in which, after recalling to their remembrance the deeds of former times, he very candidly told them they had battles to fight, and dangers to encounter, but assured them, that with steadiness and valour, victory would be theirs.

Early on the morning of the 15th of June, the French army crossed the Sambre at various places, and then directed its march upon Charleroi, where General Ziethen, with the first corps of the Prussian army, was posted. After a smart affair, the latter retired upon Fleurus, the point of assembly, whether they were pursued by the right wing, and right of the left wing under Napoleon himself. At a subsequent period of the day, the Prussians retired still farther to Ligny, followed by the enemy. The left of the French army, under Marshal Ney, moved upon the high road to Brussels, and drove back a corps of Belgians, under the Prince of Weimar, first to the position of Frasne, and latterly to Quatre-Bras.

At seven o'clock that evening. Captain H———, Lieutenant G———, and myself, strolled as far as the park to enjoy our usual promenade. We had scarcely gone half way down one of the walks, when Dr H———, who had dined with the Duke of Wellington, (or rather who did so every day,) stepped hastily up to Captain H——, who was an old acquaintance, and with considerable earnestness requested us to go home and pack up our baggage, as Napoleon was in motion. Being curious, as may be conceived, to know a few more particulars, we pressed the doctor so hard to satisfy our curiosity, that he at length informed us that during dinner, the field-marshal received a despatch from Prince Blucher, intimating that he had been attacked.

On the cloth being removed, the Duke, filling his glass, called a bumper, and then gave as a toast, "Prince Blucher and the Prussian army, and success to them." On paying this mark of respect to his gallant colleague, the field-marshal rose from the table, retired to his closet, and in a few minutes dispatched the necessary orders to every division of the allied army. The reader must remember that this was *three hours* before the ball commenced, and four before the marshal entered the ballroom, which he did but for a few minutes, a little after eleven o'clock. But more; the troops in Brussels had not only received orders of readiness, but had received six day's bread, and were actually on the streets long before the ball began. All these things, therefore, afford the most convincing proof that the whole story has been fabricated for the worst of purposes, *viz.* to injure the character of the Duke of Wellington, and by contrast to raise that of Napoleon.

Quatre Bras

Between eight and nine o'clock in the evening, the troops in Brussels received orders to be ready to fall in at a moment's notice, and at the same time six day's bread and biscuit was issued to each man. This was rather too much, for the *soft staff of life* was so bulky, that few of the men could stow the whole of it away. In many instances, therefore, the bread was either left in the street, or with those on whom the soldiers were quartered. About half-past eleven, the bugles and bagpipes gave signal to prepare for battle. At the first sounds of the warlike instruments, the Fifth Division flew to arms, and a little after mid-night was drawn up in the park and Place Royal in marching order.

At half-past three we moved out of Brussels by the Namur gate, and directed our march upon the then obscure, but now immortalized village of Waterloo. Close to this place we halted from half-past eight till nearly eleven, when we resumed our arms, and proceeded towards the enemy, followed by the Brunswick infantry. At one, we halted on a height in rear of Genappe for a quarter of an hour, and then again advanced, and on descending the height, the thunder of the enemy's artillery was for the first time heard in the distance; and about half-past two we arrived at Quatre-Bras, just in time to prevent that post falling into the hands of the enemy.

Various circumstances conspired to render the defence of this post a measure of indispensible necessity. At the village, or rather large farm-steading of Quatre-Bras, the highway from Brussels to Charleroi is intersected by another, running from Nivelles, &c. to St Amand and Ligny, where father Blucher and his gallant children had just engaged in mortal combat with their inveterate enemies. To have tamely yielded up, or abandoned this position, therefore, on the 16th, would have placed the whole of the Prussian army in a situation of great and imminent peril, for by doing so we would have left their extreme right so completely uncovered, that as soon as Ney saw us fairly out of the road, he would have carried his troops from Quatre-Bras to St Amand in a couple of hours, and in the heat of the conflict with Napoleon, attacked the right of Blucher with fatal effect. Of this there can be no doubt; and I conceive there can be as little, that had Marshal Ney been permitted to throw such a preponderating force into the scale against the Prussians on the afternoon of the 16th of June, they must have suffered a severe defeat. Their line of communication with us would, in all probability, have been cut off—the original plan of operations rendered abortive, and the allied army placed in a perilous situation.

On first coming in sight of the French, we found their right wing resting on the heights of Frasne, and their left stretching across the plain as far as the wood of Bossu. The latter skirted the right of the road from Brussels, till it passed the village about 150 yards. But although it run no farther in that direction, the wood extended a great way to the right, bounding numerous fields of wheat and rye, which lay between it and the French position, and which for some time tended to screen the enemy, not from our fire, but from our view.

The ridge on which Quatre-Bras stands runs in some degree parallel to that of Frasne, but is not so high. Perceiving it to be the marshal's intention to obtain possession of the crown of the eminence at Quatre-Bras, our general dispatched the foreign troops into the wood of Bossu, and the Eighth Brigade, 28th, 32nd, 79th, and 95th Rifles, under Major-General Sir James Kempt, into the plain on the left, to prevent the columns of the marshal obtaining possession of the road leading to Ligny. In this movement, the Eighth Brigade was supported by the Third Battalion Royals, Second Battalion 44th, and 42nd Regiment, and the 92nd Regiment was ordered to line a bank on the right of the road leading from Quatre-Bras to St Amand, on which the field marshal and his staff had taken post. The Brunswick infantry were stationed partly in rear of the left of the Highlanders, and partly in the wood on the right of the village. The Hanoverian brigade was formed on the left, and rather in rear of the 92nd, and the Brunswick cavalry took post close to the houses of Quatre-Bras.

The Eighth Brigade moved down the slope of the eminence in beautiful order, and commenced the grand struggle in fine style. But the numbers of that brigade formed such a striking contrast to those of the enemy, that many of our oldest officers looked forward with uneasiness to the issue of the conflict. But the 16th of June was not the first day on which the gallant Kempt and his brave associates had met their enemies under similar circumstances. Nothing discouraged, therefore, by the numerical superiority of their opponents, they rushed to the combat with the spirit of lions, and, after a dreadful struggle, forced the foe to retire. In a quarter of an hour the work of death was renewed on both sides with increased fury.

As before, the enemy were again on the point of yielding, when Ney dispatched fresh troops to their relief. On perceiving the marshal deploy fresh battalions towards our left, the Duke of Wellington gave orders to the Royals, 42nd, and 44th, to take part in the battle. The French infantry, assisted by a powerful and well-served artillery, and a numerous and highly equipped cavalry, displayed a considerable degree of personal bravery, fancying no doubt that a few charges of the different arms united, would either force their opponents to retire, or place them in their hands as prisoners of war. Unsupported by any artillery or cavalry, however, save a few pieces of the former, and the mounted corps of the Duke of Brunswick, our companions braved every attempt to penetrate their squares with the most unshrinking firmness, and invariably drove back the enemy with great loss.

About four o'clock the Duke of Brunswick, at the head of his cavalry, passed the right of the 92nd Regiment, to charge a body of French *cuirassiers* considerably in advance. Led by their undaunted Prince, the Brunswickers pushed forward in gallant style, and conducted themselves admirably, till, perceiving the Duke fall from his horse mortally wounded, the whole were seized with a panic, and retired towards Quatre-Bras, hotly pursued by their opponents. This unfortunate affair gave the French a temporary advantage, and inspired them with fresh courage. Elated with their success, and seeing no troops in their front to arrest their progress, the enemy advanced with all the audacity of conquerors, conceiving, no doubt, that the battle was decided. The 92nd Regiment, hitherto kept hid from (the view of the enemy, were now ordered by the Duke, to be prepared to give them a warm reception. The orders of their illustrious general, who was then along with them, were obeyed with the utmost alacrity.

Still keeping themselves out of sight of the assailants, the Highlanders permitted almost all the fugitives to pass to the rear, and then starting to their feet, they poured a most destructive flank fire upon the French cavalry, who were rapidly advancing along the highway, and laid many of them in the dust. The survivors, not expecting such a reception at a point where they imagined resistance had ceased, fled in the greatest confusion. One of their officers having advanced nearly to the houses before he discovered his danger, made an attempt to escape by the road on which the 92nd Regiment was posted. On turning the head of his horse to make a neck-or-nothing sort of a dash down the road, every one imagined his object was to find a passage for his sword to the heart of our commander. First one mounted officer, and then another, periled their lives to save that of their general, but their opponent neatly parried their cuts.

All eyes were now riveted on the Duke, confidently anticipating a fatal result. In a twinkling, the officer was within a few paces of the field-marshal, whose serenity on this, as on all other occasions throughout that day, was universally noticed, and loudly applauded. He passed, however, without even looking at the Duke, on which our eyes again glistened with joy. But in order to prevent the hair-brained youth causing a similar hubbub amongst us, a few men of the 6th and 7th Companies, 92nd Regiment, fired at him, killed his horse, and wounded himself severely, a ball passing through each foot. He was instantly removed to the rear, and afterwards to Brussels; where, being quartered in the same house with an officer of the 92nd Regiment, he candidly acknowledged that his only object was to escape.

Disappointed in his attempt upon the village, Ney again directed an attack against our extreme left. For some time his operations were all of an offensive character, and consisted of a multiplicity of attacks, sometimes with cavalry, sometimes with infantry, and not unfrequently with both, assisted in their murderous work by a numerous artillery. Having neither cavalry nor artillery to back their personal exertions, the seven British infantry regiments found it necessary to throw themselves into squares, to sustain with effect the dreadful charges of their mounted opponents. In forming square, some of them were more expert than the rest; but with one exception, none of them sustained any loss, but such as was occasioned by the fire of the enemy.

Perceiving that the British had no intention of retiring, or deploying, so long as they were surrounded with so many opponents, the French at length adopted the rather ticklish proceeding of galloping up to the muzzles of the British muskets, and endeavouring to provoke our men to throw away their fire, by discharging their carbines and pistols into the centre of our squares, to which they were most anxious to find a passage. In this, however, they were most completely disappointed; for nothing could induce our companions to depart from a system, which experience had clearly demonstrated to them was the best they could adopt, under the trying circumstances in which they were placed. All the attempts of the enemy, therefore, to induce our soldiers to part with their ammunition proving fruitless, the French, irritated at their obstinacy, attacked our squares sword in hand, but were always forced to make a precipitate flight, leaving the ground around each square, covered with their killed and wounded.

About five o'clock another attempt was made to wrest Quatre-Bras out of our hands, but with no better success than the former. Soon after this, the brigade of Guards, under Major-General Maitland, and third division, commanded by Lieutenant-General Sir Charles Alten, arrived to our assistance. Never did troops receive a more seasonable reinforcement. The Guards were thrown into the wood of Bossu, on the right of the village, and the Third Division moved along the road leading to Ligny, till they passed the Royals, &c. when they halted, and formed the left of our line. As each battalion hurried past us, it was loudly cheered by every man in the Highland corps. Yes, tears of joy bade them welcome to share our perils and our glory, and our best wishes followed but too many of them to their last and silent abode.

Leaning against a bank when the 73rd Regiment approached us, and unconscious at the time that I had the pleasure of being known to any member of that corps, I felt something like surprise when Lieutenant ——, a genuine Irishman, jumped out of his place, and grasping my hand as firmly as a vice, said, "——, how are you, my old boy? this duty is not quite so pleasant, I fear, as that in which you and I were engaged the last time we met at Athlone, devouring *poldowdies*, and swallowing whisky punch." On admitting the fact, the warm-hearted Irishman flew like lightning after his battalion, promising to call on me and renew the conversation next morning. But alas! how little do we know what is before us,—in an hour he was no more.

As the Third Division proceeded along the road to their destination, the enemy were not very sparing of their shot and shell. Their tremendous salvos, however, we could but feebly return, having received but a slender addition to our original numbers.

The enemy, conceiving that the troops composing the third division, were those who had baffled their cavalry to obtain possession of Quatre-Bras, lost no time, after the rear of the division had cleared the village, in making the necessary preparations to renew his efforts to obtain the key of our position.

Under cover of a heavy cannonade, Ney pushed forward two columns of infantry; one by the highway leading from Charleroi to Quatre-Bras, and the other by a hollow, or kind of ravine, in front of the wood of Bossu, towards the same point. On the left of, and fronting the road to Charleroi, two hundred yards in front of Quatre-Bras, there was a house of two floors, from the rear of which ran a thick hedge, a short way across a field. On the right of the road, and immediately opposite to the house, there was a garden, surrounded with a thick hedge. In the face fronting the road there was a small gate, from which a gravel walk led to a similar one on the opposite side. The house and hedge were occupied by the enemy's advanced guard, and their main body, twelve or fifteen hundred in number, had taken post about one hundred paces from the rear of the garden, when the field-marshal gave us orders to charge.

The order was no sooner given, than every man of the 92nd Regiment, about 600 in number, appeared in front of the bank, behind which they had reposed for four hours. Colonel Cameron, accompanied by General Barnes, the adjutant-general, advanced by the highway, at the head of the grenadiers and first company. The other companies, by an oblique movement to their right, directed their march upon the same points,—the house, garden, and hedge;—the enemy pouring on us a deadly fire of musketry from the windows of the house, and from the hedge on the left of it, till we succeeded in driving them from both, which was not accomplished without a severe loss. Amongst the officers who fell at this time, was the brave Cameron, who, on receiving his mortal wound, retired from the field, regretted by the whole regiment.

But, although we had forced the enemy to relinquish their hold of the house and hedge on the left of it, the principal part of our duties remained to be performed. Although their advanced guard had been driven back, the main body shewed no disposition to retire. On the contrary, they poured on us showers of musketry, sufficient to appal soldiers of more experience in those matters than one half of those who fought on the plains of Quatre-Bras. In fact it required no little exertion to keep some of the young soldiers in the ranks; for, perceiving the French so much more numerous than themselves, and that the garden-hedge, though very thick, afforded them no protection; the danger appeared to some of them so very great, that but for their veteran companions, and the attention of the officers to their duties, they might have been induced to retire.

But from this disagreeable situation we endeavoured to extricate ourselves in the following manner. The only obstacle between us and the enemy being the garden, it was proposed to move a portion of the battalion round and between it and the wood of Bossu, another division round the left, or lower side of the garden, and a third to open a passage for itself through the garden, by entering at the front gate. Being of this party, we accomplished our task of forcing the gates with some little difficulty, for the fire of the enemy was truly dreadful; and we could not take any steps to render it less effective, till the whole battalion could be brought to bear upon the enemy. At length, however, all the three columns arrived at their appointed stations. Seeing our friends on the right and left ready, we moved out at the rear gate, and quickly formed in front of the hedge. On this formation being accomplished, the signal of readiness was given, when the whole joined in three hearty cheers, and then, with the irresistible bayonet in their hands, advanced to the work of death.

Who is able to describe the feelings of the combatants at this momentous crisis? Who can paint the inward workings of every mind, when the Highlanders advanced, either to drive the enemy from the field, or leave their mangled bodies on the plains of Quatre-Bras?— language is inadequate to do it. Suffice it, therefore, to say, that for a few seconds the French appeared quite resolved to await our assault; but on perceiving that we really intended to close with them, they wheeled to the right-about, and attempted to escape by a hollow in front of the wood, along which their left column had previously advanced. As soon as they turned their backs, we poured in upon them a volley of musketry, which did great execution; and thereafter, each man did everything in his power to prevent them effecting their escape, and so well did our lads do their duty, that at every step we found a dead or a wounded Frenchman.

Many of the latter affected to treat the whole business very lightly; whilst others, even in the very agonies of death, ceased not to echo the cry of their more fortunate brethren, of *Vive l'Empereur*. Never was the fire of a body of men given with finer effect than that of the 92nd, during the pursuit of the enemy, which continued for fully half a mile, and until the advance of a corps of French cavalry rendered it prudent to retire into the wood of Bossu. In fact, before we parted, their column, at first so formidable in numbers, was reduced to a skeleton.

This was the last serious attempt made by Ney to obtain possession of Quatre-Bras, but be continued to dispute the wood, and various portions of the ground on the left, till after nine o'clock, when every prospect of victory having vanished, he withdrew his troops, *and left us in possession of the ground which they occupied at the commencement of the engagement.*

About ten o'clock, the piper of the 92nd took post at the garden in front of the village, where, after tuning his chanter, and setting his drone in order, he attempted to collect the scattered members of his regiment. Long and loud blew Cameron; but although the hills and the valleys echoed the hoarse murmurs of his favourite instrument, his ultimate efforts could not produce above a half of those whom his music had cheered on their march to the field of battle. Alas! many of them had taken leave of this bustling world. Many of them were then lying weltering in their blood in the fields or in the woods, and not a few of them in the farmyard of Quatre-Bras. Of thirty-six officers who went into action, eleven only escaped unhurt, six being killed or mortally wounded, two slightly wounded, and seventeen severely. Soon after this, the 92nd Regiment retired behind the houses of Quatre-Bras to take a little repose after the fatigues of this memorable day. The other corps remained all night nearly on the same ground they held at the close of the conflict. The field marshal retired to Genappe.

Immediately after the close of the battle, our light cavalry began to arrive in the vicinity of Quatre-Bras; and at an early hour next morning, the whole of the army had arrived at points whence they could be readily moved to wherever their services might be required.

About three o'clock in the afternoon of the 16th, Napoleon attacked the Prussian army in its position at Ligny, with the right wing and centre of his army, together with all his Imperial Guards; and after a desperate engagement of six hours, in which neither party asked or gave quarter, Bonaparte, by one of those tremendous charges of his cavalry, which on so many former occasions had commanded success, again secured the victory. The loss of each army was tremendous. But severe as the loss of the Prussian army was at Ligny, how much more would that loss have been increased, had not Divine Providence miraculously delivered their great Leader from the hands of his enemies?

On returning from an unsuccessful charge of the Prussian cavalry, the horse on which Blucher was mounted was wounded by a musket ball. Instead, however, of arresting the speed of the animal, the wound rather increased it, till it dropped down dead. Stunned with the fall, the veteran general could not remove himself from under the horse. With the animal above him, and only one Prussian officer near to render him assistance, Prince Blucher saw the enemy approach, and even pass him. It would be worth a kingdom to know what passed in the breast of the illustrious hero on this trying occasion.

The brave Prussian army defeated and annihilated—France again sole arbitress of the Continent—and himself exhibited to the gaze of a Parisian populace, as the prisoner of that individual, who, above all men on earth, he most detested, must have passed before his eyes, as some of the consequences likely to follow in the train of his misfortunes. Fortunately, however, for himself—for his country—and for Europe—the Prince was soon relieved from this distressing, and to him, humiliating situation. For, on missing their leader, the Prussian cavalry instantly turned round, and like a torrent, rushed down upon their pursuers with such fury, that a few minutes served, not only to drive back the enemy upon their infantry, but to rescue the venerable warrior, and place him once more at the head of his valiant followers.

Retreat to Mont St. Jean

On the morning of the 17th, the interior of the farmyard of Quatre-Bras presented to the eye a scene of unparalleled horror. The whole of the ground within was literally dyed with blood, and the inside of the walls was also very much stained with it. Some idea may be formed of its appearance, when I state on the authority of a surgeon who dressed a great many of the wounded, that at one period of the battle, there were nearly a thousand wounded soldiers belonging to the 3rd and 5th Divisions in that narrow space. The cries of the poor fellows were most heartrending, and the appearance of the mangled and mutilated corpses which strewed the square in every direction, was so ghastly and appalling, that he must have possessed a heart of adamant, who could have entered that place of death and lamentation, without being sensibly affected. While I live, I shall ever retain a vivid recollection of the farmyard of Quatre-Bras, on the evening of the 16th, and morning of the 17th of June 1815.

It is quite wonderful how very close a cannon-ball or a shell will sometimes pass the head of a person, without doing them any permanent injury. In the action of the 16th, at Quatre-Bras, a man named Milne, standing close to me, had his bonnet knocked off his head by a cannon shot, and carried several yards across the road. On the collision between the ball and the bonnet taking place, Milne turned quickly round to me, and with a wildness in his countenance, said, "Do you see that, Sir?" During the remainder of that day, and the two following, he exhibited a weakness of intellect, not peculiar to him, but with that exception, he sustained no other injury.

On the left side of the road leading from Quatre-Bras to Ligny, a bank rose eight or ten feet above the crown of the highway, which trifling circumstance was occasionally the means of placing a few of our men in no little jeopardy. For on hitting the bank, the shells frequently came dancing across the road to their own music, till they arrived in the ditch among the Highlanders. One of those dangerous characters having rather impudently intruded himself into our society, a few paces from where I was standing, some of my neighbours attempted to fly, but as the greater proportion preferred an extended position in the ditch, a most ludicrous scramble took place, for the honour of being undermost. In a few seconds, however, the shell exploded, without doing us any more mischief, than wounding slightly two of our men.

Almost one of the last shells fired by the enemy that evening, lighted within half-a-yard of me, and immediately exploded. But on perceiving it fall, I threw myself flat on the ground, and thereby escaped without a scratch.

Immediately after being wounded, Colonel Cameron, of the 92nd Regiment, was removed from Quatre-Bras to Genappe, where, on the wound being examined, it was discovered to be mortal. On the following morning he was placed in a waggon, with the view of being conveyed to Brussels. On the way, he complained greatly of the jolting of the carriage, and repeatedly inquired if the French had been defeated. On getting an answer in the affirmative, he said, "Then I die happy!" On receiving an answer to one of his questions, a little before his speech failed him, he added, "I hope my country will think I have done enough,—I hope she will think that I have served her faithfully." When close to the village of Waterloo, the gallant Colonel laid back his head on his servant's arm, and expired. To shew the estimation in which the services of this truly brave officer were held by his Sovereign, Mr Ewen Cameron, of Fassifern, the colonel's father, was raised to the rank of a Baronet of the United Kingdom. And on his native hills a handsome monument was erected, on which there is the following inscription, written by Sir Walter Scott,

Sacred to the memory
Of
Colonel John Cameron,
Eldest Son of Sir Ewen Cameron of Fassifern, Baronet;
Whose Mortal Remains,
Transported from the Field of Glory, where he died,
Rest here with those of his Forefathers.
During Twenty years of active Military Service,
With a spirit which knew no fear, and shunned no danger;
He accompanied or led,
In Marches, in Sieges, in Battles,
The gallant 92nd Regiment of Scottish Highlanders,

Always to Honour, almost always to Victory;
And at length.
In the Forty-second year of his age.
Upon the memorable 16th day of June, a.d. 1815,
Was slain in the command of that corps.
While actively contributing to achieve the decisive
Victory of
WATERLOO,
Which gave peace to Europe,
Thus closing his Military career
With the long and eventful struggle in which.
His services had been so often distinguished,—
He died lamented
By that unrivalled General,
To whose long train of Success and Victory
He had so often contributed.
By his Country,
From which he had repeatedly received marks
Of the highest consideration;
And
By His Sovereign,
Who graced his surviving family
With those marks of honour,
Him whose merit
They were designed to commemorate.
READER,
Call not his fate untimely.
Who thus honoured and lamented.
Closed a Life of Fame, by a Death of Glory.

Seated behind the houses of Quatre-Bras on the morning of the 17th, I received a message from a wounded soldier, named Robinson, intimating that he was in possession of a book which he was sure I would like to read. I lost no time in visiting him, and on opening the volume, was not a little surprised on discovering it to be the history of Scotland's champion. Sir William Wallace, once the property of a French soldier, whose name was inscribed on one of the blank leaves, and who had no doubt fallen in the conflict in the after-part of the 16th. At that time the histories of Wallace and Bruce were much read by the French soldiers; and I believe it is a well authenticated fact, that Bonaparte seldom went on a campaign without a copy of *Ossian's*

Poems in his possession.

Envy, we are told, is the blackest passion in the human breast, and the most prevailing infirmity to which we are subject. History affords us the most decisive proof we could desire, that it has often tarnished the character of men, who otherwise had a well-earned title to fame and renown. What, for example, has tarnished the character of Alexander the Great, so much as this unamiable passion, which reigned in his breast with sovereign authority during the whole of his extraordinary career? Since that period, how many thousands of Alexander's has this world of ours contained? How many are there even at this moment amongst us, who, like the great conqueror, ambitious of nothing so much as to rise to the first rank in the scale of human society, envy every individual who excel them in any of those arts or sciences which rivet the attention, and command the admiration of the world?

That the Duke of Wellington has been deeply indebted to the members of this rather amiable society, for the many slanderous reports circulated during the last thirty years, in regard to his military conduct in India, &c. there cannot be the smallest doubt. Like many other dupes, I gave ear to the gossip of the day, and for some time credit to it. For although courage is a most indispensable qualification in every general at the head of an army, yet history is not without examples of generals deficient in valour, not only performing their duties satisfactorily, but even raising their own and their country's glory by splendid victories. But all the doubts I had previously entertained on the subject were completely dissipated at Quatre-Bras. For there the field-marshal gave proofs to the world, which no individual, however, venomous his tongue may be, can controvert, that he possesses moral courage in as eminent a degree as any general that ever entered a field of strife.

How would His Grace's slanderers have looked, if stationed within a few yards of him, as I was for four hours on the 16th, and there beheld him, amidst showers of every description of shot, directing the movements of his columns with that firmness and coolness, so characteristic of the brave and consummate warrior? The very smile which sat on his countenance during the whole of the action, would have struck them dumb, and covered :tem with such a load of shame and disgrace, that they would have embraced the first opportunity afforded them, of hiding their convicted countenances from the stern glance of the object of their envy.

Some people seem to think, that a general at the head of an army is bound to expose himself on all occasions in the same manner as any of the junior officers. A more erroneous opinion, however, of the duties of a general, could not well be conceived; for it is the bounden duty of a general-in-chief, never, but in cases of the very last importance, to expose to unnecessary peril, a life upon which so many others depend. As a general-in-chief owes obedience to none but his sovereign, it belongs to him exclusively to judge how far he ought to expose himself, and those under him, in order to accomplish the object of his commission; and in proportion as his life is more necessary for that object than the lives of his soldiers, in the same proportion should he be more sparing of it than of the lives of his men. A general in fact ought never to expose his life without a necessary cause, or the prospect of reaping such important advantages, that the risk he runs may be trifling in comparison of the successes which he hopes to obtain by it.

About five o'clock in the morning of the 17th, the Duke of Wellington arrived at Quatre-Bras from Genappe, and the morning being rather cold, his Grace, on alighting, said, "Ninety-second, will you favour me with a little fire?" The request had no sooner escaped his lips, than a hundred men flew in as many different directions, in search of the necessary materials. On returning, the men made a fire opposite to the door of a small hut, constructed of the boughs of some trees, which the poor fellows attempted to render a residence suitable for the reception of their general. For their attention, the Duke expressed himself extremely grateful. In this splendid airy residence, the field-marshal received the Prince of Orange, Lord Hill, and many other officers of distinction; in this rural cottage he received the first tidings of Blucher's misfortunes,—and here it was that the order of retreat to the position of Waterloo was arranged.

On the arrival of Lord Hill to pay his respects to the Duke of Wellington, the whole regiment, officers and men, embraced the opportunity of testifying their regard for the character of that brave and estimable nobleman. On quitting the hut, he was greeted with loud and long continued plaudits. Turning round, his Lordship approached us hat in land, much affected, the men continuing to salute aim with cheers which proceeded from the heart, the Duke, conceiving that our cheers proceeded from a very different cause, came hurriedly out of his wooden house, but on perceiving the true one, his Grace laughed, and appeared quite delighted with the mark of respect which "her nainsel' had paid to his friend and favourite general."

Previous to the receipt of Blucher's dispatches, we were all in high spirits, anticipating a splendid victory over the french marshal before night, never doubting but Blucher would find employment for Bonaparte, while we amused ourselves with Ney. But from the moment that Blucher's retreat was known, our spirits became depressed; a gloom stole over the countenances of the whole; every individual was more or less affected; and I am inclined to think that the breast of none was more agitated than that of our illustrious chief. On receiving the unwelcome intelligence, the Duke shut himself up in the hut for some time, then came out, and walked alone in front of it for nearly an hour in deep meditation.

Now and then he was interrupted by a courier bearing a dispatch, who, on delivering it, instantly retired to some distance, there to wait his general's orders. The field-marshal walked at the rate of three and a-half to four miles in the hour. His left hand was thrown carelessly behind his back, and in his right he held a small switch, one end of which he frequently put to his mouth, apparently unconscious that he was doing so. His dress was white pantaloons, half-boots, a military vest, *white neckcloth*, blue *surtout*, and cocked-hat.

Soon after this the most exaggerated statements were circulated regarding the defeat of the Prussian army. At one time the loss was rated at 20,000 killed, wounded, and prisoners; at another, their loss in prisoners alone, exceeded that number. Everything, in short, wore the most gloomy appearance imaginable. In the full belief, therefore, that our allies had been totally routed, we commenced our retreat at ten o'clock, a.m. on the 17th of June, from the scene of our first triumph, towards the glorious plains of Waterloo.

To cover his real design, the Duke ordered the 3rd and 5th Divisions to remain in front of Quatre-Bras, till the artillery, the foreign troops, and the other divisions should be considerably advanced on their journey. This manoeuvre completely succeeded, for the retreat was never observed by the crafty Napoleon, until his equally sagacious antagonist was out of the reach of pursuit.

On perceiving us making off, the enemy pushed forward large masses of cavalry to harass our rearguard, composed of the British light and heavy dragoons. Many brilliant charges were made on the occasion, in every one of which, where the latter were engaged, the French were invariably beat back. The light cavalry were not quite so successful.

While ascending the heights in rear of Genappe, the body of the gallant Duke of Brunswick passed us stretched on a waggon, with the fatal wound in his breast, exposed to public view. To that deadly wound, the soldiers guarding the precious relic, often pointed, and swore to avenge ten-fold, the death of their lamented Prince.

On the height above Genappe, the 5th Division halted about half-an-hour. During which time, a few men were tried for wantonly firing away their ammunition. This is a common practice among foreign troops, and on occasions similar to this, it is but too much so among our own. It cannot, however, be too much reprobated, for besides being detrimental to the service, it endangers the life of many a brave soldier.

On the morning of the 17th, the weather was hazy, but before ten it had begun to clear up, and at noon the day was beautiful. About one, the air was extremely sultry, half-an-hour later, the clouds began to lour, and about two, thunder was faintly heard. In a few minutes, the horizon was darkened—the lightning flashed—the thunder rolled in terrific peals—and rain and hail poured upon us in prodigious quantities. In fine, one would have imagined that the elements had conspired with men, to render the events passing on earth the most important and dreadful recorded in history. In the midst of this tempest, we proceeded on our way, wading through mud and water to the knees.

On our arrival on the position of Waterloo, we were ordered to bivouac in a newly-ploughed field, then little better than a clay puddle. By this time we were thoroughly drenched, our baggage was not to be found, and to add to other miseries, we could not get a drop of water to quench our thirst. To procure a supply, a fatigue party was ordered to Waterloo. Being first for that duty, I proceeded as ordered, and found draw-wells in abundance, *but the ropes had all been removed*, whether intentionally or not, I cannot say, but appearances were certainly against the Belgians. As a substitute, I buckled a few canteen straps together, but even these, aided by some fathoms of rope, did not carry a can to the bottom of any of the wells.

After numerous fruitless attempts to get our canteens filled, we returned to our bivouac, where misery in its most hideous form stared us in the face. Just let any man fancy himself seated on a few small twigs, or a little straw in a newly ploughed field, well soaked with six hours heavy rain; his feet six or eight inches deep in mud, cold, wet, and hungry, without fire, without meat,—without drink, and a thin blanket his only shelter from the midnight hurricane, and he will have a faint idea of what we suffered on the night of the 17th, and morning of the memorable 18th of June.

A sound sleep being a luxury which the men could not expect to enjoy, they seated themselves in pairs, and with their blankets around them, and their backs to the storm, amused each other as they best could till morning.

The Battle of Waterloo

The storm continued to rage with very nearly the same violence till eight o'clock, a. m. About nine the clouds began to disperse, and before ten the day cleared up.

About eight, the commissary presented us with a tolerable allowance of beef, but the value of it might have been saved to the country, for few deigned to look at it. This present was soon followed by another of a more acceptable kind, however,—brandy, which met with a much more kindly welcome.

The enemy shewing no disposition to resume the offensive, we were withdrawn from our advanced position in the puddle, to a dry one considerably in rear of it. Here we lighted fires, pulled off our jackets, shoes, &c. and endeavoured to make ourselves as comfortable as existing circumstances would permit. In hopes of procuring a little repose, we had begun to construct huts, in one of which three of us were fast asleep, when the sound of the bugles called us to prepare for a renewal of the scenes of the 16th.

Hark, the din of distant war,
How noble is the clangour.
Pale death ascends his ebon car,
Clad in terrific anger.

At this interesting period of the day, the different corps of the allied army occupied the following positions:—

The road from Brussels to Charleroi, by Quatre-Bras, first traverses the forest of Soignies, then runs through the village of Waterloo, a few hundred yards in front of it. About a mile farther, the road passes the farmhouse of Mount St John, where the highway branches into two roads, the right leading to Nivelles, the other to Charleroi. At the distance of a mile from Mount St John, and on the brow of an eminence, stands the farmhouse of La-Belle-Alliance. The centre of the allied army occupied the farm of Mount St John; the right wing extended along the eminence as far as Braine-la-Leude, and the left rested on the farm of Ter-la-Haye. In front of the British position, the ground sloped gently towards the valley, from which, to the summit of the ridge on which the French army was posted, it rose in the same gradual and easy manner. The direct distance between the two positions varied from a thousand to fifteen hundred paces, and the extreme length of the field of battle was about two miles.

The first British division occupied that part of the position called the right centre, in front of which stood the *château* of Hougomont. The light companies of the Guards, some Belgic, and a few Brunswick troops, were thrown into the orchard and woods surrounding the house. The *château* and garden were occupied by the Coldstream Guards, and the remaining portions of the division were posted in rear of their companions, to support them in case of necessity.

The Third Division formed the left centre, from which some Hanoverians and light troops from the King's German Legion, were detached to the farmhouse of La Haye Sainte, situated near the bottom of the ridge, on the left of the road to Charleroi. The Second Division took post on the right of the First, and the Fourth Division on the right of the second. The latter, forming the right of the army, had its advanced posts at Braine-la-Leude. The Fifth Division was posted on the left of the Third, and crowned a height, which rose gradually from the highway for nearly half-a-mile, in the direction of Ter-la-Haye. Along the brow of the ridge run a hedge from the centre to the extreme left, behind which our artillery were stationed, completely out of the enemy's view.

In front of the hedge stood, ready for action, a brigade of Belgian infantry, each flank protected by a brigade of artillery, their rear supported by our brigade, a brigade of Hanoverian infantry, and Sir William Ponsonby's brigade of heavy cavalry. The Belgian infantry, commanded by the Prince Weimar, formed the extreme left, and were supported by the fourth brigade of British cavalry. The greater proportion of the cavalry were posted in rear of the centre, and right and left centre infantry columns, and the foreign troops were chequered with the British.

About eleven o'clock, Napoleon, with a numerous staff, appeared on the heights immediately opposite to our division. The imperial cortege was no sooner observed by our artillery, than they greeted it with a royal salute. At first the French chief seemed to relish the compliment paid him, but conceiving, no doubt, that we were rather troublesome with our *manners*, he soon turned the head of his horse and rode off.

A little after this, we were honoured with a visit from the late Duke of Richmond, who had travelled from Brussels that morning to pay his personal respects to the Duke of Wellington. After congratulating the officers present on their miraculous deliverance on the 16th, the Duke informed us that he had just seen our general-in-chief, who calculated on a glorious victory before evening, Prince Blucher and thirty-five thousand Prussians being on their march to our assistance. The effects which this communication produced on the minds of the soldiers was truly astonishing. Joy beamed on their countenances, and victory during the remainder of the day was never from their view. But it may be fairly doubted whether the speedy prospect of being succoured by the Prussians, or the two following verses, produced the most powerful effect on the hearts of the Highlanders.

Now's the day, and now's the hour,
See the front of battle lour,
See approach Napoleon's power,
Chains and slavery.
Lay the proud Usurper low,—
Tyrant's fall in every foe,
Liberty's in every blow.
Let us do or die!

These lines, chaunted by one of their own number, who altered them to suit the occasion, were received as they ought to be by every inhabitant of these realms, when threatened with the vengeance of a foreign despot.

At half-past eleven Jerome Bonaparte descended the heights on the left of La Belle Alliance, at the head of his division, and attacked our light troops in the front of Hougomont. His march was considerably retarded by our artillery, almost the first shot from which killed and wounded several of his men. Having at length arrived in the vicinity of Hougomont, the French attacked the Guards with great spirit, but for some time gained very little ground. Their assaults, which were made with great impetuosity, were met and repelled by the garrison with the most determined bravery. The foreign troops, originally associated with the British in the defence of this post, having retired, the whole duty devolved upon the Guards, who throughout the day showed that the trust could not have been reposed in better hands. Attack succeeded attack,—round shot, shell, grape shot and musketry were poured into the place in the greatest profusion, without producing any unfavourable impression on the garrison.

Every avenue to the old mansion was contested with an obstinacy seldom equalled. Every tree was contended for as if the prize had been a kingdom. No neutral walls or hedges were permitted; the one party or the other behoved to be absolute possessor. The gates of the Chateau and courtyard were assailed by the enemy with a bravery bordering on frenzy, but our troops having loop-holed the walls, fired thence on their fierce antagonists with such fatal effect, that not only were they driven back, but the ground around covered with their dead. For an hour and a-half this tragedy was acted at Hougomont. Enraged, at length, at the obstinate defence of the gallant Byng and his handful of guards, Napoleon turned his attention to the left wing and centre, with the view of wreaking his vengeance on us for his defeat at the *château*.

About one o'clock he opened a most tremendous fire upon our division, from a numerous artillery planted along the ridge on which his infantry were posted. Under cover of this cannonade, he pushed forward three columns of infantry, each from three to four thousand strong, towards the heights we occupied. With loud shouts of *Vive l'Empereur*, the left column attacked the farmhouse of La-Haye-Sainte, while the right column, supported by the third, moved against the Belgian troops, immediately in front of our brigade. The Belgians assailed with terrible fury, returned the fire of the enemy for some time with great spirit. But on the approach of the French, they shifted their ground, and retired behind the hedge, which, although it afforded them no shelter from the enemy's fire, yet concealed them from their view. Here, on seeing themselves well supported, they shewed a little more courage, and although exposed to a heavy fire, they maintained their ground with considerable firmness, until the enemy having gained possession of La-Haye-Sainte, by putting every one of the garrison to the sword, increased the numbers of the assailants.

Under cover of his artillery, Bonaparte caused the right and left columns formerly mentioned, supported by the third column, to move forward and attack the heights on which our division was posted. With drums beating, colours flying, and eagles soaring above their huge head-dresses, the enemy advanced in solid column to the attack. Their progress was considerably retarded by the fire of our artillery, and volleys of musketry from the Belgian infantry, till the enemy having almost gained the summit of the ridge, our allies partially retired from the hedge. At the entreaty of their officers, the greater part of them again returned to their posts, but it was merely to satisfy their curiosity, for they almost immediately again retired without firing a shot. The officers exerted themselves to the utmost to keep the men at their duty, but their efforts were fruitless, and at length the whole corps took fairly to their heels.

The post thus abandoned by *Les-Brave-Belges*, was instantly reoccupied by the Third Battalion Royals, and Second Battalion 44th Regiment. Those two weak battalions poured on the assailants a heavy fire of musketry, but the latter continued to advance with unflinching courage, till they succeeded in compelling our friends also to retire from the hedge.

Everyone was now convinced that our affairs had approached an important crisis, and that an attempt to arrest the torrent, must instantly be made, or the heights, and with them the victory, yielded to the enemy. The Belgians had left us; the Royals and 44th had also retired to our rear, and the 42nd Regiment being posted on an important spot considerably to our left, from which they could not move, the hazardous attempt devolved upon the 92nd Regiment, then about *two hundred and thirty strong*.

On arriving at the hedge, the enemy formed in close column, opposed to us a front not larger than our own, but then they had ten similar fronts to support the one in view. In fact, their numbers were *three thousand*, ours *two hundred and thirty*. Perceiving the urgent state of affairs, and the absolute necessity that existed of adopting some decisive measures, Sir Denis Pack, said, with much earnestness,—"*Ninety-second, you must charge! ALL the troops in your front have given way!*" To this not very encouraging address, the regiment responded with cheers, and then advanced to measure bayonets with their enemies. For some time the latter appeared resolved to give us a meeting, but on arriving within thirty paces of them, the whole column completely panic struck, wheeled to the right-about, and in the utmost confusion, attempted to escape.

But it was now too late; for on perceiving the disorderly manner in which the French infantry were retiring, Sir William Ponsonby rushed forward with the 1st, 2nd, (Scots Greys) and 6th Regiments of Heavy Dragoons, cut his way through them as far as the valley—killed and wounded an immense number—captured two eagles, and took 2000 prisoners. The Scots Greys being the centre regiment, advanced directly upon the French column, and charged past our flanks. On approaching us, the Old Greys cried, as with one voice, "Hurrah, Ninety-second, Scotland forever!" The effect produced by these heart-stirring words was astonishing. Anxious to accompany their gallant countrymen into the middle of the fight, many of the 92nd laid hold of the bridles and stirrups of the Greys, in order to be "in at the death," but "the more haste the less speed," was here fully verified; for instead of advancing at an accelerated pace, the poor fellows were thrown down, and some of them severely injured.

The whole scene was truly grand, but affecting; for around, and on every side of us, the dead, the dying, and the wounded, covered the ground. This charge was made about three o'clock. I never saw the soldiers of the 92nd Regiment so extremely savage as they were on this occasion. They repeatedly called to the cavalry to give the enemy no quarter. This feeling was produced principally by a report, industriously circulated on the previous day, that the enemy had put to death, in cold blood, all the British and Prussian prisoners who had had the misfortune to fall into their hands. Towards the close of the engagement, however, when the French were more to be pitied than feared, they assumed a very different air, and treated the prisoners with the kindness characteristic of the British soldier.

The result of this attack must have deranged the plans of Napoleon dreadfully, for an almost total suspension of hostilities on his part took place, from a quarter past three, till about twenty minutes from four. During this time, our rocket brigade attempted to break the French column of support, while the Scots Greys hovered on its flanks, to take advantage of any opening that might occur.

But their efforts were fruitless, the enemy remained firm as rocks.

Heavy as the cannonade was in the early part of the action, it was trifling in comparison to what followed. The cannon-balls were dispatched from the enemy's lines in such numbers, that it was no uncommon thing to see one rolling on the ground towards us, and two or three at the same time flying over our heads, or carrying off some of the men in the ranks.

Conceiving, no doubt, that one other effort would place Hougomont in their hands, the enemy, after pouring a terrible shower of shells into it, attempted to carry the courtyard at the point of the bayonet; but in this, as in all their former and subsequent attempts, they were signally beaten.

By four o'clock, the battle had become general. Our centre was furiously attacked by a great body of French cavalry, principally cuirassiers, supported by artillery, and a large force of veteran infantry. The French dragoons were extremely bold, galloping round the squares of British infantry, brandishing their swords, and even challenging some of the British officers to single combat,—conduct which appeared to many of us more nearly allied to frenzy than bravery. However, they succeeded in penetrating to the crest of the eminence, but being there met by the Third Division, and right of the Fifth, they were instantly sent back reeling on their reserves.

The field of battle now assumed a horrid aspect, many parts of it being so thickly strewed with the mangled corpses of the enemy, that it was scarcely possible to walk without treading on them. The wounded were in a most pitiable condition, particularly those, who, unable to remove themselves, were kept in constant terror, either of being shot, or trod to death. But all their lamentations, their prayers, and their cries for assistance, were drowned amidst the clash of arms, and the thunder of five hundred pieces of cannon, which spread death in every direction, and made the ground under our feet actually tremble.

Prince Blucher having agreed to support the Duke of Wellington with his whole army, put three corps of it in motion from Wavre at four o'clock in the morning of the 18th; two of them by the pass of St Lambert, and the third by Ohain. Knowing that the Prussians were on the march to join us, many a prayer for their speedy appearance was repeated, before their cannon began to deal death and destruction to the enemy. About four, two Prussian officers passed in front of us at full gallop, eagerly inquiring for the Duke of Wellington. On delivering their message, they returned by the same route, cheered, and cheering all the way. Soon after this, we perceived the French and Prussians engaged.

The latter were few in number at first, but as each Prussian battalion arrived it took part in the battle, so that by six o'clock, ample work was carved out for Bonaparte in that direction. Finding himself attacked by the Prussians in a much more serious manner than he had anticipated, Bonaparte caused his right to be reinforced. Between this portion of the French army, and the Prussians under General Bulow, a dreadful conflict took place, and continued till seven o'clock, by which time, all the Prussians moving by the pass of St Lambert, had arrived at the scene of active operations, and the head of General Ziethen's column, accompanied by Blucher, made its appearance about the same time near Ter-La-Haye. To prevent the junction of the two armies, Napoleon threw several considerable bodies of troops towards the extreme left of the allied army. These columns were attacked with great spirit by Blucher, who, on leaving Ohain, marched directly upon Papelotte, leaving Ter-la-Haye on his right. By this movement, the junction of the two armies was effected, and Bonaparte's object completely defeated.

Time being now of great moment to Napoleon, he, about six o'clock, pushed forward a strong body of cavalry and infantry, with orders to establish themselves at Mount St John. The column advanced under cover of a cannonade of the severest kind. For a few minutes, the shot and shell flew over, and amongst the troops in the centre, in prodigious numbers. Many of the cannon-shot, after passing our friends, skipped along the causeway, as far as the village of Waterloo, and by coming in contact with some of the poor mutilated soldiers, terminated their own career, and that of the wretched sufferers.

The French troops having reached the crest of the eminence, a report was instantly spread, that they had forced the centre of the British line, and were on the point of entering Waterloo. The village being literally filled with wounded at the time, the medical staff exerted themselves to get them sent to a place of safety, but their numbers far exceeded the means of transport, placed at the disposal of the chief medical officer. Everywhere there were to be seen soldiers without legs, without arms, and otherwise horribly disfigured, begging to be placed on a waggon, or faintly articulating, water, water!—Many who could not be accommodated with seats in the waggons, fled into the forest of Soignies, where they died, or were afterwards found, in a state too horrible to describe. The wounded in the waggons, though out of the enemy's reach, suffered severely.

The highway was so completely blocked up with baggage, stores of various kinds, and some cannon planted in battery, for the defence of the road, in case of a reverse, that the waggons crowded with wounded, could not proceed. Every minute, some new and aggravated version of the first report, was circulated by the foreign runaways. The Belgian drivers either fled from their waggons, or got intoxicated, and became unable to perform their duty; and, to crown the whole, the foreign cavalry in their flight, threatened to sabre everyone who would not, or rather could not, let them pass. The whole scene, therefore, was one of such horror, confusion, and apparent danger, that in imitation of their brethren at Waterloo, those who could crawl, quitted their seats, and sought for safety in the wood of Soignies, where many of them also perished.

Such were some of the early fruits of the enemy's operations against Mount St John, the latter may be enumerated in few words. With admirable spirit, the French ascended from the valley to the crest of our position, and for sometime seemed quite determined to retain possession of their prize. But their opponents being as fully determined that they should not, a desperate conflict ensued, which ended in the enemy being driven down the slope of the eminence with great slaughter. Never did French troops display more bravery, and never were they more signally defeated. They appeared to us at times to throw aside the character of man, and allow their courage to border on the ferocity of the tiger. It was a desperate game to be sure, which their leader was playing; and it was no doubt his best policy to employ men equally desperate as himself.

From the termination of this attack, till seven o'clock, the battle raged with great fury, from Hougomont, to the heights on which the left of the Prussian army rested. About the latter hour, Napoleon, in order to bring the conflict to a close, brought forward his guards, in number about 15,000. Placing himself at their head, he accompanied them to the bottom of the valley, but no farther; there he remained to witness the result of this awful and last struggle for victory.

Having soon after the termination of the last detailed attack, received a wound, which compelled me to quit my corps, and thereby deprived me of the honour of accompanying my friends in the last offensive movement against the enemy, I am unable to detail, from personal observation, what occurred in the latter part of the day. But the following particulars, extracted from the notebook of an old and highly valued friend, who escaped untouched, will more than supply the deficiency.

Under cover of a heavy cannonade, the Imperial Guards, who had sworn to conquer or die, ascended the heights, the thread-bare cry of *Vive l'Empereur!* issuing from every mouth. To the issue of this combat, many looked forward with emotion. The causes of their despondency were, the superiority of the enemy, and the very few British troops in the field. But although not a few despaired of victory, I am confident that not a man thought of retreating, so long as one companion remained to stand by him.

The advance of the Imperial Guards was covered by a cloud of sharpshooters, whose fire caused us considerable loss. As the enemy approached the crest of the height, the sharp-shooters were recalled to their battalions, and the fire of their artillery slackened. In a few seconds thereafter, the belligerents found themselves opposed to each other, at the distance of twenty paces, and instantly proceeded to decide the important contest.

From that time, till half-past seven, the battle raged with violence at every point, and the victory was doubtful. Soon after this, however, some little hesitation was observed in the enemy's movements; and the gallant Blucher advanced, spreading death and dismay over the field on the left of the British. The Duke taking advantage of the favourable opportunity now offered, ordered the whole allied army to advance. The charge proving irresistible, the enemy fled in confusion, and were very roughly handled by our cavalry and artillery. The carnage was dreadful;—in many places the enemy lay in heaps—their squares of infantry suffered tremendously from our artillery—and the numerous mangled corpses which strewed the field, showed, from the nature of their wounds, that our cavalry had done their duty. After a desperate resistance, the enemy were finally driven past La-Belle-Alliance; a little in front of which, we came in contact with the Prussians, who halted, and played our national air of "God save the King." Here it was also where the two illustrious commanders first met after the battle, and congratulated each other on the successful termination of their joint labours.

Hark from the gory ground,
That feeble sound,
White-robed mercy kneels amid the strife:
Sons of the true and brave.
Glory to forgive and save
The worst of fallen foes who plead for life!
Stay the arms uplifted round,
Stoop to staunch the open wound,
They are enemies no more when they yield.
Britannia! yes thy knee shall bend
To raise the vanquished foe—a friend!
Whose grateful hand thy wreath shall blend
When the lion of Old England leaves the field.

Brussels

As soon as it was known in Brussels that the allied army had retired from Quatre-Bras, and the Prussians from Ligny, the whole population was thrown into a state of agitation not to be described. The 17th was a day of alarm, the 18th one of horror. That part of the old ramparts which faces Waterloo, was crowded at an early hour with people of every description. Until nearly two o'clock, all was conjecture, but from that hour wounded soldiers arrived every minute from the field of blood. At one time it was said Napoleon had been defeated,—at another that he was victorious, and would enter Brussels in the evening. These reports threw the good people into a state of mind bordering on insanity. At first the wounded were few and far between, but in a short time the road was covered with them.

About half-past four the alarm of the citizens was at its height,—a French column having been seen on its march to Brussels, but whether as victors or prisoners none could tell, for none had ever inquired. By and bye the column entered, 2000 in number, but not as was anticipated by everybody, victors,—but as prisoners of war, being those we captured at three o'clock. Fears however still continued to haunt their breasts, for nothing could convince them but that Napoleon must be the conqueror.

On the arrival of our wounded in Brussels, all ranks vied with each other in acts of personal kindness and attention. Many of the most respectable inhabitants, ladies as well as gentlemen, waited their arrival at the gates, and to each soldier distributed wine, tea, coffee, soup, bread, and cordials of various descriptions. Those who remained at home ministered to the wants of the poor maimed houseless wanderers; dressed their wounds, and if unable, from the severity of their wounds, to proceed farther, a bed was immediately provided for them, on which they might rest their wearied and fractured limbs.

In almost every house there were wounded soldiers. In order to shew the number quartered in these houses, and the country to which they belonged, the inhabitants affixed a paper on their windows or their doors, intimating that they had four wounded English, or four wounded Scotch, &c. Nothing could exceed the attention of the ladies to their patients. In the house where I was quartered there were three ladies, the mother and two daughters. The latter always visited the hospitals morning and evening, taking with them such articles of food or raiment as they thought the sufferers required.

One morning the youngest returned in tears. Having seen a number of bad cases, the amiable and humane little creature thought that she would be able to view without shrinking the mangled frame of an unfortunate artillery officer, who had lost both his legs. But on entering his chamber, she found the poor sufferer in the agonies of death. This being more than she could bear, she burst into tears—hurried from the apartment—and returned home in the state of mind previously described.

In the Rue de l'Empereur, another family, consisting of an aged mother, a son, and three daughters, set apart two front rooms of the street floor for the accommodation of the wounded. One of them was fitted up with mattresses for those who were completely disabled, and the other as a laboratory and cooking apartment, where all those who could stroll about had their wounds dressed by the young ladies. Whatever medicines or nourishments was required, were distributed with a bountiful hand.

The French wounded were almost all placed in the city hospitals, or the houses of those who had shewn themselves to be anything but friendly to the pending struggle. Many of the poor wretches, although not able to lift their heads from their pillows, kept constantly crying, "*Vive l'Empereur!*"

One day an officer sent by Louis XVIII. went round the various hospitals to inquire into the wants of the patients, and offer assistance to all who required it. But they replied that they had no king but one, "*Vive l'Empereur*," and one of them, finding he had but a short time to live, converted the cry into a kind of song, which he chaunted as long as he could speak.

At the close of the memorable charge made by us at three o'clock, a friend of mine made lawful prize of a beautiful charger, very richly caparisoned. The richness of the furniture led him to expect a pair of handsome pistols in the holsters, but on opening them, he was most agreeably disappointed to find that a good bottle of champagne occupied the one, and the leg of a fowl and piece of bread the other. Our mouths being much parched at the time, the bottle was instantly decapitated by my friend's sword, who being of a very generous disposition, shared the wine with another officer and myself. It was, without exception, the most delicious glass of champagne I ever drank.

A French general who was made prisoner on the 18th, having on various occasions rendered himself rather conspicuous by his entire devotion to the cause of the Usurper, was very roughly treated on entering Brussels. To court the favour of the populace, the general had no sooner entered the city, than he, in a true turn-coat style, cried, "*Vive le Roi!*" But he soon found that he had committed a most egregious blunder, for, indignant at his bare-faced impudence, the people pelted him with mud and offals, till he quitted the city at the other extremity.

Immediately after the battle, the Bonapartists charged Marshals Ney and Grouchy, with all the misfortunes that had befallen the French army on the 16th and 18th of June. Ney, in a letter to Fouche, attempted to exculpate himself from so foul a charge, but his conduct to Louis XVIII. had made so deep an impression on the minds of the people, that his statement was not generally credited. With us, however, the charge was looked upon as a patched up story, to lessen the glory achieved by the allied armies on the plains of Waterloo.

The fact is, that Napoleon was not betrayed by his Marshals, but by himself. Every man who betrays a friend, is ever after deemed unworthy to associate with honourable men. How much more unworthy must that man be who betrays the interests of his legitimate sovereign, and those of thirty millions of his countrymen? This being the marshal's crime, was it possible for the French troops either to respect a man loaded with so much guilt, or to place the smallest confidence in him in the hour of danger? I should think not. And therefore conceive that Bonaparte, by appointing Ney to the command of the troops destined to act against the Duke of Wellington on the 16th, actually betrayed his own interests; for it was notorious, that it was want of confidence in their leader which made from forty to fifty thousand French soldiers, recoil before a force not more than half their number, during the struggle at Quatre-Bras.

Had the marshal's honour been as pure as in his former campaigns, the retreat of some of his troops, so far as Charleroi that afternoon, would never have taken place. No; a single word from his lips would at once have arrested any attempt of the kind. Knowing, therefore, as

Bonaparte did, that to Ney's tainted character, he owed a considerable portion of the disgrace brought on his arms at Quatre-Bras, was it not the act of a madman to appoint the same individual to a prominent command on the 18th, and thereby to prepare the way for a fresh defeat, and all its accompanying ills? But tyrants and traitors deserve no better fate than that which overtook Napoleon and his marshal on the plains of Waterloo.

With regard to the charge against Grouchy, there are no better grounds for it, than the one preferred against his brother marshal. There is not a doubt but both of them did everything in their power to secure the victory to their master. The real cause of this charge being preferred at all, may, therefore, I imagine, be traced to the following source. Calculating upon Blucher continuing his retreat, or upon his utter inability to render the Duke of Wellington any efficient assistance for some days, Bonaparte made arrangements for a general attack upon the position of the latter at Waterloo, to favour which, instructions were dispatched to Grouchy to assault that of the Prussians at Wavre with great vigour. Having made his calculations on a false data, as regarded the capabilities of the Prussians to assist their allies, and not discovering his error till on the eve of engaging the allied army, Napoleon found himself all at once placed in a ticklish, or rather in what may be termed, a false position.

To extricate himself from this dilemma, two alternatives offered—to retreat—or to endeavour to force the position of the allies, before the Prussians could arrive to their assistance. It has been shewn that he preferred the latter, and was routed. And to throw part of the blame of this step from his own shoulders, Bonaparte trumped up the charge against Grouchy, which was altogether discredited by every member of the allied or Prussian armies.

How are they bandied up and down by fate,
By so much more unhappy as they're great?

Whenever a man permits ambition to obtain such an ascendancy over his mind, as to lead him to aspire to the summit of all earthly greatness, from that moment he must be prepared to bear up against every variety of fortune that can assail the human race. To an ambitious man like Napoleon Bonaparte, who raises himself from a very humble condition, to be the arbiter of nations, the temptations of power, wealth, and pleasure, are frequently so powerful, as to urge him to put in force every species of dissimulation, and every description of treachery, rather than not accomplish the object he has in view. A man like him, previous to being placed at the helm of affairs, is continually muttering something about public liberty, and public good, but the moment he fancies himself so firmly fixed in the royal-seat that he cannot be removed, his song is instantly converted into personal honours and personal riches.

When a sovereign, like Napoleon, permits all his views to centre in family interests or personal aggrandisement,—when the sole object of his pursuit is worldly success, rank and fortune, can his people have any other feeling towards him, than unqualified hatred and contempt? Let those of a similar description, who may follow in the wake of Napoleon, reflect seriously on the course they are pursuing, before it is too late, lest, like him, they may ultimately be made to feel the weight of that irresistible arm which is continually suspended over the heads of tyrants, to avenge the cause of the injured and the oppressed.

When two nations are at war, and one of them finds it necessary to submit to the mercy of the other, it exhibits neither a prudent or magnanimous policy on the part of the conqueror, to impose dishonourable terms on the vanquished, when others far less severe may amply suffice. Few have pursued this short-sighted policy to greater lengths than Napoleon Bonaparte, and none have had greater cause to repent of their conduct. For to what else can we attribute the powerful opposition he met with on his journey towards universal dominion, in the latter years of his extraordinary reign? To what but his tyrannical and iniquitous conduct towards Spain and Portugal, did he owe the Peninsular war. To what but his insolent and domineering conduct towards all those nations who owned him as a superior or an ally, did he owe the war in Russia in 1812, and those in Germany in 1813 and 1814.

Borne to the earth by a grinding tyranny, the inhabitants of those countries, imitating the example of those who had gone before them, turned round on their oppressor at the first favourable opportunity, and with their strength and their courage, increased by despair, rushed against his legions like a torrent, and in their efforts to emancipate themselves from a degrading state of thraldom, continued to perform almost supernatural feats of personal heroism, until they either obtained their object, or died in the attempt. These facts clearly point out the course which every crowned head ought to pursue, who wishes to live respected, and die lamented—they must invariably adopt towards all nations and individuals, a line of policy governed by honour, justice, and humanity.

A charge of cowardice has been preferred against Bonaparte, and by Christian lips too, because he did not choose to die the death of a suicide on the field of Waterloo. To exculpate him from this charge, it is only necessary to remind his accusers, that—

Our time is fixed, and all our days are numbered;
How long, how short we know not: this we know,
Duty requires us calmly wait the summons,
Nor dare to stir, till heaven shall give permission.
Like sentries that must keep their destined stand
And wait the appointed hour till they're relieved.
Those only are the brave who keep their ground,
And keep it to the last.

From Waterloo, the French army retreated towards Paris, in a state of complete disorganization, hotly pursued by the Duke of Wellington and Prince Blucher. The Duke entered France by Bavay, the Prince by Beaumont. From Malplacquet, the English general, on the 21st June, addressed a proclamation to the French people, intimating that he was about to enter their country to assist them in throwing off the iron yoke of Napoleon. On the following day his headquarters were at La-Cateau. On the 24th, Sir Charles Colville captured Cambray, and on the 26th, Louis XVIII. entered it on his way to Paris. The same day General Maitland, with a brigade of Guards, took possession of Peronne, after a slight resistance.

On the arrival of the united armies in the vicinity of the capital, preparations were made to drive the remains of the French array from it, or compel the whole to surrender. Blucher, crossing the Seine at St Germain, on the 1st July, advanced towards the capital by St Cloud, on the heights of which he was warmly received on the 2nd by the enemy, but after a severe conflict, he succeeded in establishing himself in the village of Issy. Here, however, he was attacked early on the following morning, but finally beat off his assailants. Failing in this attempt, and seeing the allied army ready to storm their entrenchments on the north of the city, the enemy solicited a suspension of hostilities, and the same evening agreed to quit the capital, and retire behind the Loire. The French troops accordingly began their march on the 4th, and by the afternoon of the 6th the whole had proceeded towards their destination. The Prussian and allied armies entered Paris on the 7th, and Louis XVIII. on the following day.

Some of the regiments newly arrived from America, were thrown into Montmartre, and one brigade of British infantry occupied the Champs-Elysees. The rest of the British army were encamped in the Bois, de-Boulogne, and down the right bank of the Seine, as far as St Ouen. Several of the gates of Paris were held by British, and the remainder by the troops of the other allied powers. For some days our officers were openly insulted in the streets, and more than one of them actually spit upon from the windows of several houses near the Palais-Royal.

In company with a medical friend, I quitted Brussels in the first week of July, and proceeding by Braine, La-Compte, Mons, Bavay, Cateau, La-Chatelet, Peronne, Roya, Gournay, Pont-de-St-Maxance, and the Louvre, rejoined my corps, encamped behind the village of Clichy, on the right bank of the Seine.

Paris

On the 24th of July, the British and Hanoverian troops passed the Emperor of Russia in review, in the Place Louis Quenze: and to shew his detestation of those persons who brought Louis XVI. to the scaffold, Alexander placed himself almost on the spot where that unfortunate monarch lost his life by the hands of the executioner. In order to spare the feelings of the inhabitants, the troops were desired not to wear laurel. But the opportunity being too good to convince the Parisians that their brethren had really been worsted at Waterloo, almost the whole army hoisted the emblem of victory amid deafening cheers. Immediately after passing the Emperor, our old general (Howard) now Lord Howard of Effingham, galloped up to us in private costume, congratulated the few that were present on the additional honours which the regiment had gained, and then placing himself along-side of the commanding officer, accompanied us through various streets of Paris, on our route towards our encampment. During the time that this truly estimable and gallant nobleman commanded our brigade in the Peninsula, he was equally beloved by officers and men.

From this time, down to the end of October, the movements of the allied army were few, and with two or three exceptions, extremely unimportant. Drills, division, brigade, and regimental, we had in abundance; and often at so early an hour as three and four o'clock in the morning. Drill, when improvement is the object, is attended by all ranks with pleasure, but when its object is to harass or annoy, it is attended, but with no very friendly feelings towards the person by whom it has been ordered, and, therefore, instead of being beneficial, creates a dislike to military exercise and duty of every kind, which should invariably be avoided.

I have been led to make these remarks, in consequence of what occurred to our brigade in Clichy camp, in August 1815. Our general, who was always grumbling at something or other, and was never satisfied with the exertions of either officers or men, at length fell upon a notable plan of punishing us for our inattention, *viz.* sending us all to the balance or goose-step. At sunrise on the morning, after the promulgation of the order, our French friends beheld the no less novel than ludicrous exhibition, of two thousand men, each standing on one leg, and one or two hundred instructors bawling right, left, as if the thunders of Waterloo had deprived the men of the power of knowing their right foot from their left. In a few days, the *goose-step* was changed to squad, then to company drill, but finding us a parcel of incorrigibles, he, in a few more, finally dismissed us, conceiving, no doubt, that to continue his lessons of instructions, was something like casting pearls before swine.

On the 22nd of September, the British and Hanoverian army was reviewed on the plains of St Denis. Pursuant to the orders of the field marshal, the troops were formed by nine o'clock in the morning, with their left resting on the village of La-Chapella, and their right extending towards St Denis. The first corps, consisting of the first and second divisions of infantry, formed the left— the Second Corps, Second and Fourth Divisions, the right—and the reserve, the Fifth, Sixth, and Seventh Divisions, the centre. Colonel Estoff's brigade of cavalry, formed in rear of the Second Corps, in close column of regiments of the front of a squadron—and the cavalry brigades of Lord Edward Somerset, and Lord George Beresford, formed in a similar manner in rear of the first corps and reserve. Each division of infantry was formed in three lines of brigades, in close column of battalions right in front, with its artillery posted on the right. The colours of the regiments forming the front line—and the officers of the leading divisions were moved three paces to the front, as at open order. Drawn up in this manner, we waited the arrival of the illustrious individual, for whose amusement we had been called together.

The Duke of Wellington having arrived on the ground at an early hour, received the Emperors of Austria and Russia, and King of Prussia, about ten o'clock. On approaching the centre of the line, the front companies presented arms, the standards were lowered, and every band played "God save the King." In the suite of the allied Sovereigns on this occasion, were Prince Blucher, Prince Schwartzenberg. Field Marshal Barclay-de-Tolly, Platoff, Hetman of the Cossacks, the Arch-Duke Constantine of Russia, two sons of the King of Prussia, and a very great many more of inferior rank. The breasts of some of those individuals were literally covered with decorations, and many of their uniforms were really splendid. The three monarchs were the plainest dressed individuals in the field; the Emperor of Austria being dressed in white, and the other two wearing plain green uniforms, with a star.

This part of the ceremony being over, the field marshal summoned around him the generals commanding divisions, and gave them instructions regarding the operations of the day, which very closely resembled those of the allied army at Salamanca, on the 22nd July, 1812.

The First Corps moving to its left, passed between Montmartre and the walls of the capital, to attack the right of our supposed enemy. On arriving at the barrier of Clichy, the corps debouched on the road to that village, when, having established itself in rear of the foe, it halted.

The second corps moved forward, but obliquely to the right, and then attacked the left of our invisible enemies. In this movement, the corps was supported by the 5th Division, till the former succeeded in its object, when the latter, with the other two divisions of the reserve, advanced in column at quarter-distance; and with their light troops in front, moved round the northern base of Montmartre, to the attack of the enemy's centre. On the arrival of the second corps, in the vicinity of Clichy, and the reserve within a few hundred yards of the road leading from that village to Paris, the whole halted; and the fifth and sixth divisions formed line, the front line dressing on the 92nd Regiment. Every division now ordered arms, and stood at ease for nearly half-an-hour.

Just before moving from our original ground. Prince Blucher and staff, Platoff, &c. came forward to examine the dress of the 42nd, 79th, and 92nd Highlanders. Many a remark was made, and many a joke cracked at the expense of the philibeg; but Donald, instead of getting sulky on the occasion, took a similar method of being revenged upon the gallant body of foreigners in his front, some of them being attired in uniforms which he considered no less singular than his own.

During the temporary suspension of hostilities, the Arch-Duke Constantine of Russia walked his horse up to the left of the 92nd Regiment, and began to scrutinize the dress of the men. Having asked a young lad to show him his bonnet, the poor fellow, either not knowing the rank of the individual who was addressing him, or like some of his companions, thinking him "a queer looking chiel," actually refused. Being then with the Imperial cavalcade, a little in front of the regiment, and aware that his brother's countenance was no great introduction to him anywhere, the Emperor Alexander galloped up, and in good English, said, "Take off your cap, my lad, and show it to this gentleman."

This at once removed the bonnet from the head of the Caledonian, and placed it in the hands of the Russian Prince, who, after examining it for a little, returned it to the owner; the Emperor at the same time remarking to his brother, "*Cett un brave regiment*." On their progress towards the right, the Emperor, turning to Captain F. said, "This is my brother, Sir, will you have the kindness to show him your sword?" On examining the claymore, the royal brothers returned it, and then rejoined their distinguished friends.

On resuming our arms, the First Corps, in column at quarter distance, again manoeuvred on the right of the enemy; and the Second Corps also at quarter distance, turned Clichy, by moving between the village and the reserve. The latter advanced the Seventh Division at quarter distance, and the Fifth and Sixth Divisions in line. Soon after we moved, the heavy cavalry made a most beautiful charge past our flanks, which completed the rout of the enemy, and was the last offensive movement we made on that *memorable* day.

It now only remained for us to pay our respects to the Emperor of Austria, and for that purpose, the whole army halted, and the battalions then in line, formed column. In a few minutes, the Duke of Wellington, and the allied Sovereigns, took post on the left of the road leading from Clichy to Newilly, when the whole marched past the Emperor in column of companies at quarter-distance.

The review was attended by almost all the English nobility and gentry then in Paris. Their splending equipages added much to the interest and magnificence of the scene; for at one time almost every part of the northern slope of Montmartre was completely covered with them. As the army advanced, however, the *beaux* and the *belles* retired; and when the allied chiefs took their ground as before-mentioned, the whole group assembled around them, to witness the novel spectacle of a British army passing in review before an Emperor of Austria, under the walls of the metropolis of France.

During our stay in the camp of Clichy, my time was partly occupied in an attempt to reclaim from the paths of vice, *without the aid of the "cat o' nine tails*," six men, who had repeatedly given but too good proofs that they were ready and willing to engage in the perpetration of almost every description of crime. The measures I adopted on the occasion were the following:—

First of all I divided the company into three classes. In the *first* were placed the best men,—in the *second* the indifferent characters,—and in the *third* the very worst. On the class-rolls being made out, the company was turned out, the roll called, and each individual, on answering to his name, took post in the class to which he was appointed. The rueful countenances which those in the second and third classes exhibited on the occasion, testified at once that none of them before that moment had conceived there was the smallest shade of difference between their own, and the character of the best behaved man in the company; for, on being removed as it were from the society of the latter, I fancied I saw the tear of shame and repentance start in the eye of various individuals, and my conjecture turned out to be well-founded. On the classes being told off, the members of the first were informed that they would have themselves alone to blame, if they were removed at a future period from the proud station they occupied; and those of classes second and third, that it would be equally their own fault, if a month or two hence they should still find themselves in their degrading situations.

This preliminary step being taken, I proceeded to divide the company into six squads, corresponding with the number of desperate characters in it. Each squad, which was composed of an equal proportion of each class, was placed under the orders of a non-commissioned officer. To each squad one of the six bad characters was given in charge, with orders not to permit him to quit the camp either by night or day. This I did not conceive to be any great hardship, as they all slept in the same tents at night, and were all in camp together during the day. But the majority of the company thought otherwise, and demurred at being made responsible for the conduct of others. Being quite determined, however, to make a fair trial of the plan, I gave a deaf ear to their grumbling, and insisted on an implicit obedience to the orders I had given them.

A fortnight passed away, during which time there had been no thefts, nor plundering excursions heard of, in the company. Satisfied in their own minds by this time, that a complete remedy had been found for the evils which had arisen in the company after the battle of Waterloo, all the non-commissioned officers, and a number of the privates of the company, waited on me one morning, apologised for their previous conduct, thanked me for for what I had done, and begged me to persevere in the same line of conduct. Encouraged by the prospect of success, I, by way of an additional inducement to good conduct, placed at the disposal of the company *five prizes*, consisting of useful articles of dress, to be drawn for at the end of the first month, by all those who, during the *previous month*, had been mustered in class first.

The great amusement which the drawing of the little lottery afforded the men, and the keenness with which each individual contended for the lucky numbers, induced me to continue the same plan till relieved in the command of the company, four months afterwards, by which time my success had so far exceeded my expectation, that, previous to handing over the company to my successor, I had the inexpressible satisfaction, of enrolling *four of the bad characters in class first*, and of seeing them contend with their comrades for the monthly prizes.

Home

On the 29th of October we broke up our encampment on the banks of the Seine, and that evening our brigade occupied Saint Germain, a town which the good people declared to us Bonaparte never entered. On the 2nd of November we marched into Mountain Ville, Neuf-le-Veux, Mere, &c.; and on the 8th we removed to Montfort, and some villages in the neighbourhood.

In the vicinity of Mountain Ville, Captain H——bs and myself were billeted on an opulent and friendly family, with whom we spent two very pleasant days. The family having, unknown to us, directed the servants to have breakfast ready for us the morning we were to leave them, we were not a little surprised to find the table groaning under a load of cold fowls, veal, ham, tea, coffee, wine, &c. After doing ample justice to the viands before us, we strolled out to look after the men and baggage animals. On our return, the servants were all busy wrapping up the cold meat in strong brown paper.

Not knowing what they intended with it, we could not help smiling. By and bye, however, we were let into the secret by the butler, who respectfully inquired where he should place the parcels. On recovering from the surprise which his query occasioned, we told him that British officers never accepted presents of any kind from families on whom they were billeted; and putting a piece of money in his hand, desired him to express to the family how much we felt ourselves obliged by their kindness and attention.

Apparently astonished at our refusal, though probably more so at what we had given him, the butler remained dumb for some time, and then with a smile, said, "Oh! you British officers are not like the Prussians."

We remained very comfortably cantoned in Montfort, &c. till the following brigade order compelled us to move to Meulan.

Brigade Orders.

Port Chartrain, Nov. 29, 1815.

The Fourth Battalion of the Royals, the 42nd, and 92nd Regiments, are to march tomorrow for Meulan, on their route for Boulogne.

The corps are to march independently, under orders from their respective commanding-officers, who will please to send forward, very early, an officer to Meulan, to receive directions respecting the quartering of their corps there, and in the vicinity, for the night.

The Staff-Surgeon has been instructed to give directions respecting the sick, and the Commissary of brigade will afford all the means of transport in his power.

Major-General, Sir Denis Pack, cannot allow these corps to pass thus from under his command, without expressing his regret at losing them. The conduct of the Fourth Battalion of the Royals, both in camp and quarters, has been like that of the third battalion; and that of the two regiments, "orderly and soldierlike;" and he is confident, that from the high state of discipline the corps appears in, they would have imitated their comrades in the Third Battalion, had the same glorious opportunity teen afforded them.

The services rendered by the 92nd Regiment, in the Duke of Wellington's campaigns in the Peninsula, and his Grace's late short and triumphant one in Belgium, are so generally and so highly appreciated, as to make praise from him almost idle, nevertheless, he cannot help adding his tribute of applause. And to the 42nd Regiment, he really thinks he would seem ungrateful, as well as unmindful of the best feelings of a soldier, did he not, in taking leave, assure them that he will ever retain, with sentiments of admiration, the remembrance of the invincible valour displayed by the corps on so many memorable and trying occasions.

On the 30th of November, the 42nd and 92nd Regiments marched into Meulan agreeable to orders, where being joined by the 28th, the three corps formed into one brigade, under Sir Charles Belson, of the 28th Regiment, were ordered to move to Pont-Oise on the 1st December, and thence by Beauvais, Abbeville, Montreuil, and Boulogne, to Calais.

On our arrival before the gates of Calais, on the 17th December, we were not a little surprised to find them closed upon us, and that it was not the intention of the authorities to open them, unless our commandant would agree to make every company march at the distance of one hundred yards from the one preceding it,—the men reverse their arms,—keep their colours cased,—and prevent the bands playing on entering the town. Irritated at such conduct, instant admittance was demanded. This being refused, a second message was dispatched to the governor, giving him a quarter of an-hour to deliberate. This brought the hot-headed fool to his senses. On the gates being opened, the leading battalion entered, and was instantly followed by the others at the usual distance, with colours flying, bayonets fixed, and the bands playing the *Downfall of Paris*, all the way to the place of embarkation.

On our way from Meulan to the coast, the following General Order was issued to the different regiments. I insert it because it shews the number of British battalions which were then in France, the number retained in the country by the Duke of Wellington, and the number that he sent home.

General Orders

Headquarters, Paris, Nov. 30, 1815.

No. 1. The British troops which are to remain in France, are to be formed as follows:—

2. The 1st and 2nd Dragoon Guards, and 3rd Dragoons, are to be the First Brigade of Cavalry.

3. The 7th and 18th Hussars, and 12th Light Dragoons, are to be the Second Brigade of Cavalry.

4. The 11th and 13th Light Dragoons, and 15th Hussars, are to be the Third Brigade of Cavalry.

5. The Third Battalion 1st Guards, and Second Battalion Coldstream Guards, are to be the first brigade of infantry.

6. The Third Battalion Royals, First Battalion 57th, and Second Battalion 95th Regiment, are to be the Second Brigade of infantry.

7. The First Battalions 3rd, 39th, and 91st Regiments, are to be the Third Brigade of Infantry.

8. The First Battalions of the 4th, 52nd, and 79th Regiments, are to be the Fourth Brigade of Infantry.

9. The First Battalions of the 5th, 9th, and 21st Regiments, are

to be the Fifth Brigade of Infantry.

10. The First Battalions of the 6th and 71st, and 29th Regiment, are to be the Sixth Brigade of Infantry.

11. The First Battalions of the 7th and 43rd, and 23rd Regiment, are to be the Seventh Brigade of infantry.

12. The First Battalions of the 27th, 40th, and 95th Regiments, are to be the Eighth Brigade of Infantry.

13. The First Battalions of the 81st and 88th Regiments are to be the Ninth Brigade of Infantry.

14. Major-General Lord Edward Somerset is to command the First Brigade of Cavalry.

15. Major-General Sir Hussey Vivian is to command the Second Brigade of Cavalry.

16. Major-General Sir Colquhoun Grant is to command the Third Brigade of Cavalry.

17. Major-General Sir Peregrine Maitland is to command the First Brigade of Infantry.

18. Major-General Sir Manley Power is to command the second brigade of infantry.

19. Major-General the Honourable Sir R. W. O'Callaghan is to command the Third Brigade of Infantry.

20. Major-General Sir Denis Pack is to command the Fourth Brigade of Infantry.

21. Major-General Sir Thomas Brisbane is to command the Fifth Brigade of Infantry.

22. Major-General Sir Thomas Bradford is to command the Sixth Brigade of Infantry.

23. Major-General Sir James Kempt is to command the Seventh Brigade of Infantry.

24. Major-General Sir John Lambert id to command the Eighth Brigade of Infantry.

25. Major-General Sir John Keane is to command the Ninth Brigade of Infantry.

26. The First Division of Infantry is to be composed of the

First, Seventh, and Eighth Brigades, and is to be commanded by Lieutenant-General the Honourable Sir Lowry Cole.

27. The Second Division of Infantry is to be composed of the Third, Fourth, and Sixth Brigades, and is to be commanded by Lieutenant-General Sir Henry Clinton.

28. The Third Division of Infantry is to be composed of the Second, Fifth, and Ninth Brigades, and is to be commanded by Lieutenant-General the Honourable Sir Charles Colville.

29. Lieutenant-General Lord Combermere will take the command of the cavalry.

30. Lieutenant-General Lord Hill will take the command of the infantry.

31. The British troops to return to England, are to be brigaded as follows, for their march:—

32. The 1st and 2nd Life-Guards, Royal Horse-Guards (blue), and 3rd Dragoon-Guards, under the command of Colonel Althrope of the Royal Horse-Guards (blue).

33. The 1st, 2nd, and 6th Dragoons, under the command of Colonel Muter.

34. The 10th Hussars, 16th and 23rd Light Dragoons, under the command of Colonel Quentin.

35. The Second Battalions 1st and 3rd Guards, under Colonel Askew, 1st Guards.

36. The 36th, 38th, Second Battalion 73rd, and Third Battalion 95th Regiment, under Colonel the Honourable Sir Charles Greville of the 38th Regiment.

37. The Second Battalions 12th and 30th, and 33rd Regiment, under the command of Colonel Stirke, 12th Regiment.

38. The First Battalions 41st and 90th Regiments, and a detachment of the Royal Waggon Train, under Lieutenant Colonel Evans, 41st Regiment.

39. The Third Battalions 14th, 2nd, 35th, and 51st Regiment, under Colonel Mitchell, 51st Regiment.

40. The 54th, Second Battalions 59th and 69th Regiments, un-

der Lieutenant-Colonel Austin, 59th Regiment.

41. The Fourth Battalion Royals, the 28th, 42nd, and 92nd Regiments, under Colonel Sir C. Belson, 28th Regiment.

42. The 32nd, Third Battalion 27th, and detachment of Staff Corps, under Colonel Sir John M'Lean, 27th Regiment.

43. The 16th Regiment, 2nd, 44th, and First Battalion 82nd Regiment, under Colonel Tolley, 16th Regiment.

44. The 58th and 64th Regiments, and Second Battalions 62nd and 81st Regiments, under Colonel Walker, 58th Regiment.

45. Notwithstanding these orders, the troops are to continue with their divisions, and commanded as at present, till those ordered to England will march; and the Quarter-Master General will, in concert with the General Officers, have assembled those destined by this day's order to remain in France.

46. When the troops of the German Legion and the Hanoverians will march, it will be under the command of the officers commanding the several brigades of infantry and cavalry.

47. Major-General Sir James Lyon will be so kind as to give orders for the formation of the Hanoverian contingent, at a place which will be made known to him by the Chief of the Staff of the allied army.

48. Upon breaking up the army which the Field-Marshal has had the honour of commanding, he begs leave to return thanks to the General Officers, and the Officers, and Troops, for their uniform good conduct.

49. In the late short but memorable campaign, they have given proofs to the world that they possess, in an eminent degree, all the good qualities of soldiers; and the Field-Marshal is happy to be able to applaud their regular good conduct in their camp and cantonments, not less than when engaged with the enemy in the field.

50. Whatever may be the future destination of those brave troops, of which the Field-Marshal now takes his leave, he trusts that every individual will believe that he will ever feel the deepest interest in their honour and welfare, and will always be happy to promote either.

On the 18th, we quitted the harbour of Calais, and sailed for Dover; but the wind becoming foul, we were forced to make for the Downs, where we anchored for the night. Next forenoon we landed at Ramsgate, and proceeded to Margate. Here the late Sir William Curtis was most indefatigable during the disembarkation of the troops. He not only rendered personal assistance to the females on quitting the vessels, but placed a piece of money in the hand of each. But this was not all; the warm-hearted baronet gave all the officers a pressing invitation to dine with him. Such patriotic conduct deserves to be recorded.

On the 20th we bade *adieu* to Margate, and proceeded, the right wing to Deal, and the left to Sandwich, thence on the following day to Dover, and on the 22nd to Brabourne-Lee temporary barracks. Here we remained but a few days, when an order arrived for us to march to Colchester, where we arrived at the end of the month, and were warmly welcomed by the whole population.

On entering the barrack-gate, we were received by a guard of honour composed of wounded soldiers belonging to almost every regiment engaged at Waterloo. They were about 150 in number, and almost every one of them had lost a leg or an arm, and not a few of them one of each. Formed in two single lines, one on each side of the street through which we had to pass, the gallant fellows greeted us as we moved along with the most enthusiastic cheers, many of them actually leaping with joy. The spectacle was at once beautiful, and mournfully impressive.

A few days after our arrival at Colchester, Major-General Sir John Byng, whose defence of Hougomont will remain recorded in the page of British history, till time shall be no more, kindly agreed to forward a memorial for two months leave of absence for me, which, being granted, I quitted Colchester on the 24th of January 1816, for my native hills.

> *Around my fire an evening group to draw,*
> *And tell of all I felt, and all I saw;*
> *For as the hare whom hounds and horns pursue,*
> *Pants to the place from whence at first he flew,*
> *I still had hopes, my long vexations past,*
> *Here to return and die at home at last.*

ALSO FROM LEONAUR
AVAILABLE IN SOFTCOVER OR HARDCOVER WITH DUST JACKET

FARAWAY CAMPAIGN *by F. James*—Experiences of an Indian Army Cavalry Officer in Persia & Russia During the Great War.

REVOLT IN THE DESERT *by T. E. Lawrence*—An account of the experiences of one remarkable British officer's war from his own perspective.

MACHINE-GUN SQUADRON *by A. M. G.*—The 20th Machine Gunners from British Yeomanry Regiments in the Middle East Campaign of the First World War.

A GUNNER'S CRUSADE *by Antony Bluett*—The Campaign in the Desert, Palestine & Syria as Experienced by the Honourable Artillery Company During the Great War.

DESPATCH RIDER *by W. H. L. Watson*—The Experiences of a British Army Motorcycle Despatch Rider During the Opening Battles of the Great War in Europe.

TIGERS ALONG THE TIGRIS *by E. J. Thompson*—The Leicestershire Regiment in Mesopotamia During the First World War.

HEARTS & DRAGONS *by Charles R. M. F. Crutwell*—The 4th Royal Berkshire Regiment in France and Italy During the Great War, 1914-1918.

INFANTRY BRIGADE: 1914 *by John Ward*—The Diary of a Commander of the 15th Infantry Brigade, 5th Division, British Army, During the Retreat from Mons.

DOING OUR 'BIT' *by Ian Hay*—Two Classic Accounts of the Men of Kitchener's 'New Army' During the Great War including *The First 100,000* & *All In It*.

AN EYE IN THE STORM *by Arthur Ruhl*—An American War Correspondent's Experiences of the First World War from the Western Front to Gallipoli-and Beyond.

STAND & FALL *by Joe Cassells*—With the Middlesex Regiment Against the Bolsheviks 1918-19.

RIFLEMAN MACGILL'S WAR *by Patrick MacGill*—A Soldier of the London Irish During the Great War in Europe including *The Amateur Army*, *The Red Horizon* & *The Great Push*.

WITH THE GUNS *by C. A. Rose & Hugh Dalton*—Two First Hand Accounts of British Gunners at War in Europe During World War 1- Three Years in France with the Guns and With the British Guns in Italy.

THE BUSH WAR DOCTOR *by Robert V. Dolbey*—The Experiences of a British Army Doctor During the East African Campaign of the First World War.

AVAILABLE ONLINE AT **www.leonaur.com**
AND FROM ALL GOOD BOOK STORES

ALSO FROM LEONAUR
AVAILABLE IN SOFTCOVER OR HARDCOVER WITH DUST JACKET

THE 9TH—THE KING'S (LIVERPOOL REGIMENT) IN THE GREAT WAR 1914 - 1918 *by Enos H. G. Roberts*—Mersey to mud—war and Liverpool men.

THE GAMBARDIER *by Mark Severn*—The experiences of a battery of Heavy artillery on the Western Front during the First World War.

FROM MESSINES TO THIRD YPRES *by Thomas Floyd*—A personal account of the First World War on the Western front by a 2/5th Lancashire Fusilier.

THE IRISH GUARDS IN THE GREAT WAR - VOLUME 1 *by Rudyard Kipling*—Edited and Compiled from Their Diaries and Papers—The First Battalion.

THE IRISH GUARDS IN THE GREAT WAR - VOLUME 1 *by Rudyard Kipling*—Edited and Compiled from Their Diaries and Papers—The Second Battalion.

ARMOURED CARS IN EDEN *by K. Roosevelt*—An American President's son serving in Rolls Royce armoured cars with the British in Mesopotamia & with the American Artillery in France during the First World War.

CHASSEUR OF 1914 *by Marcel Dupont*—Experiences of the twilight of the French Light Cavalry by a young officer during the early battles of the great war in Europe.

TROOP HORSE & TRENCH *by R.A. Lloyd*—The experiences of a British Lifeguardsman of the household cavalry fighting on the western front during the First World War 1914-18.

THE EAST AFRICAN MOUNTED RIFLES *by C.J. Wilson*—Experiences of the campaign in the East African bush during the First World War.

THE LONG PATROL *by George Berrie*—A Novel of Light Horsemen from Gallipoli to the Palestine campaign of the First World War.

THE FIGHTING CAMELIERS *by Frank Reid*—The exploits of the Imperial Camel Corps in the desert and Palestine campaigns of the First World War.

STEEL CHARIOTS IN THE DESERT *by S. C. Rolls*—The first world war experiences of a Rolls Royce armoured car driver with the Duke of Westminster in Libya and in Arabia with T.E. Lawrence.

WITH THE IMPERIAL CAMEL CORPS IN THE GREAT WAR *by Geoffrey Inchbald*—The story of a serving officer with the British 2nd battalion against the Senussi and during the Palestine campaign.

AVAILABLE ONLINE AT **www.leonaur.com**
AND FROM ALL GOOD BOOK STORES

www.ingramcontent.com/pod-product-compliance
Lightning Source LLC
Chambersburg PA
CBHW031622160426
43196CB00006B/246